AMERICAN ARCHAEOLOGY
IN THE MIDEAST

CONTENTS

Preface ix
Introduction xi
List of Illustrations xiii
Map xv

CHAPTER I
BACKGROUND: THE NINETEENTH CENTURY

The Explorer-Scholar: Edward Robinson 1
Robinson's Peers 5
The American Oriental Society 6
The Palestine Exploration Fund 7
The American Palestine Exploration Society 8
The Explorer Charles Clermont-Ganneau 9
The German Society for the Exploration of Palestine 9
Parent Societies of ASOR 10
The Egypt Exploration Fund 11
The Wolfe and Nippur Expeditions 11
Biblical Scholarship in the Late Nineteenth Century 13
The Scientific Method of Excavation 17
Ecole Biblique et Archéologique Française 23
The German Institutes 24
The Lineage of ASOR 25

CHAPTER II
BEGINNINGS: 1900-1918

Charles Torrey 28
The Managing Committee 31
Political History of the Mideast 31
Annual Directors before World War I 32
Additional Field Activities before World War I 46
Back to the Jerusalem School 48
World War I 49
Post-World War I 51
William F. Albright 52
James Breasted 52

CHAPTER III
BETWEEN THE WARS: 1919-1945 (Part 1)

The Reopening of the School 55
Events of 1919-1921 57

The Archaeology of Mesopotamia 62
The Directorship of Albright 63
Bequests to ASOR 66
The Baghdad School 67
Back to the Jerusalem School 72

CHAPTER IV
BETWEEN THE WARS: 1919-1945 (Part 2)

The American School in the Late Twenties 85
Major Excavations 89
Nelson Glueck 96
Jewish Archaeologists before 1948 104
G. Ernest Wright 106
Other Notable Events in the 1930s 108

CHAPTER V
A DECADE OF DEVELOPMENT AFTER
WORLD WAR II: 1945-1955

Political Events in the Mideast 111
Directors of the Jerusalem School 112
ASOR Fellowship Program 113
The Dead Sea Scrolls 113
Millar Burrows 117
The Qumran Expedition 118
G. Lankester Harding 118
Roland de Vaux 119
Qumran Caves and the Bedouin 120
Carl H. Kraeling 121
Clark's Microfilm Project 123
The Excavation at Dhiban (Dibon) 124
Kenyon's Excavation at Jericho (Tell es Sultan) 125
Excavations at Bethel 130
Excavations at Dothan 130
The Baghdad School 131
Israeli Archaeology 134

CHAPTER VI
AN ERA OF EXPANSION: 1956-1967

Directors of the Jerusalem School from 1956 to 1961 139
Yigael Yadin at Hazor 140
G. Ernest Wright and the Shechem Excavation 141
The Expedition to Sardis 146

A. Henry Detweiler 146
James Pritchard 147
The Expedition to Beth-zur 149
The Expedition to Tuleilat el Ghassul 150
Joseph Callaway and the Excavations at Ai 150
Excavations in Jerusalem 152
Paul Lapp 153
Expedition to Gezer 168
The Baghdad School 171
Israeli Excavations 173
G. Ernest Wright's Presidency 177

CHAPTER VII
THE MODERN PERIOD: 1967-1980 (Part 1)

Politics and ASOR 181
The Six-Day War 182
ASOR and Saudi Arabia 187
Planning for a Research Center in Beirut 188
A Succession of Annual Directors 189
William G. Dever 189
The Tell Hesban Expedition 190
Excavations at Mount Gerizim 195
The New ASOR Institutes 195
The Amman Center 197
Excavations in Israel 204
The Archaeology of Judaism and Early Christianity 208

CHAPTER VIII
THE MODERN PERIOD: 1967-1980 (Part 2)

The 1973 Conflict 217
Further Excavations in Israel 217
Iraq after the War of 1967 219
Excavations in Cyprus 220
Excavations at Carthage 225
Explorations in the Buqeah Valley 228
William F. Albright 229
H. Dunscomb Colt 235
G. Ernest Wright 235
Frank Moore Cross 237
The Seventy-Fifth Anniversary of ASOR 238
Excavations in Syria 240
An Excavation in Egypt 245

CHAPTER IX
THE MODERN PERIOD: 1967-1980 (Part 3)

Excavations and Surveys in Jordan 249
Other ASOR Field Projects in Jordan 257
The Future of Jordanian Archaeology 259
Salvage Archaeology in the Negev 259
Recent Developments in ASOR 262
"Biblical Archaeology": an Anachronism? 269
Special Mentions 272
Conclusion 274

APPENDIXES

I. Presidents of the American Schools of Oriental
   Research 275
II. Directors of the Jerusalem School 276
III. Annual Professors of the Baghdad School 277
IV. Trustees of the American Schools of Oriental
   Research 278
V. Corporate Members of the American Schools of
   Oriental Research 279
VI. The Archaeological Periods of Syria-Palestine 282
VII. Examination Papers for the Thayer Fellowship
   (March 1906) 284

Index of Persons 287
Selected Index of Places 292

PREFACE

Two years before the seventy-fifth anniversary of the American Schools of Oriental Research (ASOR) in 1975, the president of ASOR, G. Ernest Wright, suggested to the board of trustees that it would be appropriate to honor the occasion by publishing a history of the organization. In promoting the project Wright pointed out there had not been a detailed study of American archaeological undertakings in the Mideast since 1903. In that year there appeared *Explorations in Bible Lands During the 19th Century*, a volume edited by Herman V. Hilprecht, which reviewed the work of the early American explorers and evaluated their contribution to Near Eastern studies. To be sure, there had been notable accomplishments in the nineteenth century, but hardly comparable to the achievements of archaeological scholars such as George A. Reisner, James A. Breasted, and William F. Albright in the twentieth century. Hilprecht's study had dealt with the infancy of archaeology; there was a need, then, for a new study of archaeology come of age. The trustees of ASOR concurred immediately with Wright's suggestion by commissioning such a work.

When I began to consult the ASOR archives as well as the voluminous literature on the archaeology of the Mideast, it became clear that only a preliminary version of ASOR's history could be ready for the seventy-fifth anniversary celebration. It was presented in summary form as part of the seventy-fifth anniversary observance in Jerusalem in June, 1975.[1] I continued the research for a year thereafter, before being elected president of ASOR. The demands of the office allowed only limited time for research; they delayed the appearance of the ASOR history but provided additional opportunity to grasp the nature of the organization through intimate association with it.

The work at hand is principally a history of ASOR, but not exclusively; ASOR is intelligible only when set in the context of the Mideast in all its aspects. This history, then, is conceived as a systematic review of American participation in the multifaceted discipline of Near Eastern archaeology (extending from prehistoric times to the Ottoman Empire), especially as it has been pursued during the past one hundred years. A review of this scope obviously must be governed by a principle of selectivity. In my conception ASOR is the center of the circle; persons and events influenced by ASOR fall within its orbit. The nearer their position to the center of activity, the more detailed the treatment; the more peripheral, the less detailed.

[1]Philip J. King, "The American Archaeological Heritage in the Near East," *BASOR* 217 (1975) 55–65.

Selection is by definition hazardous. I have aimed to be as inclusive as possible; omissions of people or events indicate no negative judgment. If all persons and events that have played a part in ASOR's history had been included, this book would have reached unreasonable proportions. As for ASOR's internal affairs, it did not seem necessary or desirable to repeat everything already recorded in official minutes. Persons and events have been included to the extent that they help to illustrate the principal developments and major achievements of this unique organization during its eighty-year history. To accomplish these purposes, I decided to follow a chronological order, making chapter divisions according to natural periods in the modern history of the Mideast.

This work does not pretend to be a social and intellectual history, but it lays the foundations for that larger objective. It is a synthetic study based on the achievements of scholars specializing in the ancient Near East, many of whom have worked within the ASOR structure. Specialists who read this history will immediately recognize the primary sources; others will have no special interest in them.

Thanks are due to many, too numerous to mention, who have helped directly or indirectly. The following must be named, however: my two immediate predecessors in the presidency of ASOR, G. Ernest Wright, who suggested the project and gave encouragement, and Frank Moore Cross, who continued Wright's support and read the manuscript with expert care. Special thanks are due to David Noel Freedman, who edited the manuscript with his well-known thoroughness and skill; he also made excellent suggestions which have been incorporated into the text. I am also grateful to his staff assistants, Marsha D. Stuckey and David F. Graf, whose careful editing improved the manuscript considerably. I wish to acknowledge the kindness of Edward F. Campbell, William Van Etten Casey, Michael D. Coogan, and Walter E. Rast, who made constructive suggestions after a careful reading of earlier drafts. The author alone bears responsibility for any errors in fact or interpretation. Finally, it is a pleasure to acknowledge the generous financial support of the Zion Research Foundation of Boston, a nonsectarian foundation for the study of the Bible and the history of the Christian Church.

INTRODUCTION

The somewhat esoteric title of the organization explains a great deal about its origins and purposes. From time to time in its eighty-year history members of the American Schools of Oriental Research have suggested a change of title so as to convey more clearly the organization's purpose, but the acronym ASOR has become such a well-known trademark, at least in the scholarly community, that there is reluctance to alter the name.

The title begins with the word "American" because most of the institutions of higher education that form ASOR's corporation are located in the United States and Canada. For "American," therefore, read "North American." "Schools" is a misnomer if its connotation is purely "institutions conducting formal classes." In the context of ASOR, "Schools" refers to overseas research centers, which sponsor lectures and seminars (seldom classes) and serve as depots for archaeological field projects.

"Oriental" is perhaps the most misleading word in the title; it is now, in fact, considered archaic. When ASOR was founded in 1900, western geographers designated as "oriental" that part of the world lying east of Europe. With an unbecoming provincialism, they divided that vast expanse into three parts—Near, Middle, and Far East—in reference from their own occidental perspective. The lands adjacent to the eastern shores of the Mediterranean Sea, roughly coextensive with the Ottoman Empire, were then known as the Near East; since World War II the term "Near East" has been supplanted by "Middle East," although in some circles they appear interchangeably (occasionally in this book). Today, Near East is restricted to use in academe, while Middle East (Mideast) is common in the political realm. This region, then, is ASOR's province. Frequent inquiries about eastern Asia directed to ASOR scholars and administrators indicate that the term "Oriental" continues to cause confusion.

The word "Research" is accurate when understood in its broadest sense, including not only the kinds of projects done in libraries and archives, but also archaeological digs, field trips, and geographical surveys. As ASOR uses the term, all of these undertakings qualify as research.

Composed of 150 institutions of higher learning, ASOR is the extension of the American scholarly community that it represents. In view of the divergence of its constituency, it is true to say that ASOR reflects the pluralistic society in which we live. The nature of this heterogeneous organization may best be understood in terms of its functions. For this reason it seemed advisable to present a history of ASOR at the end of its first eighty years, especially as it had not been done earlier.

Acting on the conviction that scholarly research is best done *in situ*, ASOR has established several overseas institutes, which serve multiple purposes. In addition to being a visible American academic presence contributing to international understanding in the host countries, they provide a base for cultural exchange between the nations of the Mideast and the United States. They also play a vital support role for field projects of all kinds, while serving as an invaluable liaison between visiting American scholars and the local governments, their Departments of Antiquities, and the national universities. These centers for advanced study and research have rightly been described as "the foreign arm of American higher learning."

Archaeology is the discipline that engages ASOR; understood in its broadest sense, it includes such fields as history, anthropology, epigraphy, linguistics, architectural history, textual and literary criticism, and art history. To limit archaeology to field excavations is to be unaware of its humanistic orientation in the historical periods and its interdisciplinary character in all periods.

These preliminary words of explanation help to prepare the way for the more detailed history of ASOR that follows, but they are not enough. To grasp the real significance of this organization it is necessary to travel back to the beginning of the nineteenth century—one hundred years before ASOR was founded. That is where this history begins.

LIST OF ILLUSTRATIONS

Edward Robinson 3
Sir Flinders Petrie and Lady Petrie 18
Frederick J. Bliss 21
Grand New Hotel 30
Nathaniel Schmidt on the way to Jericho 35
Nathaniel Schmidt on the Jordan River 36
The Jerusalem School in 1906 37
The 1906 Jerusalem School seventy-three years later 37
The logo of the American Schools of Oriental Research 61
Melvin G. Kyle 73
Clarence Fisher 75
Tell Beit Mirsim expedition camp 81
Tell Beit Mirsim dining area 81
William F. Albright shaving 82
The Jerash expedition house 88
The Jerash forum 88
Nelson Glueck 97
Atargatis at Khirbet et Tannur 99
Tell el Kheleifeh 100
The Jerusalem School in 1938 101
Nelson Glueck at Dan 102
John C. Trever 114
Dead Sea Scrolls on exhibit at Library of Congress 115
Archbishop Samuel and William Albright at Library
    of Congress 116
The Dhiban excavation camp 125
Kathleen Kenyon 126
Ernest Wright reading pottery at Shechem 142
Ovid Sellers at Shechem 143
Joseph A. Callaway 151
Joseph Callaway and Roland de Vaux at Ai 152
Paul Lapp at Araq el Emir 156
The Araq el Emir feline 157
Paul Lapp reading pottery 163
Paul Lapp at Taanach 164
The Taanach cult stand 165
Yadin, Wright, and Glueck at Gezer 169
G. Ernest Wright 178
Omar Jibrin 183
De Vaux, Lapp, and Yadin at Masada 185
Siegfried Horn at Hesban 191
Lawrence Geraty and Ernest Wright at Hesban 192

Lawrence Geraty and Ernest Wright dining at Hesban 193
James Sauer reading pottery at Hesban 194
The Albright Institute of Archaeological Research 196
The logo of the Albright Institute 197
Reconstructed Qasr at Araq el Emir 203
Tell el Hesi in 1970 205
Lawrence Stager at Hesi 206
A Mithraic medallion from Caesarea 215
The Tophet at Carthage 226
William F. Albright 230
William Albright honored in Jerusalem 234
Philip King, Frank Cross, and William Dever at the
    Albright Institute 239
Walter Rast and Thomas Schaub reading pottery at
    Bab edh Dhra 250
A Bab edh Dhra tomb 250
ASOR trustees visiting Bab edh Dhra 251

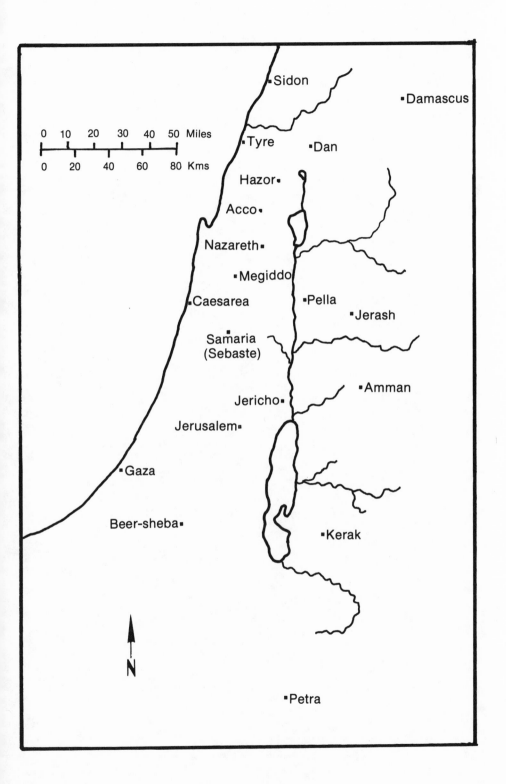

CHAPTER I
BACKGROUND: THE NINETEENTH CENTURY

Prior to the nineteenth century, hundreds of pilgrims visited what is called, by Jews, Christians, and Moslems, the Holy Land. Their travels contributed little to the scientific understanding of Palestine, however, for they were content to hear and repeat uncritically the lore emanating from local monasteries.

The reawakening of interest in Palestine and the surrounding regions dates to the beginning of the nineteenth century. At that time explorers from England, France, and Germany began to rediscover Palestine. The person who really focused international attention on the Near East in that era was Napoleon Bonaparte. In 1798, when he led a French military expedition to Egypt, he was accompanied by a corps of scholars who made a careful study of the archaeological remains of ancient Egypt and later published the results. The following year Napoleon invaded Palestine, and the geographers and engineers who accompanied him prepared maps covering Egypt and parts of Palestine.

While these developments were taking place in the Near East, biblical scholarship began to become alive in America, mostly under the influence of research done in Germany. Foremost among American biblical scholars was Edward Robinson; he had an intense interest in the geography of Palestine and a deep disdain for the fanciful stories circulated by the monks of the Holy Land.

The Explorer-Scholar: Edward Robinson

Born in Connecticut in 1794, Robinson was to become one of the leading biblical scholars of his time. After completing his undergraduate studies at Hamilton College, he continued his education at Andover Theological Seminary in northeastern Massachusetts. The center of conservative biblical studies in America, Andover was established by the Congregationalists in 1808. At Andover, Robinson came under the influence of Moses Stuart, one of America's eminent biblical scholars.

True to the tradition of Andover, which stood in sharp contrast to the liberalism of Harvard, Stuart was orthodox in theology and conservative in historical criticism. Yet he had great admiration for the German biblical scholars of his day, whose work could hardly be classified as conservative. In the course of the nineteenth century, German scholarship experienced a liberation, as it emerged from under ecclesiastical control into the university setting. Stuart, a master of the Hebrew language, was the founder of modern biblical studies in America; he also enjoyed an international reputation among his peers.

Robinson excelled in the same scholarly areas as did his mentor. Robinson's English translation of the Hebrew dictionary of Wilhelm Gesenius, a distinguished German grammarian, demonstrated extraordinary competence in the Hebrew language; at the same time this translation made a substantial contribution to the advancement of American scholarship.

Stuart was not Robinson's only teacher. Robinson continued his studies in Germany, where he came under the influence of Wilhelm Gesenius at the University of Halle and Carl Ritter,[1] the eminent geographer and historian, at the University of Berlin. Upon his return to America, Robinson became an advocate of the German scholarly method, but at the same time he remained essentially a conservative. Among his numerous literary achievements were two biblical series, which he founded and edited: *Bibliotheca Sacra*[2] and the *American Biblical Repository*. In 1837 Robinson was appointed professor of biblical literature at Union Theological Seminary in New York, a position he accepted only on the condition that he be allowed time for travel in Palestine.

Robinson's Travels

Robinson's historic travels in the Holy Land in 1838 and 1852 marked the beginning of a new era in the geographical study of that part of the world. Of his many extraordinary achievements, his exploration of Palestine and environs was by far the most important and perhaps the one closest to his heart, if one can judge from his comment in the introduction to his *Biblical Researches in Palestine*, "The following work contains the description of a journey, which had been the object of my ardent wishes, and had entered into all my plans of life for more than fifteen years."[3]

The goal of Robinson's journeys was to study both the physical and the historical geography of the Holy Land. Through a combination of philology, linguistics, and archaeology, he pursued an understanding of ancient peoples in their environment. He also hoped in the process to identify as many biblical sites as possible.

Archaeology was his weakest tool, not only because the discipline had undergone very little development in his time, but also because of his own lack of experience. In fact, he did not understand the nature of a *tell*, the Semitic word meaning "hill" or "mound" and designating those truncated cones dotting the landscape of Syria-Palestine. Composed

---

[1]Ritter was the cofounder, with Alexander von Humboldt, of modern geographical science. Although he never visited Palestine, he mastered the pertinent literature and wrote a monumental work on the geography of the land.

[2]A quarterly dealing with biblical literature and theology, *Bibliotheca Sacra* has been published continuously since 1843, by Dallas Theologial Seminary since 1934.

[3]Third edition, Jerusalem, 1970, vol. 1, p. 1.

Edward Robinson. (Courtesy of Union Theological Seminary, New York.)

of successive occupation layers containing the stratified remains of ancient cities, these tells are the archaeologist's key to the history of the Mideast. Because Robinson thought these mounds were natural formations, he failed to identify some of the more important biblical sites, such as Lachish and Jericho.

In the course of his travels through the Holy Land, Robinson was fortunate to have as his companion Eli Smith, whose prodigious knowledge of Palestine contributed greatly to the success of the exploration. A friend and former student of Robinson at Andover, Smith had spent much of his life as a missionary in the Holy Land, where he acquired such fluency in Arabic that it became his second language.[4] Smith was able to converse easily with the local population and so to learn much about the oral traditions. Aware that the modern Arabic names of villages in many cases preserve the ancient place-names, Robinson was able with the help of Smith's Arabic to identify a number of biblical sites.

Two other pioneers who had preceded Robinson and Smith in the rediscovery of Palestine also understood the importance of Arabic place-names in identifying ancient cities. They were Ulrich J. Seetzen, a German who set out for the Near East in 1802, and Johann L. Burckhardt, a Swiss who began his travels in 1809. As was true with Smith, their fluency in Arabic assisted them in toponymy and made it possible for them to wander off the well-worn tourist paths and explore more broadly than had been done before. Seetzen will always be remembered as the explorer who discovered the remains of ancient Gerasa (Jerash) and Philadelphia (Amman), while Burckhardt is best known for his rediscovery of the desert city of Petra, after it had lain hidden for over 500 years. Their work marked the beginnings of the topographical study of Palestine.

Despite the primitive conditions and inevitable hardships encountered by travelers to the Holy Land in the nineteenth century, Robinson and Smith carried out their explorations with meticulous care, taking exact measurements of all remains and making detailed notes daily. It is a great tribute to their skill and industry that they succeeded in identifying over one hundred biblical sites, an achievement reflected on every map of the Holy Land printed since their investigations. Albrecht Alt, distinguished geographer and biblical scholar of a later generation, summarized the achievements of Robinson and Smith in these memorable words, "In Robinson's footnotes are forever buried the errors of many generations."[5] It is amazing that they accomplished so much when their

---

[4]Smith spent the last years of his life translating the Bible into Arabic, an undertaking that tested his notable proficiency in the language.

[5]"Edward Robinson and the Historical Geography of Palestine," *JBL* 58 (1939) 374. (*JBL: Journal of Biblical Literature.*)

combined trips to Palestine lasted only about seven months and their scientific equipment consisted of little more than a compass, a thermometer, a telescope, and measuring tapes.

In 1841, a mere three years after the completion of their journey, Robinson published the results of the first trip in his *Biblical Researches in Palestine*. A supplement appeared in 1856, describing their second and final trip to the Holy Land. As further evidence of the importance of Robinson's achievement, *Biblical Researches in Palestine* was simultaneously published in the United States, England, and Germany; the American edition was appropriately dedicated to Moses Stuart and the German version to Carl Ritter, who called it "a classic in its own field."

Robinson's pioneer work in the historical geography of Palestine has continued to influence scholars of the twentieth century. In 1938, on the occasion of the centenary of Robinson's initial journey to the Holy Land, ASOR in conjunction with the Archaeological Institute of America, the Society of Biblical Literature, and Union Theological Seminary, sponsored a symposium in New York City. Prominent international scholars attended, and several made presentations on various aspects of Robinson's scholarly work. More recently there has been a reprinting in three volumes of Robinson's *Biblical Researches in Palestine*; it is a testimony to the continued value of this monumental study in historical geography.

Robinson's Peers

Robinson's accomplishments in biblical geography, achieved through the application of critical methods, encouraged other explorers to follow in his footsteps. In a study entitled *The Development of Palestine Exploration* (1906) Frederick J. Bliss, pioneer American archaeologist, referred to the "great quartette"—Robinson, Tobler, Guérin, and Conder. Each of these distinguished explorers built on the work of his predecessor.

Titus Tobler, often described as the father of German Palestinian research, was a historical topographer who concentrated on the scientific exploration of Judea and Nazareth; he also made a detailed survey of Jerusalem. Although he was, in fact, a rival of Robinson, he acknowledged graciously that the accomplishments of Robinson and Smith exceeded all previous contributions to Palestinian geography, including those of Eusebius and Jerome.

Victor Guérin, a Frenchman, published seven large volumes on Palestine based on his five visits to the Holy Land between 1852 and 1875. His writings provide valuable information about nineteenth-century Palestine, but they are weak in archaeological interpretation because, like Robinson, Guérin failed to grasp the key significance of Palestinian tells. Claude R. Conder, a British army officer, participated in the monumental geographical surveys of the Palestine Exploration

Fund. Despite the extraordinary achievements of this project, he also had not understood the nature of tells; he thought they were merely the sites of ancient brick factories.

The Lynch Expedition

In 1848, a decade after Robinson and Smith made their first journey to Palestine, another American, Lieutenant William F. Lynch of the United States Navy, undertook an expedition to the Dead Sea and the adjacent region of the Jordan Valley. His party sailed down the Jordan River in two metal boats, starting from the Sea of Galilee, surveying and mapping as they went.

Lynch's project was the first scientific survey of the Dead Sea. It produced, in addition to maps and drawings, reports on the flora and fauna of the Dead Sea, its geology, and an analysis of the water content. The oft-stated fact that the Dead Sea is 1,300 feet below the level of the Mediterranean was first established by the Lynch expedition. Lynch published the results of his explorations in two volumes: *Narrative of the United States' Expedition to the River Jordan and the Dead Sea* (1849) and *Official Report* (1852); the latter consists of government documentation and scientific tables. The first title is enhanced by magnificent woodcuts and drawings, which help the reader to share in the expedition.

The Explorer Renan

Among the explorers of the last century, Ernest Renan, who was also a philosopher and historian, deserves mention. Commissioned in 1860 by Napoleon III to conduct an archaeological mission to Phoenicia (modern Lebanon), Renan explored the Phoenician coast and excavated at the sites of ancient Tyre and Sidon. In the process he discovered some Phoenician inscriptions.

Renan's travels in the Holy Land inspired the work for which he is probably best known in the popular mind, *Vie de Jésus* (1863), a beautifully written account of the human Jesus. This biography makes no serious attempt to deal with the historical problems relating to the life of Jesus. Nonetheless, it is a masterpiece by a great humanist who was a towering figure in the nineteenth century.

The American Oriental Society

The American Oriental Society (AOS), one of ASOR's parent organizations, was established in Boston in 1842 for "the cultivation of learning in the Asiatic, African, and Polynesian languages." During the remainder of the nineteenth century this new society promoted interest in ancient Assyria and Babylonia, the region of Mesopotamia where the British and French were already carrying on scientific projects. From the time of the first annual meeting of the AOS in 1843 Moses Stuart and Edward Robinson were active members, and each served as first vice-president; in 1846 Robinson succeeded to the presidency of the organization.

The Palestine Exploration Fund

The scientific exploration of the Holy Land received great impetus from the establishment of the Palestine Exploration Fund (PEF) in 1865, marking the beginning of the modern period in Palestinian research. Inspired by the achievements of Robinson, the PEF was formally organized in London for the express purpose of exploring Palestine systematically and scientifically. Its founders described it as "a society for the accurate and systematic investigation of the archaeology, topography, geology and physical geography, natural history, manners and customs of the Holy Land, for biblical illustration." Although the PEF was not conceived as a religious society, one of its main purposes was to shed light on the Scriptures. As its prospectus stated, "No country should be of such interest to us as that in which the documents of our Faith were written, and the momentous events they describe enacted." In the period before the PEF was established, it was the practice for explorers to work single-handed. From 1865 on, the PEF encouraged team efforts and sponsored a number of monumental surveys.

The Wilson/Warren Surveys

Charles W. Wilson, officer of the Royal Engineers, oversaw the first scientific mapping of Jerusalem. He also launched one of the early projects of the PEF when he undertook a reconnaissance of Palestine for the purpose of identifying appropriate sites for excavation.

Sent to Palestine in 1867 by the PEF, Charles Warren, officer in the Royal Engineers and explorer, continued the surveys begun by Wilson. Warren also made soundings in the area of the temple enclosure in Jerusalem, by means of an intricate series of shafts and tunnels so as not to disturb existing structures. Because of the limitations of archaeological method in the last century, Warren and his colleagues were unable to assign accurate dates to the architecture and related artifacts that they uncovered in Jerusalem.

Contributions of Conder and Kitchener

The geographical survey of Western Palestine, which began in 1872 and continued until 1878, was by far the most lasting contribution that the PEF made to the scientific study of the Holy Land. Claude R. Conder and Horatio H. Kitchener, among others, conducted the survey, in which more that 10,000 sites were mapped. The final publication included seven volumes and a mammoth map covering an area in excess of 6,000 square miles.

Kitchener also distinguished himself in other professions, especially the military. A British field marshal, he served as Secretary of State for War in World War I; it was as the conqueror of the Sudan that he earned the title "Kitchener of Khartoum." In addition to his archaeological projects in Palestine, he made the first trigonometric survey of Cyprus in 1882 and helped to establish the Cyprus Museum in Nicosia.

In 1881 Conder directed a limited survey in Eastern Palestine, which was restricted by the Turkish government to a ten-week period and an area of 500 square miles. Conder was a prolific writer as well as an important explorer.

The American Palestine Exploration Society

The Palestine Exploration Fund served as the model for a comparable organization, known as the American Palestine Exploration Society (APES), which was founded in New York City five years after the PEF. A forerunner of ASOR, this new society enjoyed the support of leading American scholars, such as J. Henry Thayer of Harvard University and William H. Ward of the American Oriental Society. The APES had imbibed the spirit of Edward Robinson, as is indicated by the fact that its second president, Roswell D. Hitchcock, was a friend, colleague, and biographer of Robinson. The purpose of the Society was "the illustration and defense of the Bible." As its constitution stated:

> The work proposed by the Palestine Exploration Society appeals to the religious sentiments alike of the Christian and the Jew; it is of interest to the scholar in almost every branch of linguistic, historical, or physical investigation, but its supreme importance is for the illustration and defense of the Bible. Modern skepticism assails the Bible at the point of reality, the question of fact. Hence whatever goes to verify the Bible history as real, in time, place, and circumstances, is a refutation of unbelief.

The expressed intention of the APES lacked the scientific objectivity of its exemplar, the PEF; this may account in part for its early demise.

Just as the British Palestine Exploration Fund was committed to the survey of the region west of the Jordan, its American counterpart was responsible for the area east of the Jordan, Transjordan. The first attempt of the American Society to carry out its mandate produced only meager results because of lack of leadership and insufficient funding. A second expedition to Transjordan in 1875-1877, under Selah Merrill, had a more positive outcome. Merrill collected valuable data and published his conclusions in a volume entitled *East of the Jordan* (1881). A Congregational clergyman who later became the American consul in Jerusalem, Merrill was limited by the fact that he did not have adequate academic training to carry out a thorough survey.

In 1884, only fourteen years after it was established, the American Palestine Exploration Society came to an end, victimized by constant bickering among its members.[6]

The Explorer Charles Clermont-Ganneau

The history of Palestinian archaeology must include the name of Charles Clermont-Ganneau, a French explorer of uncommon ability. Beginning in 1873, he worked under the auspices of the Palestine Exploration Fund, making three significant discoveries in the realm of inscriptions. In addition to unearthing two boundary markers that established beyond doubt the location of the ancient Canaanite city of Gezer, he found a Greek inscription of the first century B.C., which warned Gentiles not to enter the court of the temple. Although he did not actually discover the Moabite Stone, or the Mesha Stele as it is often called, he was instrumental in salvaging the Moabite inscription it bore—despite the fact that a group of natives had smashed the stone to bits, hoping to realize a greater profit by selling it in fragments. Thanks to his efforts, the reconstructed Moabite Stone, which commemorates the victories of Mesha, king of Moab, over Israel in the ninth century B.C., was safely deposited in the Louvre, where it may still be viewed. The results of Clermont-Ganneau's surveys and other archaeological investigations are described in the six volumes he published between 1881 and 1905.

The German Society for the Exploration of Palestine

While biblical scholarship was flourishing on the German home front during the nineteenth century, archaeologists from that country were engaged in the exploration and excavation of Palestine. In 1877 the German Society for the Exploration of Palestine (Deutscher Palästina-Verein) came into existence, modeled on the Palestine Exploration Fund. Lutheran in origin and biblical in orientation, it provided needed support for long-term and complex projects. Gottlieb Schumacher, a German engineer living in Haifa, was one of the prominent archaeologists who worked under the auspices of this new society. During the twenty-year period it took him to complete the mapping of Transjordan (the project that both Merrill and Conder were unable to finish), he had the support of the Palestine Exploration Fund and the German Society for the Exploration of Palestine. Later, in 1903-1905, Schumacher directed a preliminary excavation at the majestic Tell el Mutesellim, the

---

[6]For those who wish to consult the records of the APES, they appear in its *Journal* for the years 1871 to 1877. They will always serve as a reminder that such a society once existed.

well-known site of ancient Megiddo; he also dug briefly at Sebastiyeh
(Samaria) in 1908. However, Schumacher was a better explorer than
excavator.

Parent Societies of ASOR

ASOR was not founded until 1900, but the establishment of two
other parent societies—the Archaeological Institute of America (AIA) in
1879 and the Society of Biblical Literature and Exegesis in 1880[7]—
prepared the way for it.

The Archaeological Institute of America

The AIA's regulations state that the organization was

> . . . formed for the purpose of promoting and directing archaeological
> investigations and research,—by the sending out of expeditions for special
> investigations, by aiding the efforts of independent explorers, by publica-
> tion of reports of the results of the expeditions which the Institute may
> undertake or promote, and by any other means which may from time to
> time appear desirable.

One of the original conveners of the Archaeological Institute of
America was Charles Eliot Norton, distinguished scholar and professor
of Fine Arts at Harvard, who also served as the AIA's energetic president
during the first eleven years of its existence. His two stated objectives
were to get Americans involved in the field work of the ancient Near
East and to acquire works of art for Americans and their institutions. In
view of Norton's own background, it is not surprising that he gave the
AIA a strong classical emphasis, evidenced by the establishment of the
American School of Classical Studies at Athens in 1882, "where young
scholars might carry on the study of Greek thought and life to the best
advantage." A School of Classical Studies was also founded in Rome in
1895, under the auspices of the AIA; in 1913 it was consolidated with the
American Academy in Rome, which had been established in 1894 as a
school of architecture dedicated to the pursuit of the Fine Arts and
humanistic scholarship.

Reporting on the progress of the schools at Athens and Rome,
which served as overseas research centers and residences for American
scholars, Norton stated, "To these Schools of Classical Studies it [the
Archaeological Institute of America] hopes that a School of Biblical
Studies, with its seat at Jerusalem, may soon to [sic] be added."[8] His

---

[7]Since 1962 the Society of Biblical Literature and Exegesis has been known officially as
the Society of Biblical Literature. (The simplified title will be used henceforth.)

[8]"The Work of the Archaeological Institute of America," an address by Charles Eliot
Norton at the opening of the First General Meeting of the AIA, held in New Haven on
December 27-29, 1899, *American Journal of Archaeology*, Second Series 4 (1900) 6.

expectation became a reality when ASOR was established in Jerusalem in 1900.

As early as 1886, the AIA began to publish its technical journal, the *American Journal of Archaeology*; in 1947 its popular journal, *Archaeology*, appeared.

The Society of Biblical Literature

Established in New York City "for the purpose of promoting a thorough study of the Scriptures by the reading and discussion of original papers," the Society appears to have been the brainchild of Frederic Gardiner, a professor of the New Testament at Berkeley Divinity School, Middletown, Connecticut. He served as secretary of the Society and also its second president. Daniel R. Goodwin, New Testament professor at the Philadelphia Divinity School, was the Society's first president, from 1880 to 1887.

From the beginning there has been a significant overlap in the membership of the SBL and ASOR, indicative of ASOR's strong biblical orientation, especially during its formative years. Similarly, the early volumes of the *Journal of Biblical Literature*, which the Society launched a year after it was founded, contained several articles with an archaeological bent, indicating the interest biblical scholars had in the archaeology of Palestine.

The Egypt Exploration Fund

In examining the nineteenth century history of the learned societies of the period one recognizes easily their concern for the Bible. The Egypt Exploration Fund (today the Egypt Exploration Society), established in Cairo by the British in 1882, was no exception. The Fund's purpose was stated as follows: "To organize expeditions in Egypt, with a view to the elucidation of the History and Arts of Ancient Egypt and the illustration of the Old Testament narrative, so far as it has to do with Egypt and the Egyptians." The *Atlas of Ancient Egypt*, which the Fund issued in 1894, gave special attention to the route of the biblical exodus, as well as to Egyptian place-names mentioned in the Bible. The eminent British Egyptologist, W. M. Flinders Petrie (1853-1942), who spent his last years as a resident at ASOR's School in Jerusalem, served as the first field director of the Egypt Exploration Fund.

The Wolfe and Nippur Expeditions

During the greater part of the nineteenth century, the British and the French were engaged in archaeological projects in Mesopotamia (ancient Assyria and Babylonia), while the Americans went unrepresented in the field. That situation changed, however, in 1884, when an American expedition set out for Mesopotamia to conduct a preliminary survey in preparation for an excavation. The American Oriental Society encouraged this pioneer project, while Catharine Lorillard Wolfe of New York, a philanthropist and art patron, provided the necessary financial support. This reconnaissance, known as the Wolfe Expedition, was under the direction of William H. Ward, who thereby became the first American explorer of Babylonia. Although by profession the editor of a New York newspaper, *The Independent*, Ward specialized in Assyrian and Babylonian seals and had sufficient scholarly qualifications to be elected president of the American Oriental Society.

Upon his return to America in June 1885, Ward recommended that an excavation be undertaken at Nippur (modern Nuffar), a prominent religious center of the Sumerians founded about 4000 B.C. and located one hundred miles south of Baghdad.[9] The Nippur excavation, which began in 1888 under the auspices of the University of Pennsylvania, was the first Amercan dig in the Near East. Over a period of several years, John P. Peters, Herman V. Hilprecht, and John H. Haynes served as successive directors of this project, while Clarence S. Fisher (who later was closely identified with ASOR) was the architect at Nippur.

Many of the scholars associated with Mesopotamian archaeology in general—and Nippur in particular—were affiliated with the University of Pennsylvania, which had a strong department of Near Eastern studies. The Oriental Club of Philadelphia, founded in 1888, cooperated with the University of Pennsylvania in fostering interest in the Near East. Several scholars who became prominent in ASOR were also associated with the Oriental Club of Philadelphia: Morris Jastrow, George A. Barton, James A. Montgomery, Edward Chiera, John P. Peters, and Albert T. Clay, to name a few.

It was mainly through the fund-raising activities of Peters, who was a professor at the Episcopal Divinity School of Philadelphia and at the University of Pennsylvania, that the Nippur Expedition became a reality; he was less successful as the director of the first two seasons of field work. Preoccupied with the budgetary aspects of the dig, he gave more attention to recovering impressive artifacts that would attract large financial donations than to observing the standards of scientific method. Peters's inability to maintain cordial relations with either his colleagues or his hired laborers exacerbated a tense situation, leading to a minor mutiny. He chose to ignore the counsel of the German-born staff Assyriologist, Herman Hilprecht, about the approach best to follow. Later he accused Hilprecht of taking credit for the discovery of tablets that, in fact, Haynes had uncovered. Hilprecht retaliated by questioning Peters's competence as an Assyriologist. University officals had to inter-

---

[9]Because it was considered the abode of Enlil, the chief god of the Sumerian pantheon, Nippur played a leading role in the religious life of Mesopotamia, but it was never a political capital.

vene. Hilprecht was eventually exonerated, but he resigned his professorship. The breach between Peters and Hilprecht never healed, and it caused hard feelings between American and European scholars. This unhappy event, remembered as the "Hilprecht Controversy," was a less than edifying episode in the history of archaeology and has become a classic example of how not to conduct an excavation. Despite these negative factors, in the course of several seasons of digging over 30,000 cuneiform tablets were recovered from Nippur, making it a primary source of Sumerian literature.

Biblical Scholarship in the Late Nineteenth Century

The biblical orientation of the various organizations that undertook exploration and excavation in the Mideast during the nineteenth century is by now self-evident. The fact that Palestine and its environs constitute the "land of the Bible" has always been a strong enticement to conduct archaeological investigations in that part of the world. Naturally, this same biblical interest played an important part in the conception and eventual establishment of ASOR as the end of the nineteenth century approached.

Johann Eichhorn and Julius Wellhausen

The critical school of biblical interpretation emanating from Germany had a more profound influence on American scholars at the end of the nineteenth century than Moses Stuart and Edward Robinson had had fifty years earlier. "Higher criticism" (in contrast to textual criticism), a term coined by Johann G. Eichhorn, father of Old Testament criticism, is a somewhat misleading name for the historical-critical method that German scholars were then applying to biblical literature. According to the humanistic presuppositions of higher criticism, the Bible must be subjected to the same kinds of analysis and interpretation as any other literature; it is to be studied and questioned openmindedly, like other ancient documents.

Julius Wellhausen was one of the great higher critics and historians of religion of the nineteenth century. Influenced by the idealistic tradition of the philosopher Hegel, but differing from Hegel in his conclusions, Wellhausen assumed a development in the religion of ancient people from primitive forms. In the case of Israel, the evolution was from a more simple form, indicated in early sources, to a more ritualistic expression presented in what was isolated as the Priestly source.

At the same time, Wellhausen was skeptical about the historical value of ancient documents in general, and he excluded from his study of Israel's religion any appeal to supernatural agency. His monumental study appeared first in 1878 under the title *Geschichte Israels I*, changed to *Prolegomena zur Geschichte Israels* in the edition of 1883. This was his statement on the higher criticism of the Old Testament, wherein he asserted that it is impossible to obtain any historical information about the patriarchs from the patriarchal narratives.

In the process of reconstructing history, Wellhausen disregarded the emerging archaeological evidence, which was beginning to shed new light on biblical religion and history. It must be acknowledged in fairness that when the *Prolegomena* was published the only city in Palestine touched by excavation was Jerusalem; on the other hand, ancient inscriptions had been unearthed in Egypt and Mesopotamia. He did, however, use the Arabic materials available; an astute philologian, he had mastered Aramaic, Syriac, and Arabic, as well as Hebrew. His primary concern, of course, was with the internal evidence supplied by the document itself; he ignored the kinds of external data made available through archaeology. The ideal approach is obviously to give balanced attention to both literary analysis and the external factors if the best understanding of ancient documents is to be achieved.

Wellhausen's contribution to the literary criticism of the Bible was immense, but his conclusions about the history and culture of biblical people were oversimplified and erroneous. As archaeology continued to develop from the end of the nineteenth century, the attitude toward the biblical narrative became more conservative; for example, some scholars of the next generation tended to view the stories about the biblical patriarchs as historical documents.

Archibald Sayce

Archibald H. Sayce, professor of Assyriology at Oxford and an Anglican priest, stated his position regarding the Bible and archaeology in 1894:

> The records of the Old Testament have been confronted with the monuments of the ancient world, wherever this was possible, and their historical accuracy and trustworthiness has been tested by a comparison with the latest results of archaeological research . . . .The evidence of oriental archaeology is on the whole distinctly unfavourable to the pretensions of the "higher criticism." The "apologist" may lose something, but the "higher critic" loses much more.[10]

Ernst Sellin

Ernst Sellin, professor of Old Testament at several universities (including Vienna and Berlin) and an archaeologist, expressed serious reservations in 1924 about Wellhausen's approach to the Old Testament. His comments, which appeared in an article entitled "Archaeology

---

[10]*The "Higher Criticism" and the Verdict of the Monuments*, London, 1894, p. 554.

versus Wellhausenism," reflect the attitude of several scholars in the early part of the twentieth century:

> I should not like to close this dissertation without having uttered this conviction: If I rightly understand our time, and especially the modern science of the Old Testament, the era of Wellhausen, in spite of all that we have learned of him, may be considered, with us in Germany, as antiquated and wholly of the past. This I deem to be proven by the generation of scholars growing up among us, who, in respect both of science and religion, are thinking from categories quite different from those of the time of Wellhausen.[11]

Archaeological Advances and Biblical Studies

By the time Hermann Gunkel, the renowned German scholar and founder of biblical form-critical research (which he called Gattungsgeschichte), reached the height of his career in the first part of the present century, field archaeology had advanced considerably in the systematic excavation of important sites and in the recovery of decipherable literary remains of the ancient Near East. The Egyptian, Babylonian, Assyrian, and Canaanite documents that became available provided the extrabiblical sources needed by scholars in comparative studies and allowed them to move beyond literary criticism to other methods such as form criticism and tradition criticism. These newer techniques required a knowledge of the larger cultural context of the biblical world. In his own research Gunkel took into consideration the results of archaeological investigations and the literature of the ancient Near East. The *Religionsgeschichtliche Schule* (the history-of-religions school), with which Gunkel's name was associated, is perhaps even more important than form criticism. In applying the historical method of analysis to the study of religion, the discipline of *Religionsgeschichte* profited from advances in archaeology, anthropology, and ethnology.

As more and more evidence was unearthed through excavations, some biblical scholars became uneasy about the growing tendency to distort the relationship between archaeology and the Bible. In 1896 Francis Brown, president of the Society of Biblical Literature, delivered an early and stern admonition to those who would misuse archaeology to confirm the biblical record:

> But one of the crudest mistakes in using Archaeology as a conservative ally is made when it is employed to win a battle in literary criticism. It is not equipped for that kind of fighting. It has its proper place in the determination of historical facts, but a very subordinate place, or none at all, in the determination of literary facts. To attempt to prove by Archaeology that Moses wrote the Pentateuch, is simply grotesque. The question is not

[11]H. M. Du Bose, ed., *The Aftermath Series*, no. 6, Nashville, 1924, pp. 270-71.

whether Moses could write, it is whether he did write certain books which there is strong internal and historical ground for holding he did not write; and on this point Archaeology has nothing to say, nor is it likely that she will have anything to say. We only discredit a most useful, often surprisingly useful, handmaid of truth, when we set her at a task for which she is in no way prepared.[12]

American Biblical Scholars

To be sure, German scholars were the leaders in biblical interpretation during the nineteenth century. As the twentieth century approached, Americans, members of the Society of Biblical Literature and later of ASOR, also began to make substantial contributions to the field. The International Critical Commentary, a series of commentaries with a critical and philological emphasis, began to appear in 1895; it was intended to provide English readers with an interpretation of the biblical books similar to the German commentaries of that day. Among the American contributors to this series were George A. Barton, Lewis B. Paton, Charles C. Torrey, James A. Montgomery, and George F. Moore.

American scholars also helped to produce *A Hebrew and English Lexicon of the Old Testament*. Francis Brown, Samuel R. Driver, and Charles A. Briggs edited this indispensable reference. Completed in 1906, it is still in use today. Besides serving as president of the Society of Biblical Literature, Francis Brown was one of the early directors of ASOR's Jerusalem School. Charles Briggs held the Edward Robinson Chair of Biblical Theology at Union Seminary, New York, and was also a leader in the field of higher criticism in America. Conservative in everything except biblical criticism, his publications on this subject unfortunately made him suspect; they led to a heresy trial by the Presbytery of New York in 1892. The result was his suspension from the ministry.

William Rainey Harper, president of the University of Chicago from 1892 to 1906 and one of the leading scholars at the end of the nineteenth century, signaled a new era in biblical studies by his inductive method of teaching Hebrew. This method stimulated large numbers of students to master the language. Archaeology was also one of his interests; he edited a magazine, *The Biblical World*, which contained a special section entitled "Exploration and Discovery."

As president of the University of Chicago, one of Harper's outstanding faculty appointments was James H. Breasted. In 1919 this distinguished Egyptologist, with the assistance of John D. Rockefeller, Jr., established at the University the Oriental Institute, which has always enjoyed a close institutional relationship with ASOR.

------

[12]"Old Testament Problems," *JBL* 15 (1896) 67.

In its Proceedings for 1906 the Society of Biblical Literature epitomized Harper's scholarly contribution in this Memorial Minute, "To President Harper, more than to any one man, is due the revived interest in Semitic and Old Testament studies which this country witnessed in the latter part of the nineteenth century."

The Scientific Method of Excavation

In the years from 1890 to 1914, just before World War I, there was such a phenomenal growth in biblical scholarship that the period has been rightly called "the golden age of Old Testament study." Americans contributed their share to this development, but their more permanent influence seems to have been felt in archaeology.

The few excavations conducted in the nineteenth century were not very productive because field techniques were still undeveloped. Unsystematic digs were little more than treasure hunts.[13] The evolution in excavation method that took place at the beginning of the present century brought about a steady improvement in archaeology as a discipline.

The first scientific excavation conducted in Palestine began in 1890 at Tell el Hesi. Even in this case, however, the adjective "scientific" has to be understood in a relative sense. Tell el Hesi is located in the foothills of the Judean mountains, roughly midway between the Philistine city of Ashdod and Beer-sheba, the modern capital of the Negev. Its excavator was W. M. Flinders Petrie, the founder of Palestinian archaeology.

Flinders Petrie

Self-taught for the most part and with little formal training in the archaeology of the Near East, Petrie at the age of twenty-seven left England for Egypt; there he launched an extraordinary career as an Egyptologist. He began his archaeological work in 1880 at Giza, where he made the first accurate measurement of the Great Pyramid; he continued to excavate in Egypt until 1926. In addition, he was the founder and director of the British School of Archaeology in Egypt. Petrie's name is associated with some of the major Egyptian sites, such as Tell el Amarna, where he excavated the ruins of Akhetaton, the royal city of Pharaoh Amenophis IV (Ikhnaton) (1377-1358 B.C.).

[13]The first excavation in Palestine dates from 1863, when Félicien de Saulcy, a French explorer, dug the so-called Royal Tombs in northern Jerusalem. The lack of excavation technique resulted in a dating error of a thousand years. He erroneously associated the tombs with the Davidic dynasty, when they properly date to the first century A.D. They have been correctly identified as the tombs of Helena, queen mother of Adiabene, a petty kingdom, vassal to the Parthian Empire in northern Mesopotamia. A convert to Judaism, Helena and her sons were buried in the Tombs of the Kings at Jerusalem about A.D. 50.

Sir Flinders Petrie and Lady Petrie in Jerusalem in 1938.
(Photo by C. C. Steinbeck.)

In 1890, after excavating in Egypt for ten years, Petrie came to Palestine under the auspices of the Palestine Exploration Fund. His purpose was to locate the site of ancient Lachish, an important biblical city in southern Judah. While searching for the remains of Lachish, he came upon Tell el Hesi, which impressed him because of the height of the tell and the pre-Greek style of its pottery. Petrie decided to dig it, despite the fact that he had only six weeks to spend in the undertaking. His efforts were also hampered by the fact that the top of the mound was under cultivation, as it is today. He was content to excavate the sides of the tell and to run tunnels through it in order to trace the walls of the ancient cities that lay within.

Petrie's pioneer dig at Tell el Hesi is a landmark in the history of Palestinian archaeology, not only because he understood the formation of a tell but also because he was able to date its ruins. Having grasped the value of pottery for dating an archaeological site during his excavations in Egypt, Petrie applied the principles of sequence-dating at Hesi and thereby established a rough ceramic chronology for Palestine.[14] He

---

[14]Simple potsherds are excellent indicators of the chronology of an ancient site, if the excavator is schooled in the development of pottery forms and carefully notes the precise level where each fragment of pottery is found. Sequence-dating is established by the

also laid the foundations for *stratigraphy* (the careful separation of occupational layers in a tell) and *typology* (the classification and comparative study of objects), the two most important principles of excavation technique. Because Petrie had correlated the soil layers and the pottery forms so well in his development of Tell el Hesi's chronology, he rightly deserved the tribute of another distinguished Palestinian archaeologist of our time, William F. Albright, "There can be no doubt that he [Petrie] was the greatest archaeological genius of modern times." It was Albright who later brought greater precision to Petrie's chronology in the process of establishing the "ceramic index," as it is called, for Palestine. Petrie's concerns on a dig went far beyond pottery. He insisted that everything had its own importance and therefore was to be recorded; likewise all artifacts were to be drawn.

Identifying an ancient site is always a haphazard undertaking. Petrie was less successful in this aspect of Tell el Hesi than he was in determining its chronology. When he left Tell el Hesi, he was satisfied that he had excavated the ruins of Lachish, and his successor at Hesi, Frederick J. Bliss, accepted Petrie's identification of the site; it turned out to be erroneous. Petrie had been influenced by Claude Conder's hypothesis that Hesi was ancient Lachish. To Petrie the presence of a water supply in the Wadi Hesi and the several occupation layers and artifacts unearthed on the tell itself seemed consistent with the history of Lachish.

Petrie published *Tell el Hesi (Lachish)* in 1891, only a year after he finished the excavation.[15] Kathleen Kenyon, noted British archaeologist, observed about Petrie, "No archaeologist has ever had such an impeccable record of rapid publication." His prompt attention to the publication of reports is evidence of the orderliness and dedication that characterized every facet of his life.

Tell el Hesi was not the only site Petrie excavated in Palestine. Toward the end of his career as a field archaeologist in the 1920s and 1930s, he moved back from Egypt to Palestine. He hoped to fill in some of the gaps in Egyptian history, and tells in the Negev seemed promising. The three he chose were all located along the Wadi Ghazzeh in the northwestern Negev: Tell Jemmeh, Tell el Farah (Tell Sharuhen), and Tell el Ajjul. These mounds have repeatedly attracted the attention of archaeologists, who have been eager to dig them in an attempt to

---

excavator's observing pottery changes in style and form as he or she moves through the strata of a tell and then places the pottery forms in chronological order. In Petrie's words, "And once settle the pottery of a country, and the key is in our hands for all future explorations."

[15]Archaeologists would understand the implication of this comment. As a group they are very dilatory in publishing the results of their field projects. Some final reports have remained unpublished for as long as thirty years after the completion of the excvation; other reports have never appeared in print.

establish their ancient identity. While directing excavations at these sites, Petrie also functioned as the field instructor of several younger British aspirants, who became distinguished archaeologists: James L. Starkey, Olga Tufnell, and G. Lankester Harding.

In his last years, Petrie had a close relationship with ASOR's School in Jerusalem, residing there from 1935 until his death in 1942. He also made the American School in Jerusalem the temporary headquarters (in exile) of the British School of Archaeology in Egypt. Nelson Glueck, the distinguished American archaeologist who directed the School in Jerusalem when Petrie was living there in retirement, evaluated Petrie's contribution to archaeology in these words:

> In many ways he [Petrie] was a giant in our own day, but particularly was he a giant of yesterday. His fame will live long after him. All of us who are engaged in archaeological pursuits stand on the shoulders of men like him, who pointed the way which we follow today.[16]

Frederick Bliss

An American archaeologist, Frederick J. Bliss, succeeded Petrie as excavator at Tell el Hesi, working there for two years under the auspices of the Palestine Exploration Fund. Born near Beirut, Bliss spent his childhood in Lebanon. There he learned Arabic, a skill that served him well as an archaeologist directing local, Arabic-speaking laborers. Bliss's father, Daniel J. Bliss, a Presbyterian missionary, had in 1866 founded the Syrian Protestant College in Beirut and was its first president.[17] Thanks to the Bliss family, a cordial relationship was maintained between the college and ASOR, with several of the early directors of ASOR's Jerusalem School spending the summer months as guests of faculty members.

Frederick Bliss's copious correspondence has provided helpful insights into both his field projects and his personality. Plagued with poor health, he found the inevitable annoyances of life on a dig hard to bear. When he reached the end of one of his dig seasons at Tell el Hesi, he wrote home, "Free for a while from all the care and worry and responsibility, dirt, dust of ages, fleas, squabbles." On another occasion, frustrated by the lack of discovery at Tell el Hesi, he referred to the site as a "fraud"; again, blinded by Hesi dust, he called the archaeologist's profession "a silly life."

---

[16]*BASOR* 87 (1942) 6.

[17]In his inaugural address President Bliss stated, "This college is for all conditions and classes of men without regard to color, nationality, race or religion." A modern center of higher education, the Syrian Protestant College was rechartered in 1920 as the American University of Beirut, a nondenominational, private, coeducational school.

Frederick J. Bliss. (Courtesy of the Palestine Exploration Fund.)

In preparation for excavating Tell el Hesi, Bliss traveled to Egypt to be Petrie's understudy at Maydum, the ancient Egyptian site near Memphis, originally a seven-stepped pyramid dating from about 2686 B.C. As Petrie's first student, Bliss learned, among other valuable skills, how to survey and photograph on a dig. During his apprenticeship he discovered from the Spartan fare that Petrie conducted his excavations very economically. On one occasion Bliss commented, "Petrie handles his workers like a good despot."

Arriving at Tell el Hesi in 1891, Bliss decided to concentrate on the northeast quarter of the acropolis, where he made a wedge-shaped cut through the mound and then dug the tell layer by layer. This cut, "Bliss's cut," distinguished Tell el Hesi from the adjacent tells in the region; it stood out even from a great distance as Hesi's trademark until the present ASOR excavators began to dismantle the tell in 1970, eighty years after Petrie's first foray there.

Bliss published the results of his four-season excavation in a book entitled *A Mound of Many Cities* (1894). It is an accurate description of Hesi's occupation layers, dating from the Early Bronze Age to the Roman period. If Petrie was a pottery expert, Bliss excelled as a stratigrapher. However, Albright lamented that Bliss had failed to correlate Petrie's pottery sequence with his own stratigraphic results. The identification of Hesi with Lachish seemed to be confirmed during the 1892 season, when Bliss unearthed a Tell el Amarna tablet. This first cuneiform tablet ever found in Palestine contained a reference to Lachish.[18]

At the completion of the Hesi dig, Bliss continued to excavate in Palestine under the auspices of the Palestine Exploration Fund. From 1894 to 1897 he and Archibald C. Dickie, a British architect, concentrated their efforts on Jerusalem, continuing the work Warren had undertaken from 1867 to 1870. In 1898 Bliss and Irish archaeologist R. A. S. Macalister joined forces for a two-year period, to work in the Philistine country of the Shephelah. There they excavated several sites in their search for Gath, the Philistine city mentioned several times in the Bible. Of the four sites they dug—Tell es Safi, Tell Zakariyeh, Tell el Judeideh, and Tell Sandahanna—the most likely candidate for Gath (as Bliss maintained at the beginning of the century) is Tell es Safi, located about

---

[18]In 1924 Albright questioned the identification of Tell el Hesi with Lachish because the history of Lachish implies that such an important city must have been much larger than Tell el Hesi. Albright went on to propose that Hesi was biblical Eglon, a Canaanite city defeated by Joshua and included among the cities of Judah. Then, in 1929, Albright suggested Tell ed Duweir as the site of Lachish. Tell ed Duweir, four times larger than Tell el Hesi, is situated near the border of the Shephelah of Judah. So far as Hesi is concerned, G. Ernest Wright, a leading American archaeologist of his generation, conjectured that this site formed part of the fortification system of the city-state of Lachish in the Late Bronze Age. Archaeologists hope that the American team presently excavating at Tell el Hesi will clarify some of the problems raised by Petrie and Bliss and may be able to establish beyond doubt the identity of the site.

twelve miles east of Ashdod. A minority opinion, following Albright, favored Tell Sheikh Ahmed el Areini as the location of Gath, but that conjecture has been disproved by subsequent excavation of this site.[19] The work of Bliss and Macalister at these four tells of the Shephelah was significant in the history of Palestinian archaeology. At Tell Judeideh they conducted one of the first stratigraphic excavations in Palestine, distinguishing three main periods: Pre-Israelite (Canaanite), Jewish (Israelite II), and Hellenistic-Roman. During these campaigns Bliss and Macalister established the chronology of Judahite pottery (today's Iron II pottery), which served later as a peg for further pottery chronology.

R. A. S. Macalister

Having gained considerable experience by excavating with Bliss, from 1902 to 1909 Macalister directed the first dig at ancient Gezer on behalf of the Palestine Exploration Fund. Working with the assistance of only one Egyptian foreman, he was his own recorder, architect, and administrator. Instead of digging the mound stratigraphically (layer by layer), he excavated Gezer by running trenches forty feet wide across the mound, a technique known as the *trenching system.* Unfortunately, this method was so unrefined that it did not allow a close inspection of a tell's stratigraphy; nor was it possible for any archaeologist to control the work when excavation was done in this way. In addition, Macalister neglected to photograph the various phases of his project, and his recording system was deficient.

Nonetheless, as early as 1912, only three years after he left the field, Macalister published a trilogy entitled *The Excavation of Gezer,* which has been of service to the American team that began digging the site anew in 1964. Judged by the standards of his time, Macalister was a competent archaeologist. While he made some errors in chronology at Gezer, he also made accurate interpretations; for example, he correctly associated the tower of ashlar masonry with the Solomonic period.

Ecole Biblique et Archéologique Française

In 1890 Marie-Joseph Lagrange, a French Dominican priest, established the Ecole Biblique et Archéologique Française in Jerusalem. Like the Palestine Exploration Fund, the Ecole Biblique helped to pave the way for the establishment of ASOR in Jerusalem, by encouraging

---

[19]Problems in identifying ancient sites can be resolved only by excavation and examination of the written sources. Tell Zakariyeh has been identified with the fortress city of Azekah, and Tell el Judeideh with Moresheth-gath, the birthplace of the prophet Micah. Tell Sandahanna is thought to be the biblical and Hellenistic city of Mareshah (Marisa). Sandahanna, the Arabic designation for the site, is a corruption of Saint Anna, the name of the twelfth-century Crusader church in the area.

American involvement in biblical and archaeological studies in the land where they can best be done. ASOR has always enjoyed a warm relationship with the Ecole Biblique, and in their annual reports the directors of the Jerusalem School have consistently paid tribute to the Dominican scholars who have generously shared their library resources and other research facilities. Today the Ecole Biblique library contains 80,000 volumes, with a concentration on biblical studies.

Marie-Joseph Lagrange

As well as being the founder of the Ecole Biblique, Lagrange was an outstanding Roman Catholic biblical scholar. His own approach to the challenges of higher criticism was positive at the very time the Roman church was showing its sense of threat in the antimodernist pronouncements of Pope Pius X in 1907. Despite official criticism of his own writings on the subject, *Historical Criticism and the Old Testament*, Lagrange inaugurated a tradition of high-level scholarship, which has characterized the research of several generations of Dominicans at the Ecole Biblique. The fact that a Roman decree condemned many of Lagrange's writings is one of several indications of Rome's handling of the modernist controversy.

In 1892 Lagrange founded a journal dealing with the Bible and archaeology, the *Revue biblique*. Then came a series of scholarly commentaries on the Bible, the *Etudes bibliques*, to which he contributed several volumes on the controversial issue of the historical-critical method as applied to the Old Testament. During his long tenure as professor in Jerusalem, Lagrange not only wrote voluminously but also trained two generations of biblical specialists, who maintained the scholarly standards he had set. One thinks immediately of Vincent, Abel, Barrois, Couroyer, de Vaux, Savignac, Dhorme, and Benoit, to name a few members of the Ecole Biblique. There is no doubt that Pope Pius XII's 1943 encyclical, *Divino afflante spiritu*—the Magna Carta of modern Roman Catholic biblical studies—traces its roots to the pioneer research of Lagrange.

The German Institutes

Just about the time ASOR was being established in Jerusalem, two German institutes came into being, based on the model of the Palestine Exploration Fund. The Deutsche Orient-Gesellschaft (German Oriental Society), founded in 1898, undertook the investigation of the Capernaum synagogue, as well as of other synagogues in Galilee. Later, in 1907-1909, this society excavated Tell es Sultan, the site of ancient Jericho, in the Jordan Valley. In 1902 the German Evangelical Church's Institut für Altertumswissenschaft des Heiligen Landes was established in Jerusalem. Gustaf H. Dalman was the first director of the institute; Albrecht Alt succeeded him. Both were leading biblical scholars and distinguished historical geographers.

The Lineage of ASOR

Several organizations working in the Mideast during the nineteenth century exerted influence that led to the establishment of ASOR; three in particular were directly involved: the American Oriental Society, the Archaeological Institute of America, and the Society of Biblical Literature. Similarly, many scholars were instrumental in ASOR's founding, but one stands above all others: J. Henry Thayer, professor of New Testament at Harvard University and president of the Society of Biblical Literature.

The twenty-ninth meeting of the Society took place at the Hartford Theological Seminary on June 13, 1895; on that occasion Thayer delivered the presidential address entitled "The Historical Element in the New Testament." In the course of his remarks he advocated that the Society take practical steps to establish an "American School of Oriental Studies in Palestine":

> But I am impatient to reach a suggestion which I will frankly confess has with me for the moment vastly more interest and attraction than any other: Is it not high time that an *American School for Oriental Study and Research* should be established in Palestine? This is no new idea. Others besides myself, no doubt, have been cherishing it as a secret hope for years. . . . Indeed, so alluring are enterprises of this sort at present, so great their promise of usefulness alike to Biblical learning and missionary work, that—as you are aware—a French Catholic School of Biblical Studies has established itself already in Jerusalem, whose quarterly "Revue Biblique," printed in Paris, is in its fifth year and deserves the respectful attention of scholars. . . . Shall the countrymen of Robinson and Thomson, Lynch and Merrill, Eli Smith and Van Dyck, look on unconcerned? Shall a Society, organized for the express purpose of stimulating and diffusing a scholarly knowledge of the Sacred Word, remain seated with folded hands, taking no part or lot in the matter?[20]

In an article entitled "The Proposed School of Biblical Archaeology and Philology in the East," which appeared in the *Presbyterian Review* (January 1887), Henry W. Hulbert, who later became a professor at Lane Theological Seminary, had pressed for the establishment of an institute in Beirut. Discussing a suitable location for such a school, he dismissed Jerusalem with this observation, "Jerusalem seems to be the sentimental

---

[20]*JBL* 14 (1895) 16. William M. Thomson, an American missionary, lived in Palestine for almost fifty years. During Robinson's 1852 journey to the Holy Land, Thomson, replacing Smith, accompanied Robinson on the latter part of the trip. Henry L. Van Dyck served as interpreter, companion, and assistant to Selah Merrill in his exploration of Transjordan.

centre, but is altogether out of the question when the matter of comfort, expense, or health is discussed." He ruled out Cairo and Damascus just as peremptorily. In opting for Beirut, he commented:

> Beirut is the only spot in the East which gives encouragement to such an enterprise. Already it is the educational and literary centre of Syria. Its situation is one of great beauty, and the climate is charming from November to June.

Thayer's forceful recommendation to establish an American School in Palestine was referred to a special committee, which had the responsibility of making it a reality. Composed of Thayer, Theodore F. Wright, Hinckley G. Mitchell, William H. Ward, and John P. Peters, the committee consulted several leading scholars and distributed a circular to theological schools and other academic institutions, with the hope of stimulating interest and support. The circular stated:

> The object of the school would be to afford graduates of American theological seminaries, and other similarly qualified persons, opportunity to prosecute Biblical and linguistic investigations under more favorable conditions than can be secured at a distance from the Holy Land; . . . to gather material for the illustration of the Biblical narratives; to settle doubtful points in Biblical topography; to identify historic localities; to explore and, if possible, excavate sacred sites.

The strong biblical orientation of this original proposal contrasted with the statement of purpose later adopted, which broadened the goals of the School to include research in areas of scholarship besides the biblical. Even so, eleven institutions and individuals responded to the solicitation by pledging one hunded dollars annually for five years. The American Oriental Society and the Archaeological Institute of America also lent their support to the proposal. Nonetheless, it took five years to raise the necessary funds for implementing the plan for a School.

CHAPTER II
BEGINNINGS: 1900-1918

The proposed American School for Oriental Study and Research in Palestine became a reality in 1900, five years after J. Henry Thayer had urged the members of the Society of Biblical Literature to take the necessary steps to establish such an institute. Thayer's committee had succeeded in interesting twenty-one universities, colleges, and theological schools in forming the core of this new organization and had raised sufficient funds to support it. The charter members of the corporation included: Andover Theological Seminary, Auburn Theological Seminary, Boston University, Brown University, Bryn Mawr College, Colgate University, Columbia University, Cornell University, Episcopal Theological School (Cambridge), Episcopal Divinity School (Philadelphia), General Theological Seminary (New York City), Harvard University, Hebrew Union College (Cincinnati), Johns Hopkins University, New York University, University of Pennsylvania, Princeton University, Princeton Theological Seminary, Trinity College (Hartford), Union Theological Seminary (New York), and Yale University. Despite the pronounced biblical component in the establishment of ASOR, the majority of incorporating schools were universities, not seminaries, just as the major excavations in the first part of the present century were sponsored by universities, not seminaries.

The organizing committee's resolutions eventually became the constitution of ASOR and provided the new organization with a broader base than envisioned in the original statement of purpose with its biblical emphasis. The resolutions also anticipated by generations the inclusive emphasis of modern times regarding race, religion, and sex. The statements follow:

(1) The main object of said School shall be to enable properly qualified persons to prosecute Biblical, linguistic, archaeological, historical, and other kindred studies and researches under more favorable conditions than can be secured at a distance from the Holy Land.

(2) The School shall be open to duly qualified applicants of all races and both sexes, and shall be kept wholly free from obligations or preferences as respects any religious denomination or literary institution.

Even before the actual establishment of ASOR, its three parent organizations—the Society of Biblical Literature (SBL), the American Oriental Society (AOS), and the Archaeological Institute of America

(AIA)—pledged their cooperation. In 1895 the SBL supported the resolution to found the School; in 1896 the AOS formally endorsed this enterprise; in 1898 the AIA guaranteed an annual subsidy to the School. The historical connection with these three associations has been legally perpetuated in the ASOR charter, which provides that each of these organizations be represented on the board of trustees by one of its own members. This regulation is in force until the present day.

From its inception, ASOR has worked closely with all three of its parent organizations, but especially with the SBL and the AIA. The following resolution governing the procedure for publishing the articles of ASOR appointees reflects the relationship:

> [Articles produced under the auspices of ASOR] may be published either in the *Journal* of the Society of Biblical Literature and Exegesis or in the *Journal* of the Archaeological Institute of America, the *Journal* of the Institute having a prior claim on such material produced by the School or as the result of its explorations as is of a distinctly archaeological and non-Biblical character.

Other resolutions for the conduct of ASOR were modeled after those of the Schools of Classical Studies in Athens and in Rome, both offshoots of the Archaeological Institute of America.

Sadly, J. Henry Thayer, the scholar chiefly responsible for the existence of the American School in Palestine, died in 1901, only one year after this dream had been fulfilled. According to J. Henry Cadbury, New Testament professor at Harvard, "At the time of his death he [Thayer] was recognized as the dean of New Testament scholars in America."

Although it was a New Testament scholar who created ASOR, ironically Old Testament specialists have always been more involved in ASOR programs than their New Testament colleagues. In the estimation of some New Testament scholars, New Testament archaeology has gotten lost between Old Testament or Syro-Palestinian archaeology on the one side and Christian archaeology on the other. Only recently have interested New Testament scholars begun to take steps toward the development of New Testament archaeology as a discipline in its own right.

Charles Torrey

Charles C. Torrey traveled to Jerusalem in the summer of 1900 to establish ASOR's first overseas institute, where he served as director for that academic year. A member of the Yale faculty for thirty-two years, Torrey was known as an original scholar whose independent views were often controversial. For example, Torrey argued that the Four Gospels were Greek translations of primitive Aramaic writings. This stimulating scholar was one of the leaders in American biblical studies.

A skilled linguist with a command of Arabic, Syriac, and Aramaic, as well as other modern and ancient languages, Torrey specialized in the era of the Babylonian exile (587 B.C.) and the postexilic period (from 538 B.C.) of the Old Testament. He proposed that the Book of Ezekiel was a pseudepigraphon written in 230 B.C. without any real historical roots. Needless to say, this view and related opinions about the dating of books and their historical value did not go unchallenged. Additionally, Torrey distinguished himself as an epigraphist in deciphering ancient inscriptions and as a numismatist in the study of coins.

Throughout his long, scholarly career, Torrey also was actively involved with ASOR, serving at various times as a trustee and also a vice-president. In recognition of his distinguished contributions to ASOR, the organization dedicated the *Bulletin of the American Schools of Oriental Research (BASOR)* 132 (1953) to Torrey on the occasion of his ninetieth birthday.

En route to Jerusalem in September 1900, Torrey stopped in Constantinople (now Istanbul) in an attempt to secure from the intransigent Ottoman Turkish government, which had jurisdiction over Palestine, the *firman* or permit required to establish an institute in Jerusalem. Impeded by the inevitable Byzantine red tape, he was unable to obtain the *firman*. So he proceeded to Jerusalem with the assurance that the United States legation in Constantinople would assist in acquiring the permit.

ASOR's first headquarters in Jerusalem were unpretentious, consisting simply of one large room in the Grand New Hotel (today the New Imperial Hotel), located near the Jaffa Gate. From the outset Torrey recognized that ASOR would need a permanent center and a long-term director, in order to compete on a scientific basis with other national overseas institutes.

In an effort to make the new headquarters a kind of research institute, Torrey began to build a library, a project continued by subsequent directors. ASOR scholars in Jerusalem also had access to the neighboring libraries of the Greek Patriarchate, the Ecole Biblique, the Franciscans, the French Hospice, and the Latin Patriarchate, since the various institutes in Jerusalem made it a practice to share their research facilities. From the beginning, ASOR enjoyed this kind of cordiality in Jerusalem; as time passed, the organization was in a better position to reciprocate. This common sharing had the effect of drawing the national scholarly centers close together.

In January 1901, a few months after his arrival in Jerusalem, Torrey received word from the Turkish government in Constantinople that the requisite permit for establishing an academic institute in Jerusalem would not be issued. Its refusal did not prove to be a serious obstacle, however. Several similar educational centers in the Ottoman Empire were able to carry on without offical approval; much of the labyrinthine bureaucracy often went unheeded.

A 1979 photograph of the south facade of the Imperial Hotel inside the Jaffa Gate; in the early days of ASOR in Jerusalem it was the Grand New Hotel and served as the residence of the Jerusalem School from 1900 to 1906. (Courtesy of Nitza Rosovsky and Lois Glock.)

Selah Merrill, the United States consul in Jerusalem, proved to be a good friend to Torrey during his early days in new surroundings. He helped Torrey to settle and to inaugurate the School program. He was also of service to the early directors of the School by lecturing on coins and pottery, drawing from his experiences as explorer for the American Palestine Exploration Society.

During his year as ASOR's first director, Torrey launched the School's archaeological program by excavating a series of Phoenician rock-tombs at Sidon, the ancient capital of the Phoenicians on the Mediterranean seacoast. A detailed, illustrated report of this field project appeared as the initial article in volume one of *The Annual of the American School of Oriental Research in Jerusalem* (1920), ASOR's first publication of research papers in its own name. In studying the materials from his pioneer excavation of the Phoenician necropolis at Sidon, Torrey had the opportunity to exercise his skills in epigraphy and numismatics. He came to the conclusion that the history of the tombs' use covered a long period, perhaps from the fifth century B.C. to the third century A.D.

The Managing Committee

During the first two decades of ASOR's history, a managing committee, led by a chairman, directed the activities of the organization. When J. Henry Thayer, the first chairman, died, George Foot Moore succeeded him in office from 1902 to 1905. The greatest intellectual among the ASOR founders, Moore was one of the eminent biblical scholars in America, on a par with Edward Robinson. Theologian, orientalist, and historian, Moore was ordained to the Presbyterian ministry in 1878. In 1902 he became professor of the history of religion at Harvard where he remained until his retirement in 1928. Before his Harvard appointment he had taught at the Andover Theological Seminary. Moore is still well known for his *Critical and Exegetical Commentary on Judges* in the International Critical Commentary series. His greatest work, however, was the three-volume *Judaism in the First Centuries of the Christian Era: the Age of the Tannaim*. His *Judaism*, based on an extraordinary knowledge of the Rabbinic sources, made him unique among Christian scholars. Moore's writings had a remarkable impact on the study of Rabbinic Judaism especially among non-Jewish scholars. In addition to his executive position in ASOR, Moore served as president of the American Oriental Society and the Society of Biblical Literature.

Three other chairmen of the managing committee followed Moore before ASOR's administration was restructured: J. Dyneley Prince of Columbia University (1905-1906), Charles C. Torrey (1907-1918), and James A. Montgomery of the University of Pennsylvania (1918-1921). When ASOR incorporated in 1921, the governing structure changed; the chief executive officer was no longer the chairman, but the president.

Keenly aware of the importance of sponsoring an excavation, the managing committee looked for a promising site. Because of its important history, Samaria, a royal city and the capital of the Northern Kingdom of Israel, was chosen as the best possibility. James B. Nies, an ordained minister of the Protestant Episcopal Church with a doctorate from Columbia coupled with a profound interest in Palestine, undertook to raise the $50,000 required to execute the Samaria project near the modern town of Sebastiyeh.

Along with raising funds for a dig and expanding the library of the School in Jerusalem, the managing committee labored to make fellowships available for qualified candidates. The Archaeological Institute of America awarded the first such grant, for $500, to Martin A. Meyer of Hebrew Union College, Cincinnati, for the academic year 1901-1902.

Political History of the Mideast

The Mideast map changes with every war, and in ASOR's history there have been five wars. Each time ASOR has had to adjust to relined borders and contend with annoying international regulations in order to secure access to the whole region. So far as ASOR's scientific work is concerned, the modern configuration of the Mideast is irrelevant, but it is the political reality and therefore must be dealt with.

In the early days of ASOR it was easy for Americans to move around the whole Mideast, not having to negotiate one border after another as is the case today. For four centuries (from 1517 to 1917) the Ottoman Turks controlled Syria and Palestine. This situation prevailed through World War I; then the British and the French divided up the territory.

By the time ASOR was established in Jerusalem at the beginning of the century, the emergence of Arab nationalism forecast the imminent collapse of the Ottoman Empire. In addition to the Arab longing for independence, Jews immigrating to Palestine from Russia and eastern Europe had hopes of creating a national home (which the Balfour Declaration of November 1917 made a reality). These and other international factors led to the disintegration of Ottoman rule at the end of World War I.

Annual Directors before World War I

From the turn of the century to the beginning of World War I, annual directors oversaw the activities of the School in Jerusalem. The fact that almost all of the directors were new to Palestine hindered the development of the program. They were unfamiliar with the land and the customs of the local people and unable to speak Arabic and Hebrew. The directors made an effort to acquire a knowledge of the spoken languages through the services of tutors and to become part of the society in which they found themselves. They spent most of each year, however, visiting sites, especially those that had been prominent in biblical history, and that activity left them little time for other undertakings. The lack of permanent headquarters for the School also hindered ASOR's progress in those early years. Each newly arrived director quickly became aware of the built-in limitations and lamented them in his official report to the managing committee. The annual reports during these years greatly resemble one another; each year the director and residents adhered to the same program. Nonetheless, the pioneer directors of the School made a contribution to the life of ASOR by helping to shape the future of the organization. Each of these early directors deserves credit for having been willing to endure hardships so that ASOR could become the influential organization it is today.

Hinckley Mitchell

Hinckley G. Mitchell, professor of Akkadian (Babylonian and Assyrian), Hebrew, and Old Testament interpretation at Boston University, became ASOR's director in Jerusalem in 1901. Despite its inadequacy, the Grand New Hotel continued to serve as headquarters for the School during this second year. In this period R. A. S. Macalister made regular use of the School library, and his constant presence helped to forge a bond between ASOR and the Palestine Exploration Fund, under whose auspices Macalister excavated.

Mitchell chose as his scholarly project a detailed study of the modern wall of Jerusalem; he published his research in *Annual* 1, with seventy-one accompanying photographs. He also conducted an extensive field trip into Transjordan, including visits to Mount Nebo, Madeba, Hesban, Amman, Jerash, and es Salt. In the vicinity of Jerusalem, on the Mount of Olives, he made a search for the remains of olive presses. He also investigated caves and tombs in the village of Silwan.

George Barton

The resident director of the School during the third academic year (1902-1903) was George A. Barton, professor at Bryn Mawr College and the University of Pennsylvania. A versatile scholar, he made an extraordinary contribution to ASOR as director of the Jerusalem School, as the first director of the Baghdad School which was established in 1921, and as secretary-treasurer of ASOR from 1918 to 1934. Towards the end of his life he made a magnificent bequest to ASOR, which continues to support resident scholars in Jerusalem, as his will specified. His commentaries, the *Book of Ecclesiastes* (1908) in the International Critical Commentary and the *Book of Job* (1911) in the Bible for Home and School, demonstrate his ability as a biblical interpreter. His popular volume, *Archaeology and the Bible*, which went through seven editions between 1916 and 1937, is eloquent testimony to his grasp of archaeology and ancient history as they relate to biblical studies.

When Barton reached Jerusalem in October of 1902, the Grand New Hotel continued to serve as the School's headquarters, although it had been expanded to accommodate the growing number of students. That year the School undertook several ambitious field trips, including visits to Transjordan and Egypt and to the following active excavations: Gezer (directed by Macalister), Megiddo (directed by Schumacher), and Taanach (directed by Sellin). During his tenure as director, Barton laid the foundations for the School's archaeological-ethnological museum by cataloguing and labeling potsherds and other artifacts donated by friends.

Lewis Paton

In 1903 another prominent Old Testament scholar and splendid teacher succeeded Barton as director in Jerusalem, Lewis B. Paton. A member of the faculty of Hartford Theological Seminary, Paton produced several useful books, including *The Early History of Syria and Palestine* (1902), *Jerusalem in Bible Times* (1908), the *Book of Esther* (1908) in the International Critical Commentary, and a key article, "Israel's Conquest of Canaan," in the *Journal of Biblical Literature* 32 (1913).

Paton and his family took up residence at the Grand New Hotel. Several students from the United States had planned to spend that year at the School, but they were deterred by reports of cholera as well as by unsettled political conditions. One of Paton's major projects was the study of the topography of ancient Jerusalem; he also found time to lead several field trips. On one such trip to Transjordan, a tragic accident occurred. He described it in these words:

> We had gone as far as Amman, and were just starting on the road to Jerash. It was a cool, cloudy morning, and we were riding slowly over a level, grassy spot, when suddenly, without any warning, and without uttering a cry, Mrs. Paton fell from her horse. Her head struck on a sharp stone, and she never regained consciousness. We were able to move her to the Amman station on the new pilgrimage railway from Damascus to Mecca, and to take her in a train to Damascus. She died on the train within two hours of Damascus, and I was obliged to bury her body in Damascus. She was the constant companion of my study and of my travels, and whatever success may have attended the work of the School during the past winter is due to her enthusiasm and brave willingness to put up with the inconveniences of life in Palestine.[1]

Nathaniel Schmidt

The director for the year 1904 was Nathaniel Schmidt, a Swede who, as professor at Colgate and later at Cornell introduced the study of Assyriology into the curriculum of each school. He was a man of great erudition and uncommon ability. Millar Burrows, one of ASOR's presidents, recalled on the occasion of Schmidt's death in 1939 this anecdote: as an undergraduate at Cornell he (Burrows) was filled with awe when an older student told him, "Professor Schmidt is a very famous scholar; he has been Director of the American School in Jerusalem!"

Like his predecessors, Schmidt took up residence at the Grand New Hotel when he arrived in Jerusalem late in November. He spent the year supervising the research of his three graduate students, who were residing at the School. Before Schmidt's arrival in Jerusalem, the students had traveled extensively in northern Syria, where they had made squeezes of about 125 inscriptions, taken over 500 photographs, and corrected errors previously recorded on published maps.

In February 1905 Schmidt fulfilled a long-standing desire which he described in these words to the managing committee:

> But I had long cherished a desire to circumnavigate the salt lake of Syria [this is the oldest and most frequently used biblical term for the lake, which may be better known to westerners as the Dead Sea, a designation dating from the second century A.D.], in order to explore a part of the

---

[1]*American Journal of Archaeology* Supplement 8 (1904) 51.

A Jerusalem School trip to Jericho during the directorship of Nathaniel Schmidt (1904-1905).

eastern coast never visited in modern times, and to seek fresh light on some recently discussed questions concerning the white line [which he described elsewhere as "a belt of foam stretching across the entire lake almost due east and west, with a peculiar haze above it toward the west"], the currents, the bottom, and the beaches . . . and on the 21st of February we floated down the Jordan. Our boat, the *Dagmar*, was about 16 feet long, had four seats, a sail, a pair of oars, and a good keel. We had supplies, consisting of bread, canned meats and fish, potatoes, rice, oats, sugar, figs, oranges, nuts, tea, and Jordan water, sufficient for three weeks . . . . In order to be able to examine the coast and photograph its most characteristic features, we did not sail or row after dark, but camped every night on the shore, each keeping watch for two or three hours, while the others slept.[2]

Schmidt and his students manifested the same indomitable courage that William F. Lynch had shown in his exploration of the Dead Sea and Jordan River fifty-seven years earlier. In the period before World War I, no group affiliated with ASOR traveled and explored so extensively as Schmidt and his student companions.

[2]*American Journal of Archaeology* Supplement 9 (1905) 29-31.

Nathaniel Schmidt and two Cornell students, Albert Olmstead and Jesse Wrench, in the Dagmar *returning from the mouth of the Jordan River. According to Schmidt, "Our boat, the* Dagmar, *was about 16 feet long, had four seats, a sail, a pair of oars, and a good keel."*

In 1905 Schmidt was the first to identify tentatively Kadesh-barnea with the modern site of the desert oasis of Ain el Qudeirat. He thought it was a likely choice for the most important station along the route of the exodus, that place where the Israelites stayed for a generation. This identification is generally accepted today because of the site's sheltered position, supply of water, vegetation, and building remains, but questions still remain.

Benjamin Bacon

In 1905 Benjamin W. Bacon, who spent thirty-three years teaching at Yale University, assumed the directorship of the Jerusalem School. Bacon became one of the ranking New Testament scholars in this country, even though he began his scholarly career in the area of Old Testament. As Jerusalem director Bacon traveled widely on both sides of the Jordan River in an attempt to resolve long-standing disputes about the location of some of the sites mentioned in the New Testament.

In January 1906 Director Benjamin Bacon acquired new rented quarters for the School outside the walls of Jerusalem. The sign over the front door read "American Institute of Archaeology."

The 1979 version of the "American Institute of Archaeology"; the current address is 6 Ethiopia Street. The porch canopy and second floor are additions since the days of ASOR occupancy. (Courtesy of Nitza Rosovsky and Lois Glock.)

Bacon succeeded in securing new temporary quarters for the School, which he described as

> . . . close to the German Institute, opposite the British Consulate, and separated only by a large vacant lot from the new German hospital. . . . At present the library occupies a large, well-lighted room on the ground floor, leaving two large and two small sleeping-rooms, parlor, dining-room, and kitchen, besides cellars and outhouses. A suitable inscription over the front door designates it as the "American Institute of Archaeology."[3]

This house still stands at number six Ethiopia Street, hidden behind another house built at a later date. Bacon's rental of this property was a positive step but not the final answer to permanent quarters for the School. The managing committee was unable to purchase this rented house, because of the owner's failure to honor the original agreement. ASOR continued its efforts to secure sufficient funds for the purchase of property in Jerusalem, but despite generous gifts from the Archaeological Institute of America and the Harvard Semitic Museum, the drive was not a great success.

In his official report, Bacon urged the managing committee to purchase the pottery collection that Selah Merrill had been acquiring over a period of years. To persuade the committee, Bacon observed that "the very alphabet of the modern excavator is the study of pottery, and it is a science which can only be studied in object lessons." Bacon obviously had grasped the significance of Petrie's work at Tell el Hesi, where the latter laid the foundations for the ceramic index of Palestine.

David Lyon

Bacon turned over the administration of the Jerusalem School in 1906 to David G. Lyon, commonly referred to as "the father of American Assyriology." Lyon's Akkadian grammar, *An Assyrian Manual* (1886), was the first of its kind published in America. Completing his studies in ancient languages at the University of Leipzig, Lyon was appointed to Harvard in 1882 as the associate of Crawford H. Toy, professor in the Semitics department; Lyon later became the Hancock Professor of Hebrew and Other Oriental Languages. It was Lyon who conceived the idea of establishing the Harvard Semitic Museum and then served as its first curator from 1891 to 1922. Jacob H. Schiff of New York, a philanthropist and member of ASOR's managing committee, financed the Harvard Semitic Museum, which has maintained a close relationship with ASOR through its directors, curators, and graduate students in Near Eastern studies.

During Lyon's year as director of the School, six students were in residence, the largest number thus far. In view of the diversity of their

[3]*American Journal of Archaeology* Supplement 10 (1906) 33-34.

interests, the director did not attempt to present formal lectures but was available as a resource for the students. As well as visiting the traditional sites, Lyon and his companions made special trips to the excavations of the British and the Germans. Lyon's report expressed dismay at the plundering and destruction of sites taking place on both sides of the Jordan, despite strict antiquities laws to the contrary.

The Excavation of Samaria

While serving as director of the School in Jerusalem, Lyon obtained permission from the Turkish government for Harvard University to excavate ancient Samaria near the modern village of Sebastiyeh, which preserves the name Sebaste, the Herodian designation of the site.[4] ASOR appointees residing in Jerusalem during the course of this excavation took an intense interest in it because of the historical importance of Samaria and because it was the first dig conducted in Palestine under American auspices. Henceforth, Samaria was included in the itinerary of every School trip.

With the financial assistance of Jacob Schiff, the imposing ruins of Samaria, located on a hill 300 feet high, were dug initially in two phases; Gottlieb Schumacher excavated briefly in 1908; then George A. Reisner, Clarence S. Fisher, and David G. Lyon directed the more extensive dig in 1909-1910.

Reisner was an outstanding scholar who began his archaeological fieldwork in 1897 in Egypt, where he concentrated on the pyramids at Giza, excavating there until the outbreak of World War II. Reisner discovered the tomb of Queen Hetepheres, mother of King Khufu (Cheops), builder of the Great Pyramid at Giza. Although he spent most of his life in the field, he also found the time to be professor of Egyptology at Harvard (1905-1942) and curator of the Egyptian collection at the Museum of Fine Arts in Boston (1910-1942).

Having interested Mrs. George Hearst, widow of the former senator from California, in archaeological research, Reisner became the director of the University of California's Hearst Expedition to Egypt (1899-1905). One of the results of this undertaking was the acquistion of the Hearst Medical Papyrus which is now housed at the University of California in Berkeley as part of a vast collection of Egyptian materials purchased by the Hearst family.

Reisner played a major role in setting the standards for excavation in Egypt, where he established a meticulous recording and classification system. A pioneer in archaeological method, Reisner's great contribution

---

[4]On rebuilding Samaria in 30 B.C., Herod the Great changed its name to Sebaste in honor of his patron, the emperor Caesar Augustus (*Sebastos* in Greek is the same as *Augustus* in Latin). The Hellenistic-Roman name of this site has been preserved in the oral tradition, while the ancient Semitic name "Samaria" has disappeared.

to the discipline was the debris-layer technique of digging, which he developed in Egypt. This technique consists of separating the occupational layers of superimposed strata of a mound, much the same way one distinguishes the layers of a cake, while noting carefully the location of artifacts. Reisner combined this method with a detailed recording system, including photographic records, a daily written report (or diary), maps and architectural plans, find-spots, and a registry with descriptions of all the artifacts. Reisner also had a well-organized staff. Each person was trained to discharge a specific responsibility, with several of the Egyptian members of his staff serving as foremen or "technical men" (as they are called today). When Reisner introduced his excavation method, recording system, and organizational structure at the Samaria dig, a new day had dawned for Palestinian archaeology, marking the beginning of the systematic excavation of Palestine.

The complexities of digging at Samaria, however, were a challenge even to Reisner's sophisticated field techniques. The layers were intricate and also disturbed by later building structures, plundering, and agricultural development. Not only did the massive stone blocks used in constructing the city make digging difficult, but successive destructions-reconstructions of the site over a long period (from Israelite occupation in the ninth century B.C. to the Arab conquest in the seventh century A.D.) made it virtually impossible to separate occupation layers, much less date them. (One archaeologist quipped that it was like digging a quarry.) The campaigns of 1908-1910 were simply a first attempt, followed by several later expeditions. Even today the tell has not yielded all its secrets.

The most noteworthy discovery of the first phase of excavation at Samaria occurred in 1910, when the team uncovered sixty-three ostraca recording the delivery of wine and oil. According to the prevailing opinion, these inscribed potsherds date to King Jeroboam II of Israel in the eighth century B.C. The ostraca played a key role in the determination of sequence-dating of Hebrew epigraphic remains and they provided the first hard data for the northern dialect (Israelite as over against Judahite). Additionally, they have shed light on the economy and the religion of the Northern Kingdom in the eighth century B.C.

Reisner, Fisher, and Lyon produced a multivolume report on their excavation at Samaria, as well as a description of the method employed, but this publication was delayed until 1924, fourteen years after they had left the field, partly because of the outbreak of World War I. The report took so long to appear that its impact on the development of archaeological method was less than it might have been. Reisner's own influence on Palestinian archaeology was channeled through his architect, Clarence Fisher, who spent his adult life in Palestine. Reisner himself dug only at Samaria and then returned to Egypt after World War I to continue his fieldwork. Fisher's careful application of Reisner's techniques of digging and recording was responsible for the coinage of the term "Reisner-Fisher method."[5]

Francis Brown

Francis Brown of Union Theological Seminary in New York, a prominent Hebrew scholar and Assyriologist, directed the School in Jerusalem during the academic year 1907-1908. He had the distinction of being the first to teach a course in the eastern Semitic language of Akkadian in America. As a scholar he was aware of the light that other Semitic languages could shed on the Bible. His judicious handling of this comparative study is apparent from the title of his inaugural lecture at Union Seminary in 1884, "Assyriology: Its Use and Abuse in Old Testament Study."

Brown and the five students enrolled at the School in 1907 resided in the house previously occupied by directors Bacon and Lyon until the lease expired in February 1908. They then moved to another building "situated very near the former one, in the same street with the British Consulate, near the Abyssinian Church, and immediately opposite the German Archaeological Institute."

In addition to the usual field trips, Brown compiled a "Book of Records" containing helpful travel information for the guidance of future appointees in planning their itineraries, a service earlier directors had apparently failed to provide. During Brown's tenure the visit to the fabulous desert city of Petra, the capital of the Nabateans, excited the most interest. Travel from Jerusalem to Petra and return was over 400 miles. Brown and his associates went on horseback, spending twenty-two days; they stayed for five and a half days in the canyon of Wadi Musa, near where Petra is located.

Acknowledging the cordial relations the School enjoyed with the other institutes in Jerusalem, especially the Ecole Biblique and the German Archaeological Institute, Brown suggested there was room for greater collaboration. At the same time he recommended increased cooperation with the Syrian Protestant College (now the American

---

[5]Later Palestinian archaeologists profited from Reisner's field methods and expressed admiration for his work. W. F. Albright considered him to be "the father of the field-methods which revolutionized the practice of Palestinian archaeology," while G. E. Wright looked upon him as "one of the greatest geniuses which field archaeology has produced in modern times." In the evaluation of field techniques before World War I, Petrie's name must be included with Reisner's. There are several parallels in their careers—both were pioneers who excavated principally in Egypt, but also in Palestine; both made a significant contribution to archaeology. But Reisner was better trained and excelled in the techniques of excavating and recording. Without question, Reisner went beyond Petrie. When they died in 1942, they were missed, and their passing marked the end of an era in archaeology.

University of Beirut), especially as archaeologist Frederick J. Bliss was
the son of its distinguished president. Brown remarked:

> No educational institution within our reach equals the Syrian Protestant
> College in the breadth and depth of its influence. Its faculty includes
> scholars of great distinction, some of them specialists in archaeological
> subjects. An alliance with it, though it may be best kept free and informal,
> cannot fail to be of much advantage to us; if by lectures from our
> Directors, or by any form of influence, our School can render the College
> some small service, so much the better.[6]

The 1908 Report of the Managing Committee

In his October 1908 report as chairman of the managing committee,
Charles Torrey noted a change in the regulations of ASOR, whereby the
annual meeting of his committee would no longer take place exclusively
in connection with the Society of Biblical Literature but sometimes in
conjunction with the Archaeological Institute of America. Torrey commented, "In this way we can better keep in touch with the work which is
being done in the wider field of archaeology, and also come into closer
association with our sister Schools in Athens and Rome." In the course
of its history, ASOR has traditionally shared the interests of the Society
of Biblical Literature, but its concerns also go beyond the biblical period
into areas proper to the Archaeological Institute of America and the
American Oriental Society. This change in the regulations anticipated
the present state of affairs; today ASOR's spectrum of interests extends
from prehistoric times to the modern period.

Torrey also reported that the Ottoman government had finally
recognized the School in Jerusalem as an institution officially based in
the Turkish Empire. The name "American School of Archaeology at
Jerusalem" then appeared on the *Official List of American Religious,
Educational, and Charitable Institutions in the Ottoman Empire*, published in Constantinople on May 17, 1907. The goal was finally achieved
seven years after Torrey had first made application en route to Jerusalem
in 1900, the year the School opened.

Robert Harper

In the autumn of 1908 Robert Francis Harper of the University of
Chicago arrived in Jerusalem to assume his duties as annual director of
the School. He has been referred to as the antithesis of his brother,
William Rainey Harper, especially in his relationship with James Henry
Breasted. The elder Harper gave Breasted strong encouragement in his
academic pursuits, while Robert Harper, threatened by Breasted's bril-
liance, treated him vindictively. Breasted incurred this enmity when he

[6]*American Journal of Archaeology* Supplement 12 (1908) 41.

and Harper were students together at Yale, and it expressed itself constantly thereafter, especially when they were colleagues on the faculty of the University of Chicago. Harper's irrational hatred for Breasted apparently stemmed from jealousy; he saw Breasted as a serious threat to his own advancement in academe.

Robert Harper's interest in archaeology dated to the Nippur excavations of 1888, where he had served as staff Assyriologist. His year as director of the Jerusalem School was uneventful with one exception—he selected the site on which the School was eventually built. In Harper's words:

> This land is without the walls of the city, in the best Mohammedan quarter, almost adjoining the properties of the Schools of the Dominicans and of the Anglican Bishop. The purchase was made through the agency of Mahmoud Effendi el-Husseini and with the assistance of that ever-ready and untiring friend of the School, Mr. Antoine Thomas Gelat."[7]

Richard Gottheil

Richard J. H. Gottheil, professor of Rabbinic literature and Semitic languages at Columbia University, succeeded Harper as director of the School in 1909. An Arabist, in the course of the year he concentrated on Arabic manuscripts and inscriptions; he also compiled a complete catalog of the Arabic manuscripts housed in the public library of the Kutainah family and in the private libraries of the Jar-Allah and al-Buderi families. This project was the first of several undertakings by ASOR in the field of Islam.[8]

The Managing Committee

In 1910 Torrey, as chairman of the managing committee, made the first ten-year review of the School's achievements to ascertain how well it had met its primary objectives. During the first decade twenty-eight regular and six special students had been enrolled at the Jerusalem School, and the directors and appointees produced in that period an

---

[7]*Bulletin of the Archaeological Institute of America* 1 (1909) 168. The name of Antoine Gelat appears frequently in the annals of ASOR. Employed as the first dragoman or interpreter in the American consulate in Jerusalem, he rendered invaluable assistance to the early directors of the School, who would otherwise have been without the guidance of a local person familiar with the languages and customs of Palestine. Gelat also held title to the land purchased by Harper on behalf of the School because Turkish law forbade a foreign institute to own property. (This law was abrogated after Palestine passed to British control in 1920.) When Gelat died in 1923, Albright, who was then director of the School, eulogized him in these words, "His death is a great loss to us all; we mourn the departure of a remarkable man, whose helpfulness and incorruptible integrity had won universal affection and respect."

[8]Confer the recent work of Oleg Grabar, his student Stephen Urice, and others who are dedicating their scholarly efforts to the study of Islamic architecture.

impressive number of books and articles. In summary, the managing committee was satisfied that the School was achieving the goals that its founders had set.

In December 1910, at the meeting in Providence, Rhode Island, of the Archaeological Institute of America, the official name of the School underwent a slight revision. Instead of the cumbersome title "The American School of Oriental Study and Research in Palestine," it was shortened to "The American School of Oriental Research in Jerusalem."

The managing committee had been working to expand the School's activities by the appointment of a field director to reside in Jerusalem. In lieu of a permanent director, such a person would provide continuity at the School from year to year and would be available to oversee multiyear field projects. Since such an appointee would have to be an experienced archaeologist, Clarence S. Fisher was the obvious candidate. A trained architect with broad field experience at Nippur, Samaria, and elsewhere, he was ready to accept the position when the University of Pennsylvania made him an attractive offer that he was unable to decline; the managing committee had to continue its search.

Charles Brown

In 1910 Charles R. Brown of the Newton Theological Institution [sic] became director of the School. A man who took his American nationality seriously, he commented:

> . . . if we can lead the way toward making distinctively American an important section of the city, we shall aid in placing the United States beside Russia, Germany, and France, in the thought of the people of Jerusalem, without presenting any sectarian or political barrier to their confidence. I recommend that the school building now contemplated be established with due regard to other possible American requirements, that the plans for it have the approval of American architects and the supervision of an American builder, and that doors, windows, wood-finish, hardware, and plumbing apparatus be purchased for it in the United States.[9]

Although he may have overstated the national aspects of the School, his full report indicated that the School was remaining true to its charter by its impartiality in the political and religious realms.

J. F. McCurdy

J. F. McCurdy of the University of Toronto assumed the directorship of the school in 1911; he was the first scholar from a Canadian university to hold this position. In his final report McCurdy noted the

---

[9]*Bulletin of the Archaeological Institute of America* 3 (1911) 34-35.

long list of visitors to the School, observing that it had become "a gathering place for English-speaking visitors and residents in Palestine who are intelligently interested in things Biblical and Oriental." The history of ASOR demonstrates that this important part of the School's life developed admirably with the passage of time.

Warren Moulton

When Warren J. Moulton became director of the School in 1912, it was a homecoming for him; he had been a student in Jerusalem in 1902. Professor of the New Testament and later president of the Bangor Theological Seminary, Moulton always found time to serve ASOR both as a trustee and as treasurer. During his tenure as director of the School, American Methodists established the Newman Biblical Institute in Jerusalem to promote biblical study in the Holy Land. This new institute found a cooperative friend in the School and its director.

The indefatigable Moulton led several comprehensive field trips, leaving over 300 photographs as evidence. He lamented the serious damage to many archaeological sites since his stay in Palestine ten years earlier. As a remedy, he advocated the establishment of a society devoted to the preservation and restoration of Syro-Palestinian antiquities. Moulton also laid the foundations for the School museum by acquiring, in his words, "some sixty pieces of Jewish pottery," which he put on display at the School.

Had it not been for Moulton's concern, the very existence of the American Palestine Exploration Society, one of ASOR's forerunners, might have faded from human memory. His article on the history of this short-lived but important organization, published in ASOR's *Annual* 8 (for 1926-1927), supplements fragmentary information garnered from other sources. Nine excellent photographs of the Transjordan survey enhance Moulton's sketch of the American Palestine Exploration Society.

George Robinson

In the academic year 1913-1914 George L. Robinson, professor at McCormick Theological Seminary, was director of the School in Jerusalem. He spent the year overseeing the travel and exploration of his students, which extended as far as the Euphrates. They also paid a visit to Petra, the ancient capital of the Nabateans, because it had a special meaning for Robinson.

Edward L. Wilson, an American editor, was the first to discover in 1882 the Great High Place of Petra. In 1900 on the occasion of his initial visit to Petra, George Robinson rediscovered the Great High Place and was the first to recognize its religious character. In 1930 Robinson published a long-delayed book on Petra, *The Sarcophagus of an Ancient Civilization.* Of special interest is his description of the Great High Place:

In a few minutes I found myself at the utmost top of the mountain, and presently stepped forth upon what was the smooth dome of Obelisk Ridge. As I advanced a few steps, there, straight before me, was a great rectangular court, cut down with striking precision into the mother rock; and close beside it, two altars with stairway approaches, a large pool also, for water, and various other cuttings, which gave all the evidence necessary that it must have been, at one time, an ancient sanctuary. There was no doubt about it. My ambition, I saw at a glance, was being realized! I had found a high place! The thrill was something glorious!

Additional Field Activities before World War I

Among the several excavations conducted in Palestine before World War I, only Samaria (modern Sebastiyeh) was dug under American auspices. The British projects of that era were sponsored by the Palestine Exploration Fund. In the same period the German and Austrian excavations took place at four prominent ancient cities: Taanach, Megiddo, Jericho, and Shechem.[10] Unfortunately, before World War I the Germans and the British were unaware of each other's projects; they worked quite independently, not even visiting one another's sites.

Ernst Sellin

Ernst Sellin, a pioneer of German-Austrian archaeology in Palestine, directed the first large-scale digs at Taanach, Jericho, and Shechem. He was both an archaeologist and a conservative biblical scholar. He repudiated the radical literary criticism of the Wellhausen School, which did not take archaeological evidence into proper account in reconstructing the history of Israel. (Archaeology has tended to support a predisposition to conservative biblical positions, and the two have worked hand in hand.)

Despite his extensive field experience, Sellin never became a leading archaeologist; he was handicapped by the inadequate methods in his day and was incapable of innovative advances. Nelson Glueck, a prominent American explorer in the 1930s and 1940s, made a harsh assessment of Sellin's work. Acknowledging Sellin's contribution to both biblical scholarship and field archaeology, Glueck deplored some of Sellin's work in both areas as "atrocious."[11]

---

[10]The importance of these sites was justification for more extensive investigation at a later period. The Americans became especially active in the reexcavation of major sites, such as Taanach, Megiddo, and Shechem; the British reexcavated Jericho.

[11]For most of the present century biblical scholars have doubled as field archaeologists in the Mideast. While this practice has worked fairly well, the extraordinary development in the fields of Bible and archaeology is making it progressively more difficult for an individual to be a practitioner of both disciplines. In the future each may have to channel

As an excavator Sellin used the trenching method, which made it virtually impossible to separate the layers of occupation debris. He also neglected pottery chronology, partly because he and several of the German excavators did not understand the importance of pottery. Furthermore, the recording system was so sketchy that it usually rendered the published reports inadequate. The German digs placed greatest emphasis on the work of the surveyor-architect to the detriment of stratigraphy and typology.

Between 1902 and 1904 Sellin conducted three campaigns at Tell Taannek, located five miles southeast of Megiddo in the Plain of Jezreel; it is the town site of biblical Taanach. Employing as many as 200 laborers, Sellin opened long trenches across the mound to locate the defenses and architectural remains. Despite the inadequacy of technique, he had some positive results; he made a historic discovery of twelve well-preserved Akkadian cuneiform tablets.

The method employed at Tell es Sultan, ancient Jericho, was a marked improvement over Taanach. Sellin and Carl Watzinger, who was trained in classical archaeology, dug at this Jordan Valley site between 1907 and 1909, with the assistance of a good staff. They produced noteworthy results. This time the plans, photographs, and architectural drawings were well done, as the final publication attests. However, their inadequate knowledge of the pottery led to serious errors in dating the remains and caused confusion in reconstructing the history of the site.

In 1913-1914, just before the outbreak of World War I, Sellin dug at Tell Balatah. Situated in the valley between Mount Ebal and Mount Gerizim in north-central Palestine, Tell Balatah is identified with ancient Shechem, made famous by the Old Testament's inclusion of the many events that happened there. In the course of the excavation Sellin distinguished four occupation levels and confirmed the identity of the site as Shechem. Again, his reports were only of limited value because of the sketchiness of his recording system.

Gottlieb Schumacher

Between 1903 and 1905 Gottlieb Schumacher directed a preliminary excavation at Tell el Mutesellim, ancient Megiddo, which is one of the most important sites in northern Palestine. While his earlier survey and mapping of Transjordan had produced positive results, his field work at Megiddo suffered from his lack of experience as an excavator; nor did he possess a comprehensive knowledge of pottery chronology.He derived minimal stratigraphic results from the long, north-south trench which he dug across the mound. These limitations were compounded by

his or her efforts in one direction or the other. (See ch. IX on "Biblical Archaeology" for further elaboration.)

financial constraints which forced Schumacher to excavate this site almost single-handed.

The Jewish Palestine Exploration Society

The Jewish Palestine Exploration Society was founded in 1914 and modeled on the foreign institutes already engaged in the exploration and excavation of Palestine. After the establishment of the State of Israel in 1948, its name was changed to the Israel Exploration Society. In its early years this Jewish organization was not involved in field archaeology; it later became very active and eventually dominated the field.

Back to the Jerusalem School

During the years preceding World War I ASOR was not actively engaged in sponsoring excavations, but the appointees of the School visited regularly all of the digs in progress. The reports of the annual directors of the School mention with gratitude the courtesy extended by archaeologists such as Bliss, Macalister, Schumacher, and Sellin on the occasion of such visits.

In Jerusalem the American scholars worked cooperatively with other national and religious institutes pursuing the same goals as ASOR. In addition to the British, French, and German schools, there was the Pontifical Biblical Institute, established by Alexis Mallon in 1913 as the Jerusalem branch of the Pontifical Biblical Institute in Rome, which had been founded in 1909. ASOR and the Biblical Institute have always enjoyed a cordial relationship, especially during Albright's tenure as director of the School.

James Montgomery

The last director of the School before World War I was James A. Montgomery, an eminent Old Testament scholar who was a professor at the Protestant Episcopal Divinity School in Philadelphia and at the University of Pennsylvania. His volumes on the *Book of Daniel* (1927) and the *Book of Kings* (1951) in the International Critical Commentary were not only among the best in that series when they first appeared but continue to be valuable today. Montgomery's esteem among his colleagues is evident in his having been elected to the presidency of three learned societies: the Society of Biblical Literature (1918), the American Schools of Oriental Research (1921-1934), and the American Oriental Society (1926-1927). During his long and productive career he edited major publications of these three societies: the *Journal of Biblical Literature* (1909-1913), the *Journal of the American Oriental Society* (1916-1921, 1924), and the *Bulletin of the American Schools of Oriental Research* (1919-1930).

In addition to his own scholarly contributions to biblical and oriental studies, Montgomery played a role in shaping the career of one who was to become the preeminent orientalist of our day; he encouraged William F. Albright to pursue postdoctoral research in Jerusalem as the Thayer Fellow. Albright's warm feelings for his mentor are reflected in the dedication of his *Archaeology and the Religion of Israel* published in 1942:

> The dedication of this book to my former chief and my friend of many years, Professor James Alan Montgomery of the University of Pennsylvania, is only a slight token of my respect and affection for him. His careful scholarship, catholic spirit and broad culture have long adorned every institution or organization with which he was connected.

The term of Montgomery's directorship in Jerusalem was reduced to less than one turbulent year by the outbreak of war in Europe in August 1914. Accompanied by his family, Montgomery arrived in Beirut in June of that year and spent most of the summer in Lebanon. There he studied Arabic and visited prominent archaeological sites. Despite expressions of concern from friends, the Montgomerys sailed from Beirut to the ancient port of Jaffa and then proceeded to Jerusalem.

World War I

The Ottoman Empire mobilized its army when World War I broke out, and it was just a matter of time before the Turks became actively engaged. When Turkey entered the war in October 1914 on the side of Germany, it became increasingly difficult for Montgomery to conduct the program of the School. With martial law in effect, the appointees of the School had to confine their activities to Jerusalem for the most part, foregoing the extensive trips that had become an integral part of the School's program.

Reflecting on the unsettled conditions in his offical report to the managing committee, Montgomery chose to see the brighter side, "But I am happy to record that we were in no way personally disturbed, the officials treating us with great courtesy, and that there was no disorder or violence." He continued in the same tone, "Mrs. Montgomery was 'at home' one day a week and this brought quite a cosmopolitan company to the School, sometimes with queer assemblages of political enemies. The School was neutral." This statement not only reflects the official posture of ASOR but also demonstrates the important mediating role it can fulfill in a part of the world often fragmented by political, religious, and ethnic parochialism.

Acting on the advice of the American consulate, the Montgomery family left Jerusalem after only three months. That day, December 14, 1914, the School closed, fourteen years after Torrey had opened it.

Montgomery spent the next three months in Cairo and then returned home via Athens and Rome, arriving in the United States in June 1915. Even though the activities of the School in Jerusalem had come to a standstill, the managing committee kept the organization alive on the home front. The members held planning sessions and designated appointees who were to travel to Jerusalem as soon as the political climate permitted. It was during this dormant period that Charles Torrey's *Report of the Managing Committee*, October 15, 1916, carried a notice that was to have wide-ranging implications for the future development of ASOR. It stated:

> The examinations for the Thayer Fellowship were held in March [1916], and the successful candidate was Mr. William F. Albright, of Johns Hopkins University. It is the understanding that his appointment is for the first year in which the School is able to resume its work.

The executive committee of ASOR in its *Report to the Managing Committee*, December 15, 1916, set forth rather ambitious plans for field archaeology and topographical survey upon the cessation of hostilities in Palestine. It listed ". . . such sites as the Temple of Eshmun in Sidon, the unexcavated portions of the mound of Samaria, and the unoccupied part of Tell el-Qadi (Dan)" as suitable for excavation.[12] In addition, the executive committee of ASOR gave priority to the conservation of antiquities, especially in view of the wanton destruction evident on every side. The report also drew attention to the necessity of photographing and drawing ancient monuments preparatory to cataloguing them.

The School in Jerusalem remained closed during the academic year 1916-1917 as the war raged; at the same time the cheerless atmosphere at home was not conducive to raising the needed endowment for the School to prosper when peace returned. Torrey's report of December 1917 reflected the melancholy of the times, but it was offset by some positive notes. The first was that British General Edmund H. Allenby captured Jerusalem on December 9, 1917. This event, along with victories in Damascus, Aleppo, and elsewhere, ended Ottoman control in Syria-Palestine. Archaeologists were pleased with the outcome, after having been obstructed at almost every turn by the Turks, who had little interest in matters relating to the life and culture of ancient times.[13] The second

---

[12]The Phoenician temple of Eshmun, the god of healing, is located north of Sidon and dates from the fifth century B.C. Samaria, of course, had already been partially dug by Reisner and Fisher on behalf of Harvard University. The site of Dan, which is located at the foot of Mount Hermon and marked the northern boundary of the land of biblical Israel, remained unexcavated until 1966.

[13]Today the situation is radically different. The Turkish Department of Antiquities, as well as the universities and museums of the country, are sponsoring excellent archaeological programs. Conditions changed for the better between World War I and II, and since

encouraging word was Mrs. James B. Nies's promise of a gift in the amount of $50,000 to erect a permanent home for the School in Jerusalem. Her generous contribution would enable ASOR to correct a longstanding deficiency, one which all the early directors of the School felt as they contended with makeshift quarters. The donor, the former Jane Dows Orr, who shared her spouse's enthusiasm for the history and culture of the Mideast, attached the following conditions to her gift:

(1) The title to the piece of land in Jerusalem purchased in 1909 must first be securely held in this country [the United States], either by the Archaeological Institute of America or by some other duly incorporated and authorized body.

(2) The sum named shall pay for the completed edifice, and is to be furnished in installments as needed for the actual work of building.

(3) The privilege of naming the building is reserved by the donor.

This momentous event marked a turning point in the history of ASOR.

Post-World War I

In 1918 James A. Montgomery succeeded Charles C. Torrey as chairman of ASOR's managing committee, a post which Torrey had held since 1907. Montgomery, cheered by the victory of the Allied Forces in Palestine, delivered a first annual report full of optimism. The demise of the Turks marked the beginning of a new era for the School; now there would be increased archaeological activity throughout the Mideast. Needless to say, new field projects were contingent upon adequate funding, so ASOR undertook to raise a million dollars. Similar earlier endeavors had not set an encouraging precedent; it is always an uphill struggle to raise money even in the best of times.

In that same report Montgomery indicated that the British were planning to establish a School of Archaeology in Jerusalem. He pledged ASOR's cooperation, which had already been extended to other national institutes in Palestine. From the beginning the Anglo-American bond was a special one, resulting in several joint undertakings.

At its meeting in December 1918 the managing committee of ASOR voted to reopen the School the subsequent year. In preparation the committee made the following staff appointments: William H. Worrell of the Hartford Theological Seminary as director, Albert T. Clay of Yale as his associate, and William F. Albright of Johns Hopkins University as Thayer Fellow.

World War II Turkish archaeologists have been taking their rightful place beside foreign teams. The University Ankara deserves special credit for many of the developments in the archaeology of Turkey.

William F. Albright

In the history of ASOR there is no question that William Foxwell Albright is the scholar who played the leading role. Born in Chile of parents who were American Methodist "self-supporting missionaries," Albright was brought up in a family that was economically poor. His incredible nearsightedness and his painful shyness would have been insuperable obstacles for the ordinary child, but Albright was not an ordinary child. These factors enhanced his bookish tendencies, and he appeased his intellectual curiosity through voracious reading. One of the books he devoured was R. W. Rogers's *History of Babylonia and Assyria*. Upon finishing it, he was impatient to get to the Mideast lest all the tells be dug before his arrival on the scene.

As a result of his steady diet of serious reading, when he entered Johns Hopkins University to pursue the doctorate in oriental studies under Paul Haupt, Albright was already well advanced in Mesopotamian history and Semitic languages. The degree was conferred upon him in 1916 after he completed his dissertation, *The Assyrian Deluge Epic*.

As a young man Albright shared the skepticism of his mentor Haupt about the historical value of the biblical traditions. In time, however, he became more conservative and repudiated the radical views of Haupt. Archaeology provided the external evidence that led Albright and others to a more positive attitude about the early traditions of Israel.

James Breasted

One of the most distinguished figures in the history of ancient Near Eastern studies was the American Egyptologist, James Henry Breasted, whose name is synonymous with the Oriental Institute of the University of Chicago. A gifted linguist, he studied first under William Rainey Harper at Yale and later pursued Egyptology with Adolf Erman at the University of Berlin. His friendship with Harper during his days at Yale led to his appointment to the University of Chicago when Harper became its president. At Chicago, Breasted held the first chair of Egyptology established in America and became a leader in this field. He compiled a record of every known Egyptian hieroglyphic inscription.

Breasted made his most enduring contribution to Near Eastern research by founding the Oriental Institute at the University of Chicago in 1919, with the financial assistance of his friend and benefactor, John D. Rockefeller, Jr. The Oriental Institute defined its purpose this way:

> . . . to trace as fully as possible the rise of man from Stone Age savagery through successive stages of advance, the emergence of civilization, the history of the earliest great civilized states, and the transmission to Europe of the fundamentals of civilization which we have since inherited.

An archaeologist, Breasted led expeditions to Egypt and the Sudan and later organized excavations at Megiddo in Palestine and at Persepolis in present-day Iran. The scientific concerns of Breasted and ASOR intersected at several points: he served as a trustee of ASOR from 1926 until his death in 1935, and the Oriental Institute and ASOR jointly sponsored several field projects, principally in Mesopotamia (modern Iraq). No one had a greater appreciation of Breasted the humanist than W. F. Albright, as his memorial tribute attests:

> With him [Breasted] is gone America's greatest Orientalist, and the greatest organizer of archaeological research whom the world has yet known—or will probably ever know. Breasted was more than these: he was the foremost humanist among students of the Orient since Ernest Renan, and the foremost humanist of our day among all specialists in the study of antiquity.[14]

[14]*BASOR* 61 (1936) 2.

CHAPTER III
BETWEEN THE WARS: 1919-1945 (Part 1)

After the defeat in World War I of Germany and Ottoman Turkey, the Ottoman territories were partitioned, and the Allied powers administered them as mandates. In April 1920 the Conference of San Remo established the French mandate for Syria and Lebanon and at the same time entrusted Great Britain with the mandate for Palestine, including Transjordan. The British mandatory government did not take effect until September of 1923. Meanwhile, a civil government replaced the British military administration in Jerusalem, and Sir Herbert L. Samuel became the first high commissioner of Palestine (1920-1925). This turn of events was good news for archaeologists. In sharp contrast to the Ottoman Turks, the British both encouraged and enabled foreigners to excavate in Palestine; they replaced the Turks' repressive regulations regarding archaeology with far more liberal antiquities laws.

From the political point of view, the period between the Wars was a time of nationalist turmoil, but from the perspective of archaeology it was the "golden age of Palestinian excavations." It was truly a formative time in Near Eastern archaeology. Having profited from the shortcomings of earlier digs through a process of experience, evaluation, reconsideration, and learning from other people's mistakes (as well as their own), archaeologists were now conducting their field projects in a more systematic manner, with greater awareness of the importance of pottery as a dating criterion. With archaeologists paying more attention to stratigraphy and typology in Palestine, archaeology was beginning to develop into a serious scientific discipline.

The Reopening of the School

The School reopened in October 1919, with William H. Worrell, a fine scholar and excellent Arabist, in charge. The managing committee back home was hoping that Worrell would be the first long-term director; all previous directors had recognized the need for the post to be held for longer periods than a year. The committee was disappointed when Worrell decided to return to the United States after only a year. While, as is well known, personal conflicts with other appointees were to some extent responsible for his disillusionment with the post, more influential, as the following letter suggests, were his economic difficulties. In correspondence of April 28, 1920, addressed to John Peters, President Montgomery wrote:

Dr. Worrell, as you may know, cabled that he did not desire a reappoint-
ment. He seems to be aggrieved over his financial support. It should be
understood that the original terms were made satisfactory to him. As to
cost of living in Jerusalem, on which he harps much, some of us here feel
we would just as lief be in Jerusalem. Prices are making life miserable.

The committee named Albert T. Clay, an Assyriologist at Yale, as
annual professor of the School in 1919, a position that had been
established when it appeared that the director would be staying on
permanently. The administrative responsibilities of the School continued
to be in the hands of the director, while the annual professor was free to
carry on personal research and participate in field trips. Clay was
ASOR's first annual professor, but his appointment was made in cooperation with the Archaeological Institute of America with the understanding that he would spend part of the year surveying Babylonia (Iraq)
in prepartion for the establishment of the School of Mesopotamian
Archaeology in Baghdad. John P. Peters, the excavator of Nippur, served
as lecturer for the School during that first year after the war, and
Albright was the Thayer Fellow. Unfortunately, Clay's and Peters's
long-standing conflict with Worrell created an unhappy situation at the
School. It was neither the first nor the last time that such an atmosphere
prevailed in an overseas institute, partly because of the restricted space
that limits the independence and privacy of the residents. The situation
must have been awkward for Albright, who was the youngest member of
the staff; he nonetheless was able to maintain cordial relations with all
parties and to profit from their experience and learning.

The British School of Archaeology

After the School reopened, it undertook a joint venture with the
newly founded British School of Archaeology in Palestine "with a view
to a close co-operation in their common works." According to the
articles of agreement, the British School was to provide the building in
which the shared offices, study halls, library, and museum were to be
housed and to maintain an inventory of all published material on the
archaeology of Palestine. The American School was to be responsible for
the development of the joint library, which already contained a nucleus
of basic research tools. While the two schools shared responsibilities,
each maintained its own identity and independence.

The Americans and the British invited the French to participate in
this cooperative enterprise, but it was impractical because the French
School was located in Syria. In 1921, however, the Dominican Ecole
Biblique was accorded the status of "official" French School in Jerusa-
lem; as before, the American School continued to work closely with the
Dominican scholars without their becoming part of the cluster.

John Garstang

John Garstang, professor at the University of Liverpool who took a very conservative approach to the history of the Old Testament, served simultaneously as the first director of the British School of Archaeology in Jerusalem and the first director of the newly established Department of Antiquities. Garstang was assisted by a British staff consisting of W. J. Phythian-Adams, C. Leonard Woolley, and E. G. H. Mackay, all archaeologists in their own right. Having trained under Petrie in Egypt, Garstang directed several excavations in Palestine. He seemed to be more interested in Turkey, however, where he later served as director of the British Institute of Archaeology in Ankara.

In 1920 and 1921 Garstang and Phythian-Adams excavated the Philistine city of Ashkelon, located on the Mediterranean seacoast. The dig was sponsored by the Palestine Exploration Fund (which later formed a joint organization with its subsidiary, the British School of Archaeology). This expedition to Ashkelon was the first excavation to take place after World War I. Both Garstang and Phythian-Adams exerted a formative influence on Albright in the course of his visits to the Ashkelon dig, as they studied together the stratigraphic section dug along the shore. Albright remarked later that his first teachers in archaeological method were Garstang and Phythian-Adams and that Phythian-Adams's knowledge of pottery had helped to clarify his understanding of the chronology of Palestine.

Events of 1919-1921

BASOR

The year 1919 marked not only the reopening of the School in Jerusalem but also the appearance of the first issue of the *Bulletin of the American Schools of Oriental Research* (better known by its acronym *BASOR*). Unpretentious, *BASOR* consisted of a mere four pages, summarizing the School's beginnings and expressing hopes for the future. This issue also described the School's cooperative efforts with its British counterpart and appealed for funds to support their joint programs. *BASOR*'s beginnings were simple but auspicious; it is now a leading journal in the field of archaeology.

BASOR 2 (1920) informed its readers that the Lord Bute House, located just inside the Jaffa Gate, was to become the common residence of the American and British Schools. The announcement proved to be premature, however, for the British were unable to secure a lease for the intended residence. Rented quarters that had housed the American School before the War had to suffice until a permanent building could be constructed.

Choosing a New Director

With the departure of Worrell, the search began anew for a long-term replacement as director of the School. Montgomery and Barton, familiar with William Albright's publications, felt he had sufficient scholarly stature to fill the position. Peters, however, had serious reservations based on Albright's inexperience as an administrator. The following letter from Montgomery to Peters indicates that the latter eventually capitulated:

> We are glad to have your favorable view of Dr. Albright. We waited a bit to hear from you on this score. But we had to proceed, and last week I wrote Albright asking him to become Acting Director next year, with, I think, a proper salary for an unmarried and economical man. Entre nous, it may be that he can prove himself as the coming Director for a term of years. Of course he would have to stay on, for we do not wish to incur further expenses in his traveling home and back again.

Albright became acting director in 1920, then director from 1920 to 1929, and again from 1933 to 1936. Apparently, to use Montgomery's word, he had "proved" himself.

The Annual of ASOR

Another highlight of the year 1920 was the appearance of the first volume of the *Annual of the American Schools of Oriental Research*, edited for the managing committee by Charles C. Torrey. All four contributors—Torrey, Mitchell, Paton, and Moulton—were former directors of the School, and each of their articles was based on research done during their time in Jerusalem.

The Appointment of Frederick J. Bliss

In his report as chairman of the managing committee, October 1920, Montgomery announced that Frederick J. Bliss, the American excavator who had dug several tells for the Palestine Exploration Fund, had been secured by the School as "Advisor on Excavations." The appointment of such an experienced archaeologist guaranteed that sites would be dug according to the best techniques and that all field projects would be coordinated—both important considerations at a time when the new government was making so many opportunities available to foreign archaeologists. Without the guiding hand of an expert, chaos might have ensued.

The Palestine Oriental Society

Another significant event took place in 1920: the establishment of the Palestine Oriental Society. On January 9, twenty-nine scholars residing in Jerusalem held a preliminary meeting to discuss the formation of a learned society. Albert T. Clay, the American Assyriologist, had taken the initiative to assemble these scholars. A tactful and charming man, Clay was well suited for organizing a community of scholars from diverse backgrounds. After having studied under Hilprecht, Peters, and Jastrow at the University of Pennsylvania and teaching there for a time, Clay became a professor at Yale. While serving as annual professor at the School in Jerusalem, he saw the advantages that would accrue from scholars working together on research and publication projects, especially under the new British administration.

Patterned on the American Oriental Society, this new scholarly organization filled a genuine need in the intellectual life of Jerusalem. The Palestine Oriental Society provided resident scholars (many of whom working in isolation were unaware of the research projects of their Jerusalem colleagues) with the opportunity to meet and to exchange ideas on subjects of common interest.

The initial general meeting of the Palestine Oriental Society took place in Jerusalem on March 22, 1920, with Marie-Joseph Lagrange (of the Ecole Biblique) serving as its first president. Ten years later the Jerusalem correspondent to the *New York Times*, Joseph M. Levy, could write:

> ... While connected with the school, the late Professor Clay of Yale University founded the Palestine Oriental Society, now a flourishing organization in its tenth year [1929], with an excellent journal. The society meets four times a year, nearly always at the American School, and papers on Biblical and Palestinian topics are presented in various languages. This year the Director of Antiquities of the Palestine Government, Mr. Richmond, is president, while a French Dominican Father and an American archaeologist are vice presidents. An Anglican authority on Jewish literature is secretary, the head of the German Protestant Mission is treasurer, while the three directors are, respectively, an Arab physician, who is the leading authority on the folklore of Palestine; a French Dominican Father, and a Jewish rabbi, who is also an eminent authority on Palestinian topography. The American School is not only responsible for the creation of this society but has also played the chief part in maintaining it.

It was an unprecedented achievement to bring together Jews and Arabs, Protestants and Catholics, for a common purpose. In so doing, Clay was helping to fulfill one of the purposes for which ASOR was founded.

The *Journal of the Palestine Oriental Society*, an international publication, began to appear in 1921, by coincidence the same year that the British government established the Department of Antiquities in Palestine. This excellent journal discontinued publication in 1941, with its nineteenth volume, although one final volume appeared in 1946.

The Legal Incorporation of the School

The year 1921 saw an event of historic significance, the legal incorporation of the School in the District of Columbia under the title

The American Schools of Oriental Research (ASOR). The plural "Schools" was deliberately chosen to encompass other institutes that might eventually arise in the Near East as the need appeared and finances permitted. The embryonic School in Baghdad, for example, was surely in the minds of the ASOR trustees at the time of incorporation. An item entitled "Incorporation of the School," printed in *BASOR* 4 (1921), shows that the ASOR officers of those days had broad vision. It stated in part, "The charter allows us to undertake archaeological works anywhere in the Orient." Until this time Antoine Gelat, a native Palestinian, had held the title to the Jerusalem property as Turkish law would not allow noncitizens to hold legal title; upon incorporation of the Schools in 1921 the title was transferred to ASOR.

The executive authority of the new corporation was held by a board of fifteen trustees, three of whom were appointed by the sponsoring institutions—the Archaeological Institute of America, the Society of Biblical Literature, and the American Oriental Society. ASOR and its founding societies, convinced that more can be accomplished through cooperation than separation, have worked to make their relationship as real as it is theoretical. In his 1918 presidential address to the Society of Biblical Literature James Montgomery reflected this spirit:

> . . . But I would remind you of an institution which, as a child of this Society, founded by its revered onetime President, Dr. Thayer, has a special claim on us. I refer to the School in Jerusalem. Its work must primarily appeal to Biblical scholarship, its support must principally be drawn from those who love and care for the Bible. Its results have been outwardly small. But its possibilities of enrichment to our scholarship have been experienced and in some cases notably demonstrated by the scholars who have gone to school at Jerusalem. An enlarged field of activity lies before it now. May I commend it to your corporate as well as individual interest?[1]

The ASOR trustees approved the seal of the corporation at their meeting in December 1923. Designed by two ASOR trustees—Edward T. Newell, president of the American Numismatic Society, and Wilfred H. Schoff, secretary of the Commercial Museum in Philadelphia—the logo was intended to represent in a general way the areas of ASOR's scholarly concerns. It is a combination of the Egyptian ankh, the emblem of life, and the Babylonian eight-pointed star, the sign of deity. Today ASOR's field operations are far-flung, but they continue to focus on Syria-Palestine without excluding the ambient cultures of the Mideast.

The incorporation of ASOR inevitably but gradually brought about changes in the organization. From 1921 to 1929 it was the custom to

---

[1]*JBL* 38 (1919) 13.

AMERICAN SCHOOLS of ORIENTAL RESEARCH

select trustees exclusively from the academic community. In 1929, however, the board was reorganized to include nonacademic or lay members as well. Since then, men and women from the business and professional spheres have been generously contributing their expertise and financial support to ASOR.

When the new corporation was organized, James Montgomery was elected the first president of ASOR in 1921. His report for November of that year provided for a change in meeting arrangements; instead of convening jointly with the Archaeological Institute of America, as had been the custom, ASOR would henceforth hold its meetings with the Society of Biblical Literature.[2]

Mesopotamia

In view of the biblical interests of ASOR members before and after World War I, not surprisingly they had a concomitant concern for ancient Mesopotamia (Babylonia and Assyria), especially for its ability to provide biblical parallels. This region is often referred to as the "land

---

[2]The scholarly concerns of ASOR in those days corresponded more closely with the Society of Biblical Literature than the Archaeological Institute of America, whose primary focus was the classical world. As the years passed, ASOR's interests broadened beyond the biblical world, and today ASOR sponsors sections at the general meetings of several cognate societies, including the Society of Biblical Literature, the Archaeological Institute of America, and the American Oriental Society.

of the Bible," as many of the discoveries there have shed light on the
biblical narrative. A note in *BASOR* 3 (1921) stated:

> The archaeological discoveries in Mesopotamia have illuminated the pages
> of the Bible more, perhaps, than those made in any other land. Discoveries
> in Mesopotamia are of greater interest to students of the Bible than to any
> one else. Assyriologists are always primarily students of the Old Testament.

That same year Mesopotamia was chosen as the regional location of
ASOR's second research institute.

The Archaeology of Mesopotamia

The excavations conducted in Mesopotamia during the nineteenth
century were, for the most part, treasure hunts for the purpose of
stocking the museums abroad, especially the Louvre and the British
Museum. At that time the French and the British were the principal
foreigners excavating in Mesopotamia; several of them were only part-
time archaeologists, serving also in diplomatic posts for their governments. Among the French who excavated in Assyria were Paul E. Botta
and Victor Place, both well known for their work at Khorsabad, the
ancient capital of Assyria founded by Sargon II. The British were
represented by the pioneer Austen H. Layard, who dug at Nimrud and
Nineveh, capital cities of Assyria, and Henry C. Rawlinson, appointed
by the British Museum to oversee several field projects. Excavators in
Babylonia included British archaeologists William K. Loftus, who dug
at biblical Erech (modern Warka), and the French archaeologist, Ernest
de Sarzec, who excavated at Lagash (modern Telloh), one of the most
important ancient cities of Babylonia.

During the early years of the twentieth century, the Germans played
a prominent role in the archaeology of Mesopotamia because they were
on good political terms with the ruling Turks. Treasure hunting had
ceased by that time and archaeology was developing into a discipline,
thanks to the meticulous methods of the German excavators. Robert
Koldewey, a German architect, was a leading archaeologist at the turn of
the century; he spent eighteen years digging at Babylon, with extraordinary results. Walter Andrae also made a significant contribution to
the beginnings of systematic excavation and recording at the site of
ancient Ashur, capital of Assyria, where he dug from 1903 to 1913.

By the end of World War I, when the British mandate was in force
in Iraq, scientific archaeology was steadily developing. After 1932, when
Iraq gained its sovereignty, this new nation undertook the training of its
own field archaeologists, enabling them to direct their projects independently. Archaeology would never again come to a standstill in Iraq,
despite the political unrest that has sporadically prevented foreigners
from working there.

As early as 1913 George A. Barton suggested the idea of establishing an archaeological institute in Baghdad, but World War I interfered. In 1920 Albert Clay, then serving as annual professor at the School in Jerusalem, visited Iraq at the request of the Mesopotamian Committee of the Archaeological Institute of America. His purpose was to determine through reconnaissance whether the time was ripe for establishing an American School of Oriental Research in Mesopotamia. Taking a long-range view, Clay reported on the opportunities for excavating in Mesopotamia:

> My own observations would lead me to believe that with ten well-equipped expeditions, working continuously in the Near East, I am sure that after a period of not twenty-five or thirty years, but after five hundred and twenty-five, there will be sufficient important tells left to keep the excavators busy for the centuries which follow.[3]

The Directorship of Albright

When Albright became director in Jerusalem, the School began to realize its potential as a research center, as his detailed annual reports attested. His influence in the scholarly community was enhanced by his marriage to Ruth Norton, which took place at St. George Cathedral, Jerusalem, in 1921. Coming from an academic background, with a doctorate in Sanskrit from Johns Hopkins University, Norton was a fitting intellectual companion during their fifty years together. Albright often remarked that without her he could not have succeeded in Jerusalem.

During his tenure as director of the School Albright and other members of the staff offered courses in archaeology, biblical studies, and the topography and folklore of Palestine. Local teachers conducted classes in modern Hebrew and colloquial Arabic to help the resident students communicate more easily with the local people.

Field Trips

As director of the School, Albright spent considerable time leading the residents on field trips; he was convinced that by direct contact with the land one best learns historical geography and topography. Albright had five categories of trips: the first included Jerusalem and immediate environs; the second, lasting one or two days, encompassed areas outside Jerusalem—places such as Shiloh, Gibeah, and Anathoth. The third type, called "tourist trips," were made by car·to outlying sites such as Jericho, Samaria, and Tiberias. The next category was scientific trips of longer duration—for example, navigating the Dead Sea by motorboat, with intermittent stops at important sites along the banks. The last class

[3]*Bulletin of the Archaeological Institute of America* 11 (1920) 62.

of trips was the most ambitious—visits to Egypt, Syria, or other countries. When the School in Baghdad was established, Iraq was added to the list of countries to visit.

Albright's field trips would never be mistaken for leisurely tourist excursions; they were very serious undertakings. En route, Albright and his companions collected artifacts of all kinds, anything that could help in the study of historical geography, especially potsherds for the purpose of dating ancient sites. Commenting on a typical field trip, Albright boasted, "This is the first long trip made by an archaeological school in Jerusalem in which potsherds have been properly studied and utilized." He had made his students aware of the value of ceramic typology as an indicator of chronology; in Albright's judgment pottery was the indispensable chronological tool. As pottery analysis has become more sophisticated, it is playing an important role in the understanding of social and economic history as well as chronological history.

In addition to collecting potsherds on field trips, participants also conducted limited surveys of many of the sites visited, and Albright was able to say in 1924, "We can now offer certain or probable identifications for over 90 of the 135 names given in the Hebrew and Greek texts of the fifteenth chapter of the book of Joshua." To make these identifications, Albright combined the results of the surveys with his considerable expertise, including his knowledge of ancient languages; he was one of the few scholars of his time who was able to complement archaeological technique with philological method and thus attain such impressive results.

These field trips were both strenuous and thorough, covering almost all the accessible sites in Palestine and its environs. At the same time they were surprisingly inexpensive, especially by today's standards. Never a spendthrift, Albright tried to keep the expenses within limited student budgets. Shoestring operations were a way of life with Albright (and with ASOR) for decades. In his words:

> The cost for each person per day, with good, if sometimes unruly, horses, satisfactory muleteers (four in number), good food, and comfortable beds, was about $3.75, which may be considered the normal minimum, if health and safety are not imperilled. It need hardly be observed that one of our principal aims is to reduce the cost of our undertakings as much as consonant with efficiency. Naturally, two of the most vital factors in efficiency are economy and simplicity.[4]

Albright's Colleagues

In the process of solidifying relationships between the School and other national institutes in Jerusalem Albright developed personal friendships with several of their staff. The Albrights and Père Louis Hugues

4BASOR 15 (1924) 3.

Vincent, Dominican of the Ecole Biblique, became such good friends that the Albrights' second son, Hugh, was named after Vincent. Arriving in Jerusalem from France in 1891, Vincent spent most of his adult life in Palestine. His own mentor and closest friend was Marie-Joseph Lagrange, who had founded the Ecole Biblique only one year before Vincent came to Jerusalem. The development of ceramic chronology in Palestine owes much to the efforts of Vincent who visited digs on a regular basis in order to coordinate the pottery from various sites. Albright called Vincent "the foremost Palestinian archaeologist of the world." The statement is exaggerated, but Vincent's comprehensive knowledge of current excavations contributed significantly to the development of Palestinian archaeology.

Albright also worked closely with Albrecht Alt, the distinguished Old Testament scholar who arrived in Jerusalem in 1922 to direct the German Evangelical School of Archaeology. After a residence of only a year and a half, he was called to the University of Leipzig, but he returned to Palestine frequently. Albright rendered an invaluable service to Alt by dating the pottery which Alt had collected in the course of his surveys. Alt's competence in historical geography, topographical research, and biblical scholarship made a profound impression on Albright, as he indicated on the occasion of Alt's death in 1956:

> With him is gone the greatest biblical historian of his time, who continued the work of his teacher, Rudolf Kittel, refining the latter's method with a learning never possessed by him and introducing brilliant new methods into a field which was in danger of stagnating.[5]

The Excavation at Gibeah (Tell el Ful)

One of the most effective ways for ASOR to fulfill the goals of its founders is to sponsor excavations. Torrey made an initial foray at Sidon in 1900, but little happened in the ensuing twenty years. In May 1921 ASOR submitted to the Department of Antiquities an application for a license to excavate Tell el Qadi, the site of biblical Dan, which is located in northern Galilee. This fifty-acre mound, first identified by Robinson in 1838, had never been excavated. Before the ASOR expedition went into the field, Gustaf Dalman, director of the German Evangelical Institute in Jerusalem, suggested to Albright that he dig instead at Tell el Ful, a smaller and more manageable project. Albright took Dalman's advice. Digging began in 1922 at Tell el Ful, only three miles north of Jerusalem. Identified by Robinson as biblical Gibeah (the capital of Saul, the first king of Israel), it was one of the first sites investigated in Palestine; in 1868 Charles Warren made soundings there on behalf of the Palestine Exploration Fund.

Albright conducted his campaigns at Tell el Ful in 1922 and 1923, and again in 1933, concentrating on the summit of the mound where the ancient fortress was situated. He also excavated on the eastern side of the tell, the location of an ancient village. Because of Albright's inexperience as a field archaeologist and the limitations of the final report of his second campaign, questions were later raised about his interpretation of some data. Paul Lapp excavated at Tell el Ful in 1964 in behalf of ASOR in order to clarify the dubious issues. Briefly, Lapp was astonished at the extent of Albright's sound conclusions when compared with the mediocre quality of archaeological work being done at that time.

Bequests to ASOR

During Albright's tenure in Jerusalem the construction of permanent quarters for the School continued to be a pressing concern and occasioned much frustration. Hopes were high in 1922, when James Nies arrived in Jerusalem to oversee the construction of the new building, to be named in memory of his spouse, Jane Orr Nies. Unfortunately, he suffered a heart attack and died two months after his arrival, but the project went forward because of the Nieses' generous bequest. In all, Nies made three bequests to ASOR: a gift of $50,000 for the building in Jerusalem, an endowment of $10,000 to support publications, and the residuary estate to assist the Baghdad School in its excavation and publication programs. Nies was not only a generous benefactor who supported Near Eastern archaeology; he was also a scholar and had served as president of the American Oriental Society. On all counts ASOR will be forever indebted to him.

The Zion Research Foundation of Boston, a nonsectarian foundation for the study of the Bible and the history of the Christian church, has been one of the strongest supporters of ASOR's work through the years. By 1921 this organization had already contributed to ASOR $1,000, to be renewed annually over a period of five years for research connected with Christian manuscripts. This initial grant helped to support a project of W. H. P. Hatch during his tenure as annual professor of the Jerusalem School in 1922-1923. On leave from the Episcopal Theological School in Cambridge (Massachusetts), Hatch was searching for ancient manuscripts in St. Catherine monastery on Mount Sinai and the monasteries in the Nitrian Desert of Egypt.

Through its continuing generous grants the Zion Research Foundation has enabled numerous graduate students to undertake research or participate in excavations in the Mideast, opportunities that they might otherwise never have had. Several scholars have made their first trip to the Mideast with the financial assistance of the Zion Research Foundation. Additionally, the Foundation has subsidized several of ASOR's publications, particularly the *Biblical Archaeologist*, ASOR's popular quarterly.

In the 1930s the Rockefeller Foundation made a munificent grant to ASOR, to be paid over a period of seven years; it was an outright gift intended for offsetting ASOR's annual operational budget. The Rockefeller Foundation also offered to underwrite a challenge grant as a way of creating an endowment for ASOR. The trustees put forth a vigorous effort to raise the necessary funds to meet this challenge, but the response from ASOR's friends and supporters was not so generous as first hoped; nor was the financial climate of the United States in that era congenial to fund raising.

The Baghdad School

By the time the Jerusalem School got its feet on the ground, the School in Baghdad was just being born. Originally known as the American School of Mesopotamian Archaeology, the School appointed as its first director George A. Barton, with Albert T. Clay as resident professor. Unlike the practice in Jerusalem, Baghdad's long-term director was to be based in the United States, where he would oversee the general policy of the School and provide continuity, especially as the resident professor in Baghdad was to be appointed on a yearly basis. The unsettled political climate in Iraq made it impossible to open the new Baghdad School officially until 1923. There was a formal inauguration in November of that year at the Iraq Army Officers' Club with American consul Thomas R. Owens presiding. The event marked the establishment of the first American academic institution in Baghdad; the Archaeological Institute of America referred to the founding of the Baghdad School as "an epoch-making advance in the great program of enlarged oriental research."

The School was established during the period of the British mandatory government before Iraq became a sovereign state. A representative of the Ministry of Education by the name of F. B. Riley gave this estimate of the Baghdad School:

> It cannot be too much emphasized that work of this nature appeals to the people of Iraq, because it is felt to be disinterested. It has no suggestion of either political or economic exploitation; it is a work beneficial to all parties concerned, for the uncovering of buried cities which will reveal an early history common to all—be they Occidentals or Orientals. In such work, co-operation is both possible and desirable and, so far as they can, the Iraqis will be only too willing to co-operate.[6]

The American consulate provided office space for the Baghdad School as it did not have its own building. As a sign of Iraqi support, the local government set aside a plot of land to be used for the eventual construction of a permanent residence for the School. The Baghdad

[6]*BASOR* 17 (1925) 11.

School's never having had its own quarters partly explains its not having kept pace with the Jerusalem School. The fundamental problem, however, has been lack of adequate financial support; ASOR has not been in the position to support both Jerusalem and Baghdad at the same level.

Gertrude Bell, the honorary director of antiquities in the kingdom of Iraq, played her part in forming cordial relations between the Baghdad School and the host country; in recognition, ASOR placed her among its honorary members. British by birth, she studied at Oxford and afterward spent much of her life traveling in the Mideast. Especially devoted to Iraq, she was instrumental in establishing the National Museum in Baghdad, where ASOR had its headquarters. She also drafted the country's antiquities law. At the time of her death in Baghdad in 1926, she bequeathed funds to inaugurate the British School of Archaeology in Iraq, which became a reality in 1932. Bell may be better known in some circles for her involvement in politics; she played a principal role in the establishment in Baghdad of the Hashemite dynasty.

Another benefactor to archaeology in the Mideast was the explorer William H. Ward, who at the time of his death in 1916 left his considerable library to ASOR for use in Iraq. The bequest had one proviso: that an institute be established in Baghdad within ten years of his demise. That condition fulfilled, the Ward library, together with the library of another Assyriologist, Morris Jastrow of the University of Pennsylvania, constituted an impressive resource at the Baghdad School. Also, the archaeological section of John Peters's library was a valuable addition. When this entire collection was shelved in a special room of the American consulate, it formed the first research library in Iraq. Today the library of the Baghdad School, still intact, is housed in the National Museum in Baghdad where it is at the disposal of Iraqi scholars.

From the outset the Baghdad School welcomed all serious students interested in pursuing research on Mesopotamia regardless of their nationality. The School was eager to provide training in archaeological field methods, to ensure that all projects would yield as many scientific data as possible. The first appointees to the School conducted archaeological surveys combined with a careful study of all excavated sites in order to familiarize themselves with the topography of the land and its history.

Edward Chiera

Edward Chiera, an Italian by birth, was annual professor of the Baghdad School in 1924. A leading Assyriologist, he taught first at the University of Pennsylvania and later at the University of Chicago, where he edited from 1927 to 1933 the monumental *Chicago Assyrian Dictionary*. In addition to being a dictionary, this work is a thesaurus and an encyclopedia. In the field of Assyriology Chiera was distinguished by his ability to copy cuneiform texts with great accuracy and skill.

Chiera learned his archaeological techniques from two British excavators who were digging in southern Iraq (ancient Sumer), Ernest Mackay at the city of Kish and C. Leonard Woolley at the city of Ur. Woolley encouraged Chiera to undertake a long-term project consisting of surveying and mapping ancient sites in Mesopotamia; he called it the most meaningful contribution the Baghdad School could make to the history of the region between the Tigris and Euphrates.

The Excavations at Yorghan Tepe and Khorsabad

As annual professor, Chiera was prepared to begin the survey, but he altered his plans when the Iraqi government asked him to excavate Yorghan Tepe, the ancient Hurrian city of Nuzi, situated about twelve miles southwest of modern Kirkuk in northeastern Iraq. Preparatory to the dig, Chiera surveyed the Kirkuk region in the spring of 1925.

The excavation of Nuzi was a joint project of the Iraq Museum and the Baghdad School; Harvard University's Semitic and Fogg Art Museums also cooperated in this multiseason project, which not only cemented good relations with the local authorities but also produced impressive results. Edward Chiera and Robert H. Pfeiffer directed the first two seasons of digging, and Richard F. S. Starr of the Fogg Museum the last two. Pfeiffer, who was teaching at Boston University at the time, served as annual professor of the Baghdad School during the academic year 1928-1929. He played a prominent role in the excavations at Nuzi both as an organizer and as a director of the project. During the first season Chiera discovered the private archive of a wealthy person; it contained cuneiform tablets that were business documents dating from about 1500 B.C. This good fortune stimulated further digging, which continued until 1931 and resulted in the recovery of several thousand clay tablets dating as far back as 2500 B.C.[7]

Biblical scholars of the past generation were inclined to exploit the Nuzi materials somewhat uncritically in pursuit of parallels to the social customs of the patriarchal age; for example, inheritance and birthright. The question of Nuzi parallels vis-à-vis the biblical narrative is under reevaluation at present, and the tendency is to discount earlier conclusions regarding the Book of Genesis.

---

[7]Reports on the specific number of tablets or manuscripts unearthed at any site are invariably vague and inaccurate because of the difficulty involved in determining whether one is dealing with integral epigraphic remains or fragments. Usually the initial estimate will be very high; after examination and study the number may be considerably reduced. The discovery of the Ebla tablets at Tell Mardikh in northern Syria is a typical example. The original inventory was an inflated 14,000 to 18,000; the more realistic number of complete tablets and large, readable fragments may be closer to 2,500.

From 1928 to 1929, on behalf of the Oriental Institute Chiera excavated at Khorsabad, the site of the Assyrian capital under Sargon II (721-705 B.C.). Here the French had dug as early as 1842. It was at Khorsabad, famous for monumental finds, that Americans recovered the king-list, which was an important key to establishing the dynastic chronology of Assyria. The Oriental Institute continued digging the site through 1936 with Henri Frankfort as director.

Raymond Dougherty

Raymond P. Dougherty of Goucher College and later of Yale, a good cuneiformist and an excellent copyist, was the annual professor at the Baghdad School in 1925. He spent the year making an archaeological survey in accordance with the overall plan adopted by the School. In a report on his work in southern Babylonia, he observed:

> The officials of the Kingdom of Iraq are exceedingly interested in such a survey and are ready to cooperate to the fullest extent. Another favorable circumstance is the fact that conditions are settled among the Arab tribes. Hence the time is ripe for a systematic surface examination and preliminary sounding of all the ruins in the land where the Sumero-Babylonian and Assyrian cultures prevailed.[8]

Ephraim Speiser

Ephraim A. Speiser of the University of Pennsylvania was professor at the Baghdad School in 1926 and spent the year directing the survey of northern Mesopotamia. From this time on, Speiser did his scholarly work in close association with ASOR. Born in Polish Galicia, he made his early studies in Austria and then came to the United States when he was eighteen. He spent the greater part of his life at the University of Pennsylvania; shortly before his death in 1965 he was appointed a Distinguished University Professor. While filling several important posts at the University, he found time to be the stateside director of the Baghdad School as Barton's successor from 1934 to 1947; later he served as an ASOR vice-president (1948-1965). He was also an active member of the American Oriental Society, serving both as president of the society and editor of its journal. But his administrative commitments did not prevent him from publishing significant books and articles. For example, his commentary on the Book of Genesis, the initial volume of the Anchor Bible series and one of its best, was the fruit of his lifetime research in ancient Near Eastern studies, especially Mesopotamian civilization. Reviewing Speiser's career at the time of his death in 1965, A. Henry Detweiler, president of ASOR, rightly observed that Speiser "received his start, as so many of us have, in the service of the Schools."

[8]*BASOR* 23 (1926) 15.

In the 1930s Speiser directed excavations on two mounds in northern Mesopotamia for ASOR and the University of Pennsylvania Museum: Tell Billah and Tepe Gawra, both in the neighborhood of ancient Khorsabad. Tell Billah, the site of an Assyrian royal palace of King Asshurnasirpal II (884-860 B.C.), is one of the largest mounds in Iraq, but not so important as Tepe Gawra.

The Excavation at Tepe Gawra

Tepe Gawra (meaning "the great mound") is located fifteen miles northeast of modern Mosul, the largest city in northern Iraq. When Speiser made a sounding there in 1927 with the financial support of Dropsie College in Philadelphia, he stated, "It is the first time that a site in Northern Iraq has been opened, which must have been completely abandoned as early as 2000 B.C." A key mound for determining the stratigraphy of northern Mesopotamia, Tepe Gawra warranted the six seasons spent in excavation, five directed by Speiser and one by Charles Bache of the University of Pennsylvania Museum. Cyrus H. Gordon, another prominent ASOR scholar, served as epigraphist for this dig and had responsibility for all the inscriptions.

Albright summarized the significance of the Tepe Gawra expedition in these words:

> Suffice it to say that the stratification alone now makes Tepe Gawra the most important prehistoric excavation in northern Mesopotamia, while the buildings of the early fourth millennium B.C. are the oldest architecturally respectable constructions hitherto discovered in the world.[9]

Achievements of 1927-1928

During the academic year 1927-1928 the appointees at the Baghdad School were busy excavating. Edward Chiera, designated as field director of the School that year, led the joint expedition to Tarkhalan on behalf of the Baghdad School and Harvard University. The site is situated about eight miles southwest of Kirkuk. Like the other ruins in that region Tarkhalan yielded an impressive cache of tablets.

At the same time Leroy Waterman of the University of Michigan, annual professor at the Baghdad School, excavated at the Tell Omar complex of mounds on the western bank of the Tigris, opposite Ctesiphon. Waterman identified Tell Omar with Babylonian Opis, where Cyrus of Persia decisively defeated the Babylonian army of Nabonidus in 539 B.C. It may also have been the site of Seleucia, which Seleucus I Nicator founded in 312 B.C. and intended as his Mesopotamian capital, replacing Babylon as the center of Hellenistic culture in that region.

[9]*BASOR* 66 (1937) 37.

In 1927 Edward Chiera's first volume, *The Joint Expedition with the Iraq Museum at Nuzi*, appeared as a publication of the Baghdad School; this volume contained information on one hundred of the tablets found in 1925. To undertake publications of this nature was an ambitious step on the part of the Baghdad School. While the pace has slackened over the years, the Baghdad School has made a notable contribution to Mesopotamian scholarship.

Chiera's brilliant career as a cuneiformist and an archaeologist came to a premature end in 1933, when he died after a long illness at the age of forty-eight. Before his death he produced three volumes of Nuzi texts in the Baghdad School series and one in the Harvard Semitic Museum series.

Back to the Jerusalem School

Between World Wars I and II the number of excavations in Palestine increased noticeably and standards of digging improved significantly, although room remained for betterment. The Jerusalem School was not directly involved in all the American field projects of the twenties, but it provided support services for several, including hostel accommodations for the staffs. In this way the School was "a real social center for American archaeologists in Palestine," according to Albright, and helped to foster a greater degree of cooperation among the excavators.

The Excursion to the Southern Ghor

In Albright's ambition to get to know the land of Syria-Palestine very well, he was not content with field trips alone, which can be somewhat superficial; he also undertook larger expeditions, such as his famous survey of the region adjacent to the Dead Sea in 1924. This excursion to the Jordan Rift Valley or Souther Ghor (as it is called in Arabic) was organized under the joint sponsorship of ASOR and the Xenia Theological Seminary in order to learn more about the "cities of the plain," especially Sodom, Gomorrah, and Zoar.[10] Among the members of the expedition were Melvin G. Kyle of Xenia, Alexis Mallon of the Pontifical Biblical Institute, and Eliezer L. Sukenik of the School in Jerusalem, with Albright in charge.

It was during this survey that Mallon discovered by accident the incredible site of Bab edh Dhra, a Bronze Age town with a mammoth cemetery situated just east of that tongue of land, known in Arabic as the Lisan, which protrudes into the Dead Sea at the southeast side. Judging

---

[10]These cities are mentioned frequently in the Old Testament. It has traditionally been assumed that they were located at the southern end of the Dead Sea, although their exact whereabouts remains a mystery. Respectable claims have also been made for the north, the southwest, and elsewhere, although the southeast quadrant of the Dead Sea seems more convincing.

Melvin G. Kyle as a member of Albright's expedition to Moab and the Dead Sea in 1924.

from the pottery strewn about, Albright dated the site to the third millennium B.C. The presence of a group of stone pillars (called *masseboth* in the Hebrew Bible) led him to the conclusion that Bab edh Dhra was a holy place, the scene of annual pilgrimages. This extraordinary ruin has occupied the attention of ASOR archaeologists for many years, each new phase of excavation shedding additional light on this site.

The 1924 expedition to the Dead Sea and surrounding region of Moab was important for ASOR not only archaeologically but also organizationally; it was a cooperative venture in which Xenia provided the funds and ASOR the expertise. It has been a long-standing policy of ASOR to join forces with institutional members of its corporation in fielding excavations and surveys. Kyle of Xenia was especially helpful in making such joint arrangements. In commending Kyle's efforts in support of the Dead Sea expedition, Albright commented:

> Let us hope that other institutions will see the opportunity for similar joint expeditions, where we can promise scientific results and interesting experiences quite out of proportion to the modest expenditures. . . . In this connection it may not be amiss to emphasize the fact that the American School in Jerusalem is a strictly scientific institution, which endeavors to

cooperate with all, Protestant or Catholic, Jew or Gentile, liberal or conservative, on the basis of the same friendly reciprocity.[11]

The New Jerusalem Headquarters

The most memorable event of the academic year 1924-1925 was the completion of the permanent headquarters of the School in Jerusalem, the Jane Dows Nies Memorial Building. Its completion coincided with the twenty-fifth anniversary of ASOR's founding, although the director's wing was not finished until 1931. Following is a description of the complex:

> The new School is actually a group of three buildings set about an inner quadrangle. Each of the three buildings has its length along one of the sides of the quadrangle, and they are connected by a loggia running around the inner court and flush with it. This provides a passage between the several buildings and is a pleasing architectural feature.[12]

A competition among students at the Yale School of Architecture produced the preliminary plans for the new building. However, the winning proposal had to be revised in Jerusalem, as the number of entrances provided on the plans would have made it impossible to secure the buildings. Elias T. Gelat, son of the late Antoine Gelat, was the contractor for the project, while Friedrich Ehmann of Jerusalem served as architect.

The architectural plans provided for further development of the Jerusalem property, namely a fourth building to enclose the quadrangle, but it has not yet been constructed. Landscaping and other improvements over the years have enhanced the appearance of the property; they have made it more functional and increased its value.

Activities under Albright

Albright generated extraordinary activity at the School in Jerusalem, as his annual reports attest. They are in reality more than reports; they are detailed accounts that record the main events in the life of the School and also chronicle the progress of archaeological scholarship in Syria-Palestine. Not satisfied simply to list all the current digs, Albright added his critique of the projects, often comparing one with another. Young scholars in residence during Albright's directorship were indeed fortunate, for he took a personal interest in them, advising them regularly about their projects—all this in addition to giving formal lectures at the School. Because of Albright's rapport with the other national institutes in Jerusalem, appointees of the School were welcome to make use of those schools' resources. As an additional service to ASOR members,

[11]BASOR 14 (1924) 12.
[12]BASOR 15 (1924) 2.

Dr. Clarence Fisher working on his Corpus *of Palestinian Pottery at the Jerusalem School.*

Albright established a summer program at the Jerusalem School beginning in 1925. It consisted of a lecture series on archaeology and related topics; field trips to ancient sites in Palestine and Syria supplemented the formal lectures.

Clarence Fisher

Clarence S. Fisher, a trained architect from the University of Pennsylvania and a member of the staff of the Nippur excavations (1888-1890), played a leading role in Palestinian archaeology between the World Wars. His vast field experience had been gained in Iraq, Egypt, Palestine, Transjordan, and Syria. After World War I he participated in almost every dig conducted under American auspices, including Bethshan, Megiddo, Jerash, and Beth-shemesh. In addition, from 1925 until his death in 1941, Fisher was professor of archaeology at the American School in Jerusalem, a position described in this way:

> He [Fisher] will act as our adviser in all matters of field work, will conduct or supervise any excavations made by the Schools; and at the same time will be free for service to any archaeological enterprises, between which and the Schools, as we trust, he may act as a bond.[13]

[13]*BASOR* 18 (1925) 19.

From 1908 to 1910 Fisher had worked at Samaria (Sebastiyeh) with George Reisner; the experience made him the proper person to help systematize the field work of archaeologists with regard to the methods of digging and recording and of classifying architecture and pottery. No scholar had synthesized the results of the excavations that had taken place before World War I. Fisher was eager to improve archaeological method; he was keenly aware of areas where improvement was needed. Convinced that the Jerusalem School should be the clearinghouse for all future excavations, Fisher issued "A Plan for the Systematic Coordination of Archaeological Research in Palestine and Syria." He conceived the purpose of his plan as "the rebuilding of the archaeological history of the country [Palestine]" through the cooperation of all the dig directors. This objective was entirely consonant with ASOR's own statement of purpose.

Fisher's elaborate program, the first attempt to organize digs and standardize procedures, dealt with every phase of field archaeology from funding the excavation, organizing the staff, acquiring the equipment, maintaining the records, and establishing the techniques of digging to publishing the final reports. The coordination which Fisher advocated was bound to improve Syro-Palestinian archaeology and to eliminate the duplication that was prevalent. Even today excavators working in the Mideast could profit from a review of Fisher's guidelines.

Albright, who called Fisher "one of the most thorough scientific archaeologists of America," learned a great deal from him about excavation technique, pottery chronology, and several other aspects of field archaeology; on many occasions Albright acknowledged his gratitude to Fisher. Ephraim Speiser, who got his first taste of field archaeology at Megiddo under Fisher, observed, "With the kindness and patience that are so characteristic of him, Professor Fisher encouraged me to draw freely upon his unparalleled archaeological experience." According to American archaeologist James Kelso, Fisher was often heard to say, "Never discourage a young archaeologist."

Nelson Glueck admired Fisher's human qualities, saying, "He was the most faithful friend of the underprivileged in Jerusalem." Those who knew Fisher spoke of his kindness but mentioned an enigmatic quality of his personality. Living apart from his family, he was a lonely man; apparently he found it difficult to maintain personal relationships.

During his professional life Fisher prepared material for his magnum opus, his three-volume *Corpus of Palestinian Pottery*. Publication of this mammoth project, commissioned by the Oriental Institute of the University of Chicago, was announced several times, but each time it failed to materialize. It would have been a landmark in the history of Palestinian archaeology. Once Albright had become established in Jerusalem, the pace of development in ceramic typology so accelerated that Fisher was unable to keep abreast of it. Falling behind, he was ready to learn from Albright.[14] Fisher made his lasting contribution to the development of excavation methods and recording techniques. A good summary of the Fisher method appears in William F. Badè's *A Manual of Excavation in the Near East* (1934), which served as a handbook for a generation of archaeologists.[15] In the final analysis Nelson Glueck's summary evaluation of Fisher seems to be the most accurate, "His name will always be linked with the names of Schliemann, Petrie, Reisner, and Vincent as among the most original of Near Eastern archaeologists."

The Excavation at Beth-shan (Tell el Husn)

It was Fisher who initiated the first American excavation after World War I. In 1921 he undertook a large-scale dig at Tell el Husn on behalf of the University of Pennsylvania Museum. This strategic and imposing site, situated fifteen miles south of the Sea of Galilee at the foot of Mount Gilboa, is identified as Beth-shan, to whose city wall the Philistines affixed the bodies of King Saul and his sons after their defeat in battle on Mount Gilboa. Fisher directed this project until 1923, when he resigned; the two succeeding directors, Alan Rowe and Gerald M. Fitzgerald, had both been trained by him.

In the course of ten campaigns (1921-1933), the excavators distinguished eighteen occupation levels, dating from about 3500 B.C. to the early Arab period. Among the notable discoveries at Beth-shan was a succession of Egyptian temples of the Late Bronze Age, which the Philistines later transformed to suit their own worship. In one of these temples Saul's armor (perhaps also his head) was put on display to dishonor him.[16]

Despite the fact that Fisher's methods were utilized in the excavation of Beth-shan, errors continued to be made. Rowe, for example, seriously misdated some of the strata. Tardy publication of results also made it difficult to assess several aspects of the Beth-shan dig. Some preliminary reports appeared, but it took four decades to complete the final report.

The Excavation at Megiddo (Tell el Mutesellim)

In 1925, with the financial assistance of John D. Rockefeller, Jr., James Breasted of the Oriental Institute (University of Chicago) organized an expedition to Tell el Mutesellim, the site of ancient Megiddo. Schumacher had dug at this site earlier (1903-1905) and was himself interested in completing the project, but after World War I Germans were not

---

[14]From 1922 Albright could date Palestinian sites by the excavated pottery, an ability that most of his peers including Fisher lacked.

[15]Also, Clarence S. Fisher, *The Excavation of Armageddon*, Chicago, 1929, ch. 3.

[16]In the 1960s the Israelis working at Beth-shan cleared a Roman theatre, which they dated to A.D. 200; it had a seating capacity of 8,000.

welcome in Palestine. At the request of Breasted, Clarence Fisher served as director of the new project from 1925 to 1927.

Breasted himself had planned in advance not only the techniques for digging and recording the mound but also all the details associated with putting a dig staff into the field. His organization of the Megiddo excavation contrasted sharply with other projects of that day, which lacked Breasted's skills and resources. In many ways the Megiddo project became a model for future archaeologists; perhaps it should not have been because it was too big to be efficient and too destructive.

Breasted intended to dig the whole mound layer by layer down to bedrock, a herculean undertaking to extend over twenty-five years. Instead of employing unskilled laborers, he preferred salaried professionals—a luxury few expeditions could afford. He also provided a field library for his staff and made comfortable accommodations available to them (instead of the traditional tent camps of less affluent digs), as they spent most of the year at the site. However, even good housing did not prevent malaria from striking the entire staff. Breasted's carefully planned budget also included a line for the publication of final reports—an indispensable item often neglected by current expeditions.

From 1927 to 1935 the Megiddo excavations were directed by Philip L. O. Guy. A Scotsman by birth, he had in 1922 been appointed chief inspector in the Department of Antiquities of the mandatory government of Palestine. Later, in 1938, he became director of the British School of Archaeology in Jerusalem. A strong supporter of the State of Israel, he was prominent in the Israel Department of Antiquities after 1948.

As head of the Megiddo dig, Guy was a pioneer in aerial photography; he suspended an electrically-controlled plywood camera from a hydrogen balloon. Even today after extraordinary developments in technology, photography by balloon is in some ways superior to photography by airplane or helicopter; a plane cannot zoom in close enough to provide the desired detail, and a helicopter, stirring up clouds of dust, may disturb the artifacts.

Gordon Loud succeeded Guy as director of the Megiddo excavations, continuing in that position until 1939, when events leading to World War II brought the ambitious project to a close. By that time the work had already suffered from the economic pinch of the depression of the 1930s, which even Rockefeller's resources could not forestall. That the Megiddo expedition had three directors in fifteen years accounts for some of the staff's problems in interpreting the stratigraphy of the site.[17]

---

[17]In the sixties Yigael Yadin, distinguished Israeli archaeologist of Hebrew University in Jerusalem, made soundings at Megiddo in an effort to clarify some of the earlier confusion in the stratigraphy of the Solomonic city, including a reexamination of the casemate wall. Breasted's archaeologists had dated the critical stratum IV A to the time of Solomon, but Yadin demonstrated that it was in fact related to the dynasty of King Omri, specifically to his son Ahab, who reigned almost a century later than Solomon. (Albright and Wright had shown earlier that strata V A-IV B were Solomonic.)

In summary, the Chicago expedition identified more than twenty strata representing occupation from about 3300 to 300 B.C.

Excavations at Tell en Nasbeh and Tell Beit Mirsim

In 1926 the Jerusalem School cooperated with two institutions affiliated with ASOR in excavating at Tell en Nasbeh and Tell Beit Mirsim; the Pacific School of Religion at Berkeley sponsored the first dig, and Xenia Seminary of St. Louis the second.

William F. Badè, professor and dean at the Pacific School of Religion, directed the dig at Tell en Nasbeh, located eight miles north of Jerusalem and regarded by some as Mizpah of Samuel. Rejecting this provisional identification, Albright suggested to Badè that he excavate the site to answer the question of its ancient name, but identification is not yet certain. Badè graciously acknowledged his indebtedness to both Albright and Fisher for their assistance:

> I believe their generous spirit of helpful encouragement to be typical of the management of the American Schools of Oriental Research, and I wish I could add the word that would call forth the more adequate financial support of which it is worthy.[18]

Of Fisher's archaeological expertise Badè observed:

> The writer considers himself particularly fortunate in being able to gain a practical acquaintance with Dr. Fisher's archaeological technique. It is a field in which he is an acknowledged master, and in the interest of science it is greatly to be hoped that his methods may prevail more and more widely.[19]

Tell en Nasbeh, a small mound, was the first Palestinian site to be dug completely when Badè directed five campaigns there between 1926 and 1935. Following Fisher's method, he established that the predominant occupation of this tell fell between 1100 and 300 B.C.; he uncovered the massive fortifications of the city and dated them to about 900 B.C. Though Badè died shortly after the final dig season (probably because of the strenuous work involved), publication of the excavation report was not neglected. Chester C. McCown, a colleague at the Pacific School of Religion, prepared two large volumes on the excavation and they

---

Yadin also corrected the chronology of Megiddo's spectacular water system, which consisted of a vertical shaft 120 feet deep and a horizontal tunnel 215 feet long. This extraordinary engineering feat also dated to the Omride dynasty—probably to Ahab, in Yadin's estimation—and not to the twelfth century B.C., as the Chicago archaeologists had thought. Other questions still remain, despite the number of years spent excavating Megiddo; for example, the nature of the "stables" which Pritchard identified as barracks and Aharoni as storehouses. Yadin also dated these structures to Ahab's reign.

[18]*BASOR* 23 (1926) 31.
[19]*BASOR* 26 (1927) 2.

appeared in 1947. In spite of the positive results of this dig, it suffered like many digs of the twenties and thirties from the excavator's lack of expertise in pottery classification and stratigraphy.

Albright directed four seasons of excavation between 1926 and 1932 at Tell Beit Mirsim. He was assisted by Melvin G. Kyle, then president of Xenia Seminary, the institution that financed the project. The mound, situated about twelve miles to the southwest of Hebron on the edge of the Shephelah (the foothills of the central mountain range of Judah), was in the estimation of Albright the site of Debir (originally called Kiriath-sepher), the largest Canaanite city south of Hebron. It was Albright's tentative identification that interested Kyle in digging at Tell Beit Mirsim. As Kiriath-sepher means "city of the scribe," Kyle may have been expecting to find an archive of cuneiform tablets there. Archibald Sayce had suggested to Albright that the site should contain valuable archives of cuneiform tablets. Several scholars following Kurt Galling, former head of the German Evangelical Archaeological Institute in Jerusalem, reject Albright's proposal and suggest instead Khirbet Rabud as the site of Debir. Located about eight miles southwest of Hebron, it seems to accord better with the biblical account of Debir's history.[20]

Tell Beit Mirsim has been referred to as the "type-site" for the chronology of Palestine because Albright, building on the results of Petrie's work at Tell el Hesi, used it to develop and refine the ceramic index for the whole country, especially in the second millennium B.C. By classifying the stylistic changes in potsherds, he constructed a ceramic typology, which he then correlated with the stratigraphy of the tell. Through a combination of stratigraphy, typology, and other means, he was able to assign relative dates to the occupational levels of the site. The pottery chronology of Palestine that Albright established at Tell Beit Mirsim has been published in *Annuals* 12 (1932) and 13 (1933) of ASOR; even today they serve as ideal ceramic textbooks for students of Palestinian archaeology.

In commenting on Tell Beit Mirsim as the type-site for the ceramic index of Palestine, Albright said:

As will be seen, we have an extraordinary opportunity here for highly interesting discoveries, and best of all to the archaeologist, excellent conditions for the study of pottery, since the strata are horizontal and exceptionally well defined.[21]

In his excavation of Tell Beit Mirsim Albright was fortunate to have the valuable assistance of Fisher as adviser and coordinator; he readily

---

[20]The Bible describes Debir as the west boundary of the tribe of Judah, located in the hill country. Khirbet Rabud fits that definition, but Tell Beit Mirsim is located in the Shephelah. Moshe Kochavi of Tel Aviv University excavated Khirbet Rabud in 1968-1969, but he failed to convince Albright.

[21]*BASOR* 23 (1926) 6.

The expedition camp at Tell Beit Mirsim.

The "mess hall" at Tell Beit Mirsim in the 1930 season; left to right: Bulos el Araj (surveyor), A. Saarisalo (University of Helsinki), N. Glueck, J. Kelso, M. Kyle, W. Albright, Mrs. Kyle, O. Sellers.

*William Albright's morning ablutions in preparation for a
day on the dig at Tell Beit Mirsim in June 1930.*

acknowledged his dependence on Fisher, "whose plan of operation and
methods of work were followed as closely as possible."

Melvin Kyle

Melvin Kyle's long association with ASOR began in 1912 when he
was a resident of the School in Jerusalem. Before joining Albright in the

expedition to Moab and the Dead Sea and in the excavation of Tell Beit Mirsim, Kyle worked with Petrie in Egypt. For several reasons, Kyle and Albright were unlikely colleagues. A lecturer in biblical archaeology and later president of the Xenia Theological Seminary (now Pittsburgh Theological Seminary), Kyle was the author of several conservative books and articles on the Bible and archaeology, emphasizing their relationship. The titles of three of Kyle's writings illustrate his position on the relationship between the Bible and archaeology: *The Deciding Voice of the Monuments in Biblical Criticism* (1912), *The Problem of the Pentateuch: A New Solution by Archaeological Methods* (1920), and *Moses and the Monuments: Light from Archaeology on Pentateuchal Time* (1920). Kyle attempted to establish from archaeological evidence the Mosaic authorship of the Pentateuch as well as the historical reliability of the first five books of the Bible. It was Kyle's assumption that if it could be proved that something might have happened, it was thereby proved that it had happened.

George A. Barton and others seem to have had a less benign attitude toward Kyle the biblical scholar than did Albright. Barton made a pointed response to Kyle's *The Deciding Voice of the Monuments in Biblical Criticism* when he wrote:

> In conclusion the fact should be noted that it is not the function of archaeology to deal with criticism at all, and it is but rarely that an archaeological fact has any vital bearing upon a critical theory. Any attempt to reconstruct ancient history must take into account both the facts of archaeology and of criticism, if the reconstruction is to have any hope of accurately representing the facts of ancient life. Both external and internal evidence must be taken into account. Archaeological objects and ancient documents must both be put upon the witness stand. One must cross-question them both, and not blindly accept the first impressions given by either one. It is as necessary to criticize the archaeological data, i.e., to seek to understand them from every point of view, as it is to criticize documents, i.e., really to understand them.[22]

According to Albright, Kyle's conservatism was rational and open-minded. Albright explained, "He [Kyle] possessed that rarest of all qualities, the instinct and art of befriending those whose religious and scholarly views diverged sharply from his." Albright's "In Memoriam" on the occasion of Kyle's death revealed much about Kyle, Albright, and ASOR:

> We seldom or never debated biblical questions, but there can be no doubt that our constant association with ever-recurring opportunity for comparing biblical and archaeological data has led to increasing convergence between our views, once so far apart. To the last, however, Dr. Kyle remained staunchly conservative on most of his basic positions, while the

---

[22] "'Higher Archaeology' and the Verdict of Criticism," *JBL* 32 (1913) 259-60.

writer has gradually changed from the extreme radicalism of 1919 to a standpoint which can neither be called conservative nor radical, in the usual sense of the terms.

Just as the School is supported by Catholics, Jews and Protestants, by conservative and liberal religious bodies, so it may point with pride to a long line of Protestant, Jewish and Catholic directors, trustees and staff members. Among the Protestants, who naturally form the majority, we are proud of such friends as B. W. Bacon and J. M. P. Smith, on the liberal side, and as A. T. Clay and M. G. Kyle, on the conservative side. May the School ever remain common ground for both sides, meeting here in their search for a common truth.[23]

This ASOR policy of evenhandedness caught the attention of *New York Times* foreign correspondent Joseph M. Levy, who filed the following report in the July 7, 1929 issue of the newpaper:

To one who reads and hears constantly about the bitter strife between different religions and sects, and between conservative and liberal members of each sect, the very existence of such an institution [the American School in Jerusalem] may seem incredible. Yet such an American institution is now approaching its thirtieth anniversary, after a history unmarred by a single dispute of a religious nature.

[23]*BASOR* 51 (1933) 6-7.

CHAPTER IV
BETWEEN THE WARS: 1919-1945 (Part 2)

The American School in the Late Twenties

After spending seven years as director in Jerusalem, Albright returned to America for a year's sabbatical leave in 1926-1927. A good part of that time was devoted to lectures: he spoke to over a hundred groups on the activities of ASOR. As a result of the publicity, enrollment in the Jerusalem School increased from that time.

In the absence of Albright, Romain Butin, professor at the Catholic University of America, served as the Jerusalem School's acting director. An interesting discovery was made on land abutting the School property during Butin's tenure—while repairing the street in front of the School, the municipality uncovered some large blocks, which could be the continuation of the Third Wall of Flavius Josephus, so called because he spoke of Jerusalem's three walls that stood in A.D. 70.[1] To avoid damaging the exposed masonry, the School, responding to the proposal of the mandatory government, relocated its own wall so as to enclose the ancient wall within the School property. The question of the precise location of the walls of Jerusalem is being debated to this day because the evidence is inconclusive. The present walls of the Old City date only as far back as the sixteenth century A.D.; they were built by the Ottoman Sultan Suleiman the Magnificent, although they often rest over long stretches on Herodian foundations.

The year 1929 signalled the end of an era in the history of the School in Jerusalem. In July, Albright completed his term as director and returned to America to begin a new phase of his academic career as the W. W. Spence Professor of Semitic Languages at Johns Hopkins University. Paul Haupt, Albright's teacher, had occupied that chair until his death in 1926. Albright did not immediately succeed Haupt but was appointed to the Spence professorship only in 1929. There was no question about Albright's ability, but he was still a young man, and his youth raised questions about his maturity. His departure from Jerusalem was a great loss to ASOR. In a decade the School had been transformed from mediocrity to excellence under Albright's extraordinary leadership. The ASOR trustees expressed their profound appreciation for his services in these words:

---

[1] Also called Agrippa's Wall, attributed to Herod Agrippa I (A.D. 41-44).

Throughout his long term of office, his devotion to the best interests of the School and of the scholarly aims for which it stands was unswerving. . . . By his energy and prudence in directing the routine work of the students, arranging and conducting expeditions, exploring and excavating ancient sites, and publishing the results of the School's scientific work, the good name of our institution has been preserved and its prestige steadily increased.

Dr. Albright has maintained excellent relations with the officials and residents of Jerusalem, and with the various learned institutions in Palestine and Syria. The important aid which he gave toward the erecting and furnishing of the School building; . . . and the generous sacrifice of time and labor in our interests, we acknowledge with gratitude.[2]

In order to keep Albright permanently related to the School in Jerusalem, the trustees appointed him adjunct professor in 1930; from 1933 to 1936 Albright served both as professor at Johns Hopkins and director of the Jerusalem School in alternating semesters. He had become so closely identified with the School that it was difficult to think of him apart from it, or it apart from him. In a sense the School was an extension of Albright; it continued to reflect his pervasive influence long after he ceased to reside in Jerusalem. Of course, Albright was deeply involved with ASOR in several other capacities for the rest of his life.

Chester McCown

Chester C. McCown, dean of the Pacific School of Religion and a New Testament scholar of unusual breadth, succeeded Albright as director of the School in 1929. The fact that McCown was a New Testament specialist with a strong interest in the Hellenistic and Roman periods of Syro-Palestinian history broadened the scholarly horizons of ASOR. Now the School focused attention on these areas of research. Although Albright had certainly not neglected the later historical eras, they were not his major concern.

As director of the Jerusalem School, McCown placed special emphasis on field trips, which he considered an excellent learning experience for the appointees. He expressed his conviction in this way:

The field trips of the School at Jerusalem serve five purposes: (1) in the course of the year they bring the members of the School to all sites where excavation is in progress; (2) they provide for a general survey of the topography and geography of the land; (3) they present to the student a series of typical sites covering all phases of the cultural history of the Near East from prehistoric times down to the present; (4) they give some conception of life in its primitive aspects as seen in the simple agricultural village and the Bedouin encampment, including incidentally modern

[2]*BASOR* 33 (1929) 13.

developments and Zionist enterprises; and (5) they offer opportunity for the study of unsolved problems and the making of topographical and archaeological discoveries.[3]

McCown also emphasized other goals of the School, which he described as follows:

> It must always be the task of the School to stand for the most creative as well as the most exact scholarship, to bring to American religious and educational leadership fresh and revealing contacts with the interpretative values of oriental research in all its multitudinous ramifications, and to serve as a center of study and a clearing-house of ideas and discoveries for the widest possible circle.[4]

The Expedition to Gerasa (Jerash)

During his tenure as director, McCown undertook with Fisher an expedition to Gerasa (modern Jerash), one of the confederation of ten cities known as the Decapolis. Situated in Transjordan about twenty-five miles north of Amman, Gerasa in New Testament times was a Roman provincial city; it is often referred to as the "Pompeii of the Near East" because of its extraordinary architectural remains. Ulrich Seetzen was the first to discover Gerasa, in 1806; later other explorers visited its ruins. Between 1925 and 1928 John Garstang and George Horsfield of the Department of Antiquities were engaged in the excavation and conservation of this site.

John W. Crowfoot, director of the British School of Archaeology after Garstang, began the systematic excavation of the imposing city-state of Gerasa in 1928, under the joint sponsorship of the British School and Yale University. Yale had become involved at the encouragement of Benjamin W. Bacon, the Yale faculty member who had been an early director of the Jerusalem School (1905-1906).

In 1930, when Crowfoot went to Samaria to begin a new excavation at that site, McCown and Fisher assumed the directorship of the Gerasa project under the auspices of ASOR and Yale. Nelson Glueck of ASOR and G. Lankester Harding of the Department of Antiquities also served as directors of this expedition through 1935.

In recent times the Jordanian Department of Antiquities has been continuing with the excavation, conservation, and restoration of Gerasa, developing it into one of the most impressive tourist attractions in the Kingdom of Jordan. Comparable in magnificence to Baalbek, Palmyra, and Petra, Gerasa ranks among the prized monuments in Syria-Palestine.

Altogether the remains of more than a dozen churches have been unearthed at Gerasa, the oldest dating to about A.D. 400. Crowfoot's team

---

[3]*BASOR* 43 (1931) 23.
[4]*BASOR* 44 (1931) 27.

The ASOR expedition house at Jerash in the 1930s.

Nelson Glueck, director of the Jerusalem School, pays a visit in 1946 to Jerash, where he had directed an ASOR field project earlier. The School vehicle is parked in the street of the columns leading to the forum.

cleared nine of them. Restricted by the Department of Antiquities to the investigation of churches, Crowfoot concentrated on the basilica of St. Theodore, which was built in A.D. 496.

Although the Americans were granted a concession to excavate the entire area of the city, Fisher and McCown focused their efforts on the temple of Artemis, the female deity who was the patroness of the city. This temple dates to the second century A.D.; it is without question the most imposing building at the site.

In 1938 Carl H. Kraeling of Yale edited a splendid volume on these excavations, *Gerasa, City of the Decapolis*. Several ASOR members, as well as scholars from other national institutes, contributed to this book, which was described at the time as "the most elaborate publication which has yet been issued by the Schools."

McCown's "Retirement"

The ASOR board of trustees had hoped that McCown would be a long-term director of the Jerusalem School; they were disappointed when he retired at the end of his two-year term. He did, however, return to the School as its annual professor in 1935. One of his well-known books, *The Ladder of Progress in Palestine* (1943), in its day a valuable introduction to the archaeology of Palestine, benefited from firsthand experience in the Mideast, which his ASOR appointment made possible. In the preface to this volume McCown acknowledged his indebtedness to ASOR and to the excavators of that era, who took the time to explain their field projects to ASOR appointees on the occasion of visits to the sites.

Major Excavations

The Excavation at Beth-zur

McCormick Theological Seminary in Chicago joined ASOR in sponsoring the excavation of the frontier city of Beth-zur in 1931. Ovid R. Sellers of the Seminary faculty directed the project, and Albright acted as scientific adviser. The site, about four miles north of Hebron, is identified with modern Khirbet et Tubeiqah. While sporadic occupation of the city can be traced to the Early Bronze Age, the most important period in its history was the second century B.C. This was the era of the Maccabees, the sons of the priest Mattathias who revolted against the Seleucid kings because they were persecuting the Jews. Here Judas Maccabeus fought a great battle against Lysias, an officer of the Seleucid king Antiochus IV Epiphanes, and defeated him.

During the first campaign the excavators were able to trace the history of the site with the help of the potsherds they unearthed. In Albright's words, "Since the pottery of Beth-zur is identical in type with that of Tell Beit Mirsim, where conditions of stratification are ideal, we

were seldom in any doubt as to our dating." In addition, the archaeologists uncovered the fortress at Beth-zur. Dating to the Maccabean
period, it had been built and destroyed three times. Despite the positive
results of the dig, many questions remained to be answered in a future
season.[5]

The Excavation at Bethel

In 1934 ASOR and the Pittsburgh-Xenia Theological Seminary
jointly sponsored a full-scale campaign at Bethel; this was the ninth
cooperative undertaking of the two institutions. In 1927 Albright had
made soundings at the ancient site of Bethel, which Edward Robinson
had located at the modern village of Beitin, ten miles north of Jerusalem.
At Bethel, one of the cities most frequently mentioned in the Bible,
Albright had uncovered evidence dating to the Canaanite and Israelite
periods, He described the comparative method used to establish the
chronology of sites such as Bethel:

> The collection of pottery and sherds in the American School from the
> excavations in such well-stratified sites as Gibeah and Tell Beit Mirsim, in
> addition to the material from Shiloh, etc., places us in a unique position
> of vantage with respect to dating the strata at Bethel. Père Vincent of the
> French School, who is the unrivalled master of Palestinian archaeology,
> was also so kind as to examine our pottery, and his dating proved to agree
> in every detail of importance with that which we had previously deduced
> from a careful comparison with the results of our previous excavation. It
> cannot be emphasized too strongly that the ceramic chronology of Palestine
> is now on a firm basis back to about 2000 B.C.[6]

Albright directed the 1934 project, named the Kyle Memorial Excavations at Bethel, with the assistance of James L. Kelso of the Seminary.[7]
Later Kelso returned to the site three times—in 1954, 1957, and 1960—to
continue the excavation. Albright reported that the 1934 season had
yielded important stratigraphical results, extending in time from the end
of the third millennium to A.D. 69. Through the systematic excavation of
Bethel and the other sites described, Albright was inductively developing
the scientific discipline of Palestinian archaeology; each of these projects
was contributing to the refinement of pottery chronology for the region.

The Excavation at Beth-shemesh

Between 1928 and 1933 Elihu Grant of Haverford College, assisted
by Fisher, directed five campaigns at Beth-shemesh.[8] This town is

---

[5]Sellers returned to Beth-zur in 1957 to conduct a final season of excavation.

[6]*BASOR* 29 (1928) 10-11.

[7]Other American members of the staff who later figured prominently in Syro-
Palestinian archaeology were John Bright, James B. Pritchard, and G. Ernest Wright.
Hans Steckeweh also participated in this dig.

[8]The name Beth-shemesh, meaning "house of the sun," suggests a Canaanite temple
dedicated to the sun god.

identified with the modest mound called Tell er Rumeileh, or Ain Shems, situated about twelve miles west of Jerusalem in the northeastern Shephelah. Duncan Mackenzie of the Palestine Exploration Fund had excavated this frontier post, located on the border between Philistia and Judah, in 1911-1912. During his campaign he traced the Bronze Age city wall and excavated Israelite tombs and the remains of a Byzantine monastery on the site. Grant's expedition established that the occupation of Beth-shemesh had extended from the Middle Bronze Age to Byzantine times, with the town flourishing between 1500 and 918 B.C. In preparing the multivolume publication of his results at Beth-shemesh, Grant was indeed fortunate to have the assistance of G. Ernest Wright, who was to become one of the leaders in Palestinian archaeology. Wright's real contribution to the Beth-shemesh publication project was to rescue what could be educed from chaos.

In addition to excavating at this biblical site, Grant served as the annual professor of the Baghdad School during the academic year 1937-1938. Affiliated with the Society of Friends, Grant was concerned for the Palestinian Arabs and openly supported their cause.

The Jericho Dig

Between the World Wars the British were also actively engaged in excavations, attempting to clarify some inconclusive results of previous digs by reexamining those sites. Between 1930 and 1936 John Garstang resumed the Jericho project undertaken by Sellin and Watzinger at the beginning of the century. As director of the Neilson Expeditions to Tell es Sultan (Old Testament Jericho), Garstang's great achievement was the discovery of the prepottery Neolithic occupation (7000 B.C.) beneath the Bronze Age levels; it established Jericho as one of the oldest continuously inhabited cities on earth.

In some other matters, especially his interpretation of the defense systems of the Bronze Age (which he had assigned to the period of Joshua's invasion), Garstang had to be corrected. When Kathleen M. Kenyon, director of the British School of Archaeology in Jerusalem, dug at Jericho between 1952 and 1958, she clarified the stratigraphy of the mound; in the process she demonstrated that the assumed "Joshua walls" dated to the Early Bronze Age, roughly a thousand years before the Israelite conquest under Joshua. No trace of a city wall of the Late Bronze Age (1550-1200 B.C.) remained.[9]

Garstang's unfamiliarity with the Reisner-Fisher stratigraphic method may account for his inability to make sense of the stratigraphy of Tell es Sultan. Glueck's evaluation of Garstang's field work was harsh but somewhat justified, "An ideal example of how not to proceed."

[9]Scholars who accept as historical fact an Israelite conquest of Canaan rather than a peaceful settlement there date the conquest to the latter half of the thirteenth century B.C. According to Kenyon, Jericho was desolate in that period.

Albright's estimate of his colleagues was usually more benign: of his friend Garstang, he said, "While he cannot be rated as an original genius like Petrie and Reisner, he stands very high in the annals of field archaeology."

The Excavation at Ghassul

Alexis Mallon of the Pontifical Biblical Institute in Jerusalem was a tireless explorer of Palestine, and he often accompanied Albright on the School trips. From 1919 until his death in 1934, Mallon directed the excavation at Tuleilat el Ghassul, a series of low mounds located a few miles northeast of the Dead Sea. It is such an important Chalcolithic settlement (about 4200-3300 B.C.) that in the language of archaeologists "Ghassulian" and "Chalcolithic" have become interchangeable terms. Mallon was attracted to this desolate site during a field trip when he spotted huge quantities of flints, implements, and handmade pottery strewn on the ground.[10]

The Excavation at Samaria (Sebastiyeh)

In 1931 a joint British-American-Hebrew University team undertook excavation at Samaria (Sebastiyeh), the site of the first American dig in Palestine between 1908 and 1910. Crowfoot directed this new phase of the work, assisted by Eliezer Sukenik and Kathleen Kenyon. Clarence Fisher's acting as an adviser to the team provided continuity between the major campaigns at Samaria despite the two decades separating them. Crowfoot's team enlarged the earlier excavations, especially in the fortress area of the Israelite kings. Because of advances in field methods between 1908 and 1931, Crowfoot was able to correct some erroneous conclusions of the Reisner-Fisher campaign, especially concerning the dates of various occupational levels. The combined efforts of the two expeditions helped in clarifying the complex history of the tell. Fixing the site's chronology, which spans about 1500 years, was made more difficult for the archaeologists by the confused stratigraphy of the mound. During the first phase of excavations (1908-1910) the team made the exciting discovery of sixty-five ostraca (inscribed potsherds) of the eighth century B.C.; it was matched on the second expedition by the unearthing of abundant, finely carved, ivory fragments.

The two modern methods of digging, the Reisner-Fisher and the Wheeler-Kenyon systems, were employed successively on the Samaria excavations; both Reisner and Kenyon dug at Samaria, albeit at different

---

[10]Robert Koeppel succeeded Mallon as director of the project; then after a lapse of twenty-two years Robert North, professor of archaeology at the Pontifical Biblical Institute in Rome, resumed excavations at the site in 1959 and 1960. The most recent work there was done under the direction of J. Basil Hennessy on behalf of the British School of Archaeology.

times. Despite the different designations, these two techniques are basically alike, each concerned with the removal of debris in the sequence of strata within a well-defined area. In many ways the Reisner-Fisher system anticipated the fundamentals of the Wheeler-Kenyon method, although Kenyon did not acknowledge the fact.[11]

The Excavation at Shechem (Tell Balatah)

The Germans participated to a limited degree in field archaeology between the Wars. Ernst Sellin, who had dug briefly at Tell Balatah in 1913-1914, returned to that site for a third campaign in 1926. From then until 1934, Sellin, Gabriel Welter, who was trained in Greek archaeology, and Hans Steckeweh, an architect, directed successive excavations at this important city of ancient Palestine. The serious personality conflicts between Sellin and Welter resulted in the removal of Sellin as director. Welter succeeded to the position; then he was dismissed for failing to publish the results of his work. This unhappy situation was compounded by inadequate excavation techniques; running trenches the length of the tell confused the stratigraphy. In addition, the recording system was deficient and the analysis of pottery neglected.

Steckeweh achieved far more satisfactory results with the stratigraphy during the 1934 season, when he was in charge. Two decades later, when G. Ernest Wright led the American expedition to Tell Balatah beginning in 1956, Steckeweh was chosen as a member of the new staff to provide continuity with the earlier campaigns. Unfortunately, Sellin's field records and his excavation reports on Shechem were destroyed when Berlin was bombed in 1943. As Sellin's work at Tell Balatah had not been published, Wright decided to make up this deficiency. First he had to reexcavate the site in order to clarify its history; only then could he publish a final report.

The Excavation at Shiloh

Edward Robinson had identified the Israelite central shrine of Shiloh with the Arab village of Seilun, which is situated about twenty miles north of Jerusalem. Two Danish archaeologists, Hans Kjaer of the National Museum of Copenhagen and Aage Schmidt, began systematic excavation at this site in 1926, with Albright and later Glueck serving as archaeological advisers. The Danes worked slowly and meticulously

[11]The best laboratory for the Wheeler-Kenyon method was Tell es Sultan (Old Testament Jericho), where Kenyon dug in the fifties. (Ch. V contains a discussion of the various field techniques.) From 1965 to 1967 Fawzi Zayadine of the Jordan Department of Antiquities carried out excavation and clearance at Samaria, especially in the area of the theatre. Support came from the United States Agency for International Development (USAID), whose concern was to develop the site for tourism. In 1968 J. Basil Hennessy of the British School of Archaeology directed an additional season of digging at Samaria, exposing strata of the Hellenistic and Roman periods in the western sector of the tell.

until 1932, when the dig came to an end with the sudden death of Kjaer—some say from overwork on the dig.

In 1963 S. Holm-Nielsen carried out a brief supplementary campaign at this Israelite-sanctuary site and called for a revision of the conclusions reached by his predecessors in their preliminary reports. They had stated that Shiloh was destroyed in the Iron I period—apparently by the Philistines about 1050 B.C., after they captured the Ark of the Covenant—and that it never completely revived. Holm-Nielsen asserted, "There is no evidence of a regular destruction in the Iron I period, and ceramics from Iron II are abundant." In other words, Shiloh continued to be inhabited in the Israelite period, before being destroyed about 600 B.C.; afterward it was reoccupied in the Roman and Byzantine periods to the time of the Islamic conquest, when it ceased to be important. The final word has not yet been said on Shiloh; the site requires further excavation.

The Excavation at Lachish (Tell ed Duweir)

Tell ed Duweir, thirty miles southwest of Jerusalem, is one of the most imposing mounds in the Shephelah. Strategically located on the main route from Egypt to Hebron and central Palestine, it was occupied from the Chalcolithic to the Hellenistic period. Albright's identification of the site in 1929 as the ancient fortress-city of Lachish is generally accepted, although it is occasionally questioned. British archaeologist James L. Starkey directed six seasons of excavation at Tell ed Duweir between 1932 and 1938. Like Petrie, with whom he worked in Egypt, Starkey was a self-made archaeologist—well organized at all times and a genius in the field. He maintained high standards in every aspect of his excavation: surveying, photography, pottery, epigraphy, etc. In Albright's estimation Starkey's dig at Tell ed Duweir was the best planned and executed project in Palestine. It also should be noted that Starkey's work at Tell ed Duweir did not reflect the Wheeler-Kenyon influence, though Kenyon was digging at Samaria during the years Starkey was at Tell ed Duweir.

Of the several important discoveries made at Tell ed Duweir, the inscriptions were the most remarkable, especially the Lachish Letters or Ostraca; a group of eighteen jar fragments with messages in ink was found in the guardhouse at the city gate in 1935, three additional ones in 1938. The first cache, dated to 589-588 B.C., was composed of letters written to the military governor of Lachish by a subordinate officer stationed at an outpost. Composed in ancient Hebrew script, these letters provide valuable information about the Hebrew language and script in use at the time of Jeremiah and about the history of the last days of Judah.

Were it not for the skill and dedication of British archaeologist Olga Tufnell, who dug with Starkey at Lachish, the final results of this project might never have been published. Committing twenty years to the preparation of the material, she brought it to publication in 1958.[12]

Starkey was prevented from completing the report himself because he was murdered in 1938, at the age of forty-three, while the dig was still in the field. Albright described the circumstances of the tragic death in these words:

> Mr. Starkey left Tell ed-Duweir (Lachish) about 4:30, January 10th, on his way to attend a preview of the opening of the Palestine Museum the following morning. He had been warned against travelling so late through the rugged hill-country around Hebron, but with his usual rather rash courage, he waited until the end of the day's work before leaving camp. About half-past five, when dusk had already settled, he was stopped by armed bandits at a point just before the Beit Jibrin road joins the Hebron-Jerusalem one. The bandits ordered him out of the car, riddled him with bullets, and crushed his head.[13]

This was a rare instance of an archaeologist being killed by local people. It was not politically motivated but resulted from a purely private grievance on the part of the assassin, so far as can be ascertained. The tragic event is not to be misconstrued as a political struggle between Arabs and Jews, with the British in the middle. There have been enough documented incidents attributable to internecine warfare in the Mideast without adding alleged ones.

The Excavation at Ai (et Tell)

According to Albright the biblical city of Ai is located at et Tell, a mound situated near ancient Bethel. Ai, about eight miles north of Jerusalem, is often linked with Bethel. From 1933 to 1935 Judith

---

[12]In 1966 and 1968 Yohanan Aharoni, with the sponsorship of several Israeli institutions, excavated the area of Starkey's "Solar Shrine," which dates to the Hellenistic period. Starkey identified the structure as a Jewish temple on the basis of the architecture. Aharoni also thought it may have been a Jewish temple or sanctuary. Albright and Cross disagreed, stating there is no evidence that the structure is a Jewish temple, certainly not the inscription on the cosmetic burner found in the vicinity. In 1973 David Ussishkin of Tel Aviv University began a new phase of excavations at Lachish, conceived as a long-term study of this key site. In addition to digging the Late Bronze temple on the crest of the tell and other installations, Ussishkin has concentrated on the Iron Age city-gate complex, in an effort to clarify its successive destructions (especially the date of stratum III, which has been the subject of a long-standing scholarly dispute). Like Tufnell and Aharoni before him, Ussishkin has concluded from stratigraphic evidence that stratum III represents the destruction by Sennacherib, king of Assyria, in 701 B.C., while stratum II is to be attributed to the Babylonian conquest under Nebuchadrezzar in 588-586 B.C. Not all scholars have been ready to concur. Kenyon, for example, on the basis of the excavations at Samaria, identified stratum III with the destruction of 597 B.C., the year Nebuchadrezzar besieged Jerusalem, and Yadin agrees. Scholarly debate continues despite the fact that Ussishkin's data and argumentation are convincing.

[13]*BASOR* 69 (1938) 6.

Marquet-Krause of France directed three campaigns at et Tell on behalf of the Rothschild Foundation. She concluded that the site was a flourishing city in the third millennium but unoccupied from about 2200 to 1200 B.C. This conclusion meant that there was no settlement at Ai when, according to the traditional understanding of the Book of Joshua, the Hebrew conquest of Ai is supposed to have taken place. Marquet-Krause's death in 1936 brought the project to an abrupt end.

Marquet-Krause's conclusion contradicted Garstang's; running a trial trench at the site in 1928, he judged from recovered pottery that the town had been destroyed at the time of the Israelite invasion, which he dated about 1400 B.C. Both Garstang and Albright had misread the evidence, however; they dated the Early Bronze pottery much too late. Albright changed his opinion later and acknowledged that there had been a large gap in occupation from about 2200 to 1200 B.C.[14]

Nelson Glueck

The history of ASOR attests that its institutes abroad flourish when long-term directors are in residence. Albright's tenure as director of the School in Jerusalem is the classic example. Nelson Glueck, whose scholarly career was profoundly shaped by Albright, was the second director to spend several years in succession in Jerusalem. An explorer of Palestine in the tradition of Edward Robinson, Glueck was a religious man whose life was deeply influenced by the Bible. Born in Cincinnati in 1900, he was ordained a rabbi in 1923. He earned his doctorate at the University of Jena, now in East Germany, where he wrote his dissertation on the biblical concept *ḥesed*. After meeting Albright, Glueck combined his traditional interest in the Hebrew scriptures with a lively concern for biblical archaeology.

Glueck came under the influence of Albright for the first time in the late 1920s at Tell Beit Mirsim, where he learned the techniques of digging and the intricacies of ceramic chronology. Glueck's rapid progress in field archaeology obviously pleased his mentor, who commented:

Nelson Glueck was the first of my students to master the then obscure art of dating Palestinian pottery by use of its many typological differences as well as by careful analysis of changes of form in each type from first introduction to vestigial remains—which often last through several cultural phases. This he accomplished by working through the pottery of each day, recording its features and regularly attending our informal sessions on the stratigraphy and typology of the pottery which had emerged during a given period or in a given locus. While he learned the principles of archaeological stratigraphy it was as a typologist that he distinguished himself.[15]

---

[14]This site required further study to clarify both its identification and chronology. In 1964 Joseph A. Callaway reopened the excavations at et Tell on behalf of ASOR in an effort to resolve these problems.

[15]*BASOR* 202 (1971) 3.

Explorer Nelson Glueck, the friend of the Bedouin, during one of his surveys in Transjordan.

Glueck manifested his innate love of the land by undertaking on behalf of ASOR his monumental explorations of the formerly unknown lands of Transjordan, the Negev, and adjacent areas of the Mideast. Between 1932 and 1947 the mapping, photographing, and surveying of Moab, Ammon, and Edom—complemented by aerial reconnaissance—consumed most of his time. Later, from 1952 to 1964, he explored the Negev. In all, Glueck visited more than 1500 sites, and most of his identifications are still accepted in the scholarly community. Unlike earlier explorers, Glueck had an extensive knowledge of pottery chronology, a knowledge which enabled him to determine quite accurately the periods of occupation of any site.

Even though several archaeologists have conducted more recent surveys of the vast areas covered by Glueck, his comprehensive geographical, historical, and demographic studies of the ancient kingdoms of Transjordan, especially the Nabatean civilization, have not been surpassed. Naturally, the use of sophisticated techniques in the present day has occasioned some revisions in Glueck's conclusions. Glueck's hypothesis, for example, of an occupational gap east of the Jordan between about 1900 and 1200 B.C. has been disproved by recent surveys in which evidence to the contrary has been uncovered. (To Glueck's credit, it should be observed that he later modified his thesis, admitting that the decline in sedentary occupation for this period was not as radical as he had once assumed.)

Excavations at Tannur and Kheleifeh

Glueck supplemented his explorations by excavating two sites in Transjordan: the ruins of a Nabatean temple at Khirbet et Tannur, in 1937, which shed new light on the religion and culture of the Nabateans;[16] then Tell el Kheleifeh, from 1938 to 1940, which Glueck identified as Solomon's seaport of Ezion-geber.

The German Fritz Frank of Jerusalem was the first to discover Tell el Kheleifeh, near the head of the Gulf of Aqaba. Frank proposed that this low mound with Iron Age and Persian remains was the site of Ezion-geber, today a doubtful identification. Initially Glueck designated a large mudbrick building at the northwest corner of the tell as a Solomonic copper smelter because of the presence of two horizontal rows of apertures on each of the building's walls. When other archaeologists challenged his interpretation, Glueck reconsidered and then suggested that the building had served as a storehouse or granary; he theorized that the apertures had held wooden cross beams as a support for the installation.

A study of Glueck's excavation technique would lead to the conclusion that he was a more competent explorer than excavator. His

---

[16]The Nabateans, originally a nomadic desert tribe of hardy Arabs, had settled all the territory of Edom and Moab in Transjordan by the fourth century B.C., with Petra, the wonderful "rose-red city half as old as time," as their capital. Their temple at Tannur, dedicated to Atargatis and Zeus-Hadad, is situated on the peak of Jebel Tannur, southeast of the Dead Sea, not far from Petra. Atargatis, the goddess of foliage and fruit and one of the mother-goddesses of Asia Minor, was the chief deity in the pantheon at Khirbet et Tannur; Zeus-Hadad, the storm god, was her consort. (Atargatis is a composite of Canaanite Ashtart and Anat, a fertility goddess, developing in Aramaic paganism from Canaanite borrowing. Some have suggested that she is a merger of all three Canaanite goddesses, that is, including Asherah as well.) The temple at Tannur, the scene of a fertility cult, underwent several phases of rebuilding from the first century B.C. to the beginning of the second century A.D., until it was destroyed, probably by an earthquake. The various adornments and sculptured objects of the temple attest that the religion of the Nabateans was syncretistic, combining in its worship both Semitic and Hellenistic deities.

Atargatis as dolphin goddess at Khirbet et Tannur.

misunderstanding of the installation at Kheleifeh and his confusion about the stratigraphy of the site are the bases of this judgment. Furthermore, he did not find time to publish the results of this excavation in final form.[17] It is difficult to have access to Tell el Kheleifeh today because it lies in a sensitive military area—in the middle of no-man's-land between Jordan and Israel.

Political Unrest in Jerusalem

Glueck served as director of the Jerusalem School from 1932 to 1933, 1936 to 1940, and 1942 to 1947, the same years he conducted his surveys

[17]However, publication plans under ASOR auspices are now in place; Gary Pratico of Harvard University has undertaken the project as his doctoral dissertation. In addition to studying the field records of Glueck, he has visited Tell el Kheleifeh several times to check them for accuracy. The new study of the materials indicates that the ceramic corpus dates between the eighth century B.C. and the Hellenistic period, in contrast to Glueck's tenth-century B.C. dating. Pratico's reappraisal of Glueck's work at Kheleifeh undermines Glueck's identification of the site as biblical Ezion-geber. According to Pratico's survey of the site, there is no evidence of tenth and ninth century pottery of Solomon and Jehoshaphat. The difference between Glueck and Pratico is the refinement that has taken place during the past four decades in excavation method and ceramic typology.

Nelson Glueck measuring bricks in the guardroom on the east side of the gateway of Tell el Kheleifeh, while an Arab boy holds the tape and the architect notes the measurements.

The Jerusalem School in 1938.

of Transjordan. During his tenure in Jerusalem there were serious political disturbances and civil disorders sparked by the enmity now accepted as commonplace between Jews and Arabs. In the midst of the political tension the School remained neutral, according to Glueck's own testimony, "We are partisan only to scientific research. No other attitude can be tolerated." He reported in 1937:

> It is worth chronicling that although serious disorders occurred all around the area in which the School is situated, not a single act was directed against the School or any of its members. During the height of the riots, at a time when few if any cars moved except in armed convoy, the Director, accompanied only by the faithful and capable Ilias Tutunjian of Jerusalem as chauffeur, travelled constantly up and down the Jericho road in the conspicuous School car, without the slightest harm ever being threatened. We attribute our safety to the well-known, strenuously maintained, and generally respected political and religious neutrality of the School.[18]

Glueck expressed the hope in the midst of perennial political turmoil that "representatives of the three great faiths, whose substance is of the soil of Palestine, may come together in council tempered with reason and charity, and bring peace to this sadly tried land." The present generation, buoyed by the 1979 peace accords between Egypt and Israel,

[18]*BASOR* 68 (1937) 33.

Director Nelson Glueck refreshing himself at the spring of Dan during a School field trip in 1947. Mrs. Jeffery, wife of Annual Professor Arthur Jeffery of Columbia University, in background.

looks for the fulfillment of Glueck's hope, but this may still not be the time.

Glueck's professional work in Palestine brought him into close contact with the local Arab population, and he was proud of his friendship with them. His explorations in Transjordan were successful because he maintained such a good relationship with the Bedouin, speaking their language and sharing their proverbial hospitality. The Arab staff at the School in Jerusalem remember Glueck with affection. Omar Jibrin, the School's long-term majordomo, referred to Glueck as one of the finest directors he knew during his own forty-year tenure—a tribute not lightly bestowed.[19]

Glueck's Newsletter

When Nelson Glueck was director of the Jerusalem School, he used to circulate occasional letters among his friends to keep them abreast of developments in the archaeology of the Mideast. These private communications were so exciting and informative that Millar Burrows, the ASOR president at the time, decided to circulate widely one such letter from Glueck. The reception was so enthusiastic that Glueck agreed to have his letters distributed to the ASOR membership. This was the origin of the *ASOR Newsletter*, which became a regular feature of the organization in 1948. The format of the *Newletter* has changed from time to time, but it continues to be informative.

Glueck's Other Achievements

While persistently pursuing his archaeological interests, Glueck still found time for the Hebrew Union Colleges of American Reform Judaism. In 1928 he joined the faculty of Hebrew Union College in Cincinnati; twenty years later he became its president. In 1963 he established the Hebrew Union College Biblical and Archaeological School (HUCBAS) in Jerusalem. Glueck's personal involvement in the two American archaeological institutes in Jerusalem—ASOR and HUCBAS—forged a friendly relationship between the schools. The expedition to Tell Gezer (1964-1973), for example, was sponsored by HUCBAS and staffed by ASOR-trained archaeologists.

In addition to acquitting his administrative responsibilities as president of the Hebrew Union Colleges, Glueck devoted considerable time to lecturing and writing—and he did both effectively. Participants in the

---

[19]By compromising his political evenhandedness during World War II, Glueck lost the confidence of Arab friends. In that period he was engaged by the Office of Strategic Services (OSS) as an observer in Transjordan while carrying out his archaeological surveys. It is an unwritten law in the Mideast that archaeology and politics should never be mixed; when they are, it is always to the detriment of archaeology.

Gezer dig in the sixties will recall Glueck's stirring annual presentation, the highlight of each dig season, when he would share with them his own love for the romance and adventure of archaeology, as well as his deep affection for the land of the Bible. He had the rare ability to make digging, which is sometimes boring and always tedious, sound glamorous. His prolific writings centered for the most part on his surveys of Transjordan and the Negev; they have inspired many others to follow in his footsteps. Today regional surveys are a way of life on both sides of the Jordan, thanks in part to the precedent set by Glueck.

Glueck's colleagues paid a lasting tribute to him in two volumes— one a Festschrift, the other a memorial. On the occasion of his seventieth birthday (1970) he was presented a series of essays, *Near Eastern Archaeology in the Twentieth Century*, edited by James A. Sanders. His Israeli friends prepared a comparable collection on Syro-Palestinian archaeology; it is part ·of the Eretz-Israel series and is entitled *The Nelson Glueck Memorial Volume* (1975). Both are fitting tributes to the scholar who was the first Jewish American archaeologist to work in Syria-Palestine. His example has encouraged countless Jewish scholars— American and Israeli—to work there also.

Every encomium on Nelson Glueck must include a word about Eleanor K. Vogel, his long-time archaeological research assistant at the Hebrew Union College in Cincinnati, who helped with the preparation of his several books. Without her, later generations might never have seen the results of Glueck's prodigious explorations. She also produced her own *Bibliography of Holy Land Sites* (1971), a useful reference for archaeologists that is in constant demand; it has been updated to 1980.

Jewish Archaeologists before 1948

Between 1920 and 1948 large numbers of Jews, escaping persecution in Germany, Poland, and Russia, fled to Palestine. Before the establishment of the State of Israel in 1948, Jewish residents in Palestine undertook archaeological projects only occasionally. Although the Jewish Palestine Exploration Society (later the Israel Exploration Society) was established in 1914, the unstable political climate created by the increasing hostility between the Jewish and Arab communities in the late twenties, thirties, and forties, was not conducive to major work in archaeology.

Nahum Slousch

Nahum Slousch was the first Jewish resident in Palestine to conduct an excavation; in 1921 he uncovered the Hammath Synagogue south of Tiberias on the shore of the Sea of Galilee, erroneously dating it to the

Early Roman period.[20] In the Kidron Valley there are some monumental tombs ascribed to prominent persons in history. In 1924 Slousch cleared the so-called "Tomb of Absalom"; in Hebrew it is known as *Yad* (Hand of) *Absalom*. On the basis of architectural style scholars were inclined to date these tombs in the second century B.C.; today Avigad, Rahmani, and other Israeli scholars assign a date in the first century A.D. (before A.D. 70).

Eliezer Sukenik

Albright, in his role as director of the Jerusalem School, assisted in the training of local Jewish archaeologists. In 1923 Eliezer L. Sukenik spent a year studying at the School; Vincent of the Ecole Biblique had also been one of his teachers. In 1926 Sukenik received his doctorate from Dropsie College in Philadelphia and then returned to Palestine, where he became a specialist in Jewish tombs and their inscriptions and in ancient synagogues. Assisted by Nahman Avigad, he began excavations in 1929 at the ancient synagogue of Beth Alpha, at the foot of Mount Gilboa, on behalf of Hebrew University. The site is best known for its magnificent colored-mosaic floors, which, according to the accompanying inscription, date to the sixth century A.D.

When Sukenik was appointed professor of archaeology at Hebrew University in Jerusalem in 1938, he was the first teacher of archaeology at that institution. One of the early scholars to recognize the Dead Sea Scrolls as authentic, Sukenik was instrumental in acquiring three of the scrolls for the State of Israel. He spent the rest of his life studying these manuscripts, and before his death in 1953 he published some of this material. Sukenik was a leading Palestinian archaeologist, but his most enduring contribution to the field was to convey his interest in archaeology to his son, the distinguished Yigael Yadin.

Benjamin Mazar (Maisler)

Benjamin Mazar (Maisler)[21] was also associated with the American School in Jerusalem through his participation in Albright's dig at Tell Beit Mirsim. It was Mazar's distinction to have been both president and rector of Hebrew University at the same time. This was an unusual responsibility and honor, for normally the positions are held by different people. Mazar is perhaps the best known of Israeli archaeologists (along

---

[20]On the basis of later research a fourth century A.D. date has been assigned to this synagogue. In 1961, forty years after the pioneer dig of Slousch, Moshe Dothan of the Israel Department of Antiquities excavated at the same site and uncovered a number of superimposed synagogue buildings.

[21]With the establishment of the State of Israel its Jewish citizens hebraized their family names, for example, from Maisler to Mazar, Bergman to Biran. For this reason Yadin has a different name from his father.

with Yadin) and is rightly considered the doyen of this distinguished guild. Among Mazar's earlier field projects were the excavations at Beth Shearim and Beth Yerah; from 1948 to 1950 he dug at Tell Qasile.[22]

Mazar's excavations in 1936 at ancient Beth Shearim (known in Arabic as "Sheikh Abreik"), located in Lower Galilee, marked an important step in the history of Jewish archaeology in Palestine. The results were a major contribution to modern knowledge of ancient Jewish life, especially during the Roman period. The largest Jewish necropolis ever unearthed in Palestine was discovered at this site. Dating to the third or fourth century A.D., it served as the burial place for Jews of Palestine and the Diaspora. Mazar dug here for four seasons on behalf of the Jewish Palestine Exploration Society and was assisted by Jacob Kaplan, another early Jewish archaeologist, who became the director of the Museum of Antiquities in Tel Aviv-Jaffa.[23]

In 1944 Mazar was associated with the excavation at Khirbet el Kerak, also known as Beth Yerah, along the southwestern shore of the Sea of Galilee. This site is the source of the famous "Khirbet Kerak ware," Albright's designation for Early Bronze Age III pottery. Burnished with red and black, this pottery was first discovered here and subsequently found at other sites in Syria-Palestine. The Israel Department of Antiquities and the Oriental Institute continued work at this site in the 1950s and 1960s.

G. Ernest Wright

In its eighty-year history ASOR has numbered among its members several distinguished scholars; G. Ernest Wright is surely among the outstanding. Born in 1909, he received sound biblical training in the Presbyterian tradition. After completing his courses at McCormick Theological Seminary in Chicago, Wright pursued his doctorate in ancient Near Eastern studies at Johns Hopkins University under W. F. Albright. Because of Wright's archaeological interests, he over the years became more closely identified with his mentor than did any other of Albright's students.

Wright was a versatile scholar who distinguished himself in both biblical theology and biblical archaeology. The convergence of these two disciplines was central to his conception of biblical studies. Holding to

---

[22]In 1968 Mazar undertook the ambitious dig along the western and southern walls of the Temple Mount in Jerusalem, a project that continued year-round for a decade. He recovered remains of Jerusalem's history as early as the Iron Age to the period of the Ottoman Empire; discoveries from the Herodian period (36 B.C.-A.D. 70) were the most exciting.

[23]Nahman Avigad directed additional work at this site from 1953 to 1958. A professor of archaeology at Hebrew University for many years, Avigad is counted among Israel's distinguished scholars. He worked in conjunction with Sukenik in his early career; after the War of 1967 Avigad excavated in the Jewish Quarter of the Old City (Jerusalem).

his basic position that revelation comes through event, Wright understood biblical faith as rooted in history and saw it as archaeology's function to recover the historical foundation of the Judaeo-Christian tradition.

Convinced that the meaning of the Bible could best be realized through the complementary roles of theology and archaeology, Wright contributed valuable books and articles to both areas of scholarship. His doctoral dissertation, *The Pottery of Palestine from the Earliest Times to the End of the Early Bronze Age* (1937), was a critical synthesis of pottery sequence-dating. His final work was theological, *The Old Testament and Theology* (1969). In addition to these two significant works he wrote a number of important articles and books, including *Biblical Archaeology*, which became a standard text of introduction to the subject. His successive writings are an index of his development during his professional career; they reveal that he had moved considerably from earlier positions through his receptiveness to new ways and fresh ideas.

The Biblical Archaeologist

Wright gained his initial field experience in archaeology in the 1930s at the Bethel dig; in addition, he assisted with the publication of the Beth-shemesh project. As early as 1938 Wright made an enduring contribution to ASOR and the biblical world by launching a popular journal entitled the *Biblical Archaeologist*. The *Bulletin of the American Schools of Oriental Research* (*BASOR*), which began to appear in 1919, and the *Annual*, inaugurated in 1920, were serving scholars well. They were too technical, however, for the average reader interested in following developments in biblical archaeology. Millar Burrows, president of ASOR at the time, pointed out the need for a more popular, general publication to serve the layperson. Ernest Wright was the ideal person to fill the vacuum, for he was a scholar who always maintained the common touch and was able to translate the results of scientific research into the language of the ordinary reader.

The first issue of the *Biblical Archaeologist* consisted of a mere four pages. Appearing in February 1938, the journal stated that it would be published quarterly, with a subscription rate of fifty cents a year. Despite its unpretentious format, the *Biblical Archaeologist* was readable and reliable. As editor, Wright was assisted by Albright, as well as Millar Burrows of Yale and Ephraim A. Speiser of the University of Pennsylvania. Emily Wright, the editor's spouse, rendered invaluable assistance in launching the journal and continued to help with the pasting, typing, and mailing.

Wright's article in the first issue, "Herod's Nabataean Neighbor," was probably occasioned by Glueck's excavation of the Nabatean temple at Khirbet et Tannur, southeast of the Dead Sea. This article was the first of thirty-six which Wright contributed to the *Biblical Archaeologist* in as many years. Through the years many scholars in addition to Wright have been responsible for the growth of the *Biblical Archaeologist*. In 1959 Edward F. Campbell of McCormick Theological Seminary, a former student of Wright who shared his teacher's interests in both the Bible and archaeology, became editor of the journal. Campbell like his teacher Wright was also a pupil of Albright and was in the last generation of Albright-trained scholars. Wright continued to be a member of the editorial board until 1962, when he resigned after twenty-five years of service to the *Biblical Archaeologist*. Other members of the editorial board were Frank M. Cross, Floyd V. Filson, Lee Ellenberger, and H. Darrell Lance. Lance served as editor with Campbell for several years, and in that period the journal carried some excellent articles which informed the public but also found their way into the footnotes of more specialized publications.

Other Notable Events in the 1930s

Excavations were not the only factor contributing to the growth of archaeology in Palestine before World War II. The Palestine Archaeological Museum in Jerusalem also played a major role, as a result of the beneficence of John D. Rockefeller, Jr. In 1929 he donated one million dollars for the construction of the building and an additional million as an endowment to provide for acquisitions and maintenance. When the museum officially opened in 1938 the legal title was consigned to the British mandatory government with responsibility for the administration of the museum.[24]

In 1934 Millar Burrows of Yale University succeeded James Montgomery as president of ASOR. Although he was not trained in archaeology, Burrows knew ASOR very well through several of his teachers who had served as directors of the Jerusalem School. At Cornell, where he did his undergraduate work, Burrows studied with Nathaniel Schmidt; at Union Theological Seminary (New York) he made the acquaintance of Francis Brown. At Yale he studied with Benjamin Bacon and Charles Torrey. Burrows was primarily a student of Torrey, who directed his doctoral dissertation, *The Literary Relations of Ezekiel*. His first faculty appointment was at Brown University, where he taught biblical studies from 1925 to 1934. He spent the next twenty-four years teaching at Yale. Meanwhile Burrows served as director of the Jerusalem School in the academic year 1931-1932, and again in 1947-1948. During his first term

---

[24]Just before the mandate ceased in 1948, the title was turned over to an international board, which included an ASOR representative. In 1966 the government of Jordan nationalized the Palestine Archaeological Museum; less than a year later, as an aftermath of the Six-Day War, the State of Israel assumed jurisdiction over the museum. Since then it is commonly referred to in Israel as the Rockefeller Museum.

as director of the School he made a stong appeal for American participation in the archaeology of Palestine:

> One thing which strikes an American visitor to the excavations in Palestine
> is the dearth of American archaeologists, even on what are known as
> American expeditions. Money from America is making possible much of
> the work that is being done, but it is being done and even directed all too
> largely by men of other nationalities. Science, of course, is interna-
> tional. . . . One does not like to think, however, that America can furnish
> only money and must draw upon other countries for the brains and
> ability. . . . The American School of Oriental Research offers an opportu-
> nity for young Americans who would like to take up this fascinating
> work.[25]

During the era between the Wars, ASOR grew in stature in the
Mideast and at the same time made its presence felt in scholarly circles at
home. At the annual meetings of learned societies, such as the Society of
Biblical Literature and the American Oriental Society, ASOR members
were active participants. For example, at the meeting of the Society of
Biblical Literature in 1936, almost half the papers and addresses were
presented by scholars affiliated with ASOR. By the outbreak of World
War II, then, ASOR was playing a major role in Near Eastern studies,
including languages, literature, and archaeology.

[25]*BASOR* 45 (1932) 31-32.

CHAPTER V
A DECADE OF DEVELOPMENT
AFTER WORLD WAR II: 1945-1955

Political Events in the Mideast

The fourth period in the history of American archaeology in the Mideast fell between 1945 and 1955, an era of rising nationalism. At the end of World War II, the central political issue became the establishment of Israel as a Jewish state on formerly Palestinian soil, an event that served to heighten Arab hostility. In 1947 the United Nations partitioned Palestine into two sections, one Arab and the other Jewish, thus sparking the Arab-Jewish War. A battlefield for centuries, the Mideast has perhaps witnessed more wars than any other area of the world. Although it would be difficult to identify the period of greatest political turbulence, the years immediately before and after the division of Palestine would seem to qualify for the dubious distinction. The Arabs finally signed armistice agreements in 1949 but refused to recognize the sovereignty of the new Jewish state.

Between 1939 and 1945, when Arab and Jewish extremists were battling the British, the conflict made it impossible to conduct classes at the School or to secure a resident annual professor. However, these interruptions in the academic routine, in addition to minor damage inflicted on the School property, were insignificant when compared to the casualties suffered by both warring factions. It is hard to believe that the intense fighting in the immediate vicinity of the School during the Palestine War did not cause more serious destruction.

The fighting in Palestine became extreme during the directorship of Ovid R. Sellers in the academic year 1948-1949. In fulfilling his responsibilities he excelled in courage and dedication. On a flight from Beirut to Jerusalem in September 1948 he suffered severe burns when the aircraft was shot down. Having survived the plane crash he proceeded to Jerusalem and continued to direct the School "with cheerful courage and wise ability shown in spite of serious danger and difficulty." His official report to the ASOR trustees made no mention of this near-fatal incident, but it did contain a description of the effect the strife had on the School property:

> The School's position near the front lines made it the target for a great deal of small arms fire and mortar shells. Many windows were broken and every room in the buildings received smoke damage. It is remarkable that while some thirty mortar shells fell in the grounds, not one struck the

buildings. The greatest harm was done by a mortar shell which tore a hole in the front fence and by a mine which was placed in the vestibule of the main building.[1]

During the troubled period of 1948-1949, the doors of the School were open to refugees in need of shelter, and the United States consulate used the building for a year as its headquarters on the Arab side of Jerusalem. With the cessation of hostilities and a return to relative normality, the ASOR property had to be repaired as the first step toward reestablishing the School as a scholarly institution.

As a result of the partitioning of Palestine, the School found itself in the Arab sector of the divided city of Jerusalem; this situation required adjustment to new borders. Transjordan, the region east of the Jordan River, had originally been included in the area of the British mandate for Palestine. In 1923 formal recognition of the independent government of Transjordan under Emir Abdullah, King Hussein's grandfather, was proclaimed; in 1946 the Hashemite Kingdom of Jordan become a sovereign state as a hereditary constitutional monarchy. In 1949 eastern Palestine (including Arab Jerusalem), commonly known as the West Bank, was joined to Transjordan to form the Hashemite Kingdom of Jordan. The Jerusalem School had access to that whole region but was totally isolated from the northwestern section of Jerusalem and the rest of Israel to the west; the new division put an end to the scholarly collaboration that had taken place regularly with Jewish colleagues.

Before the War of 1948 the School was surrounded by open space, unhampered by neighboring buildings (as earlier photographs illustrate). By 1952 East Jerusalem was burgeoning with new developments, and the School no longer enjoyed the luxury of seclusion. As the immediate vicinity became the business center for Arab Jerusalem, the School's directors fostered cordial relations with the Arab neighbors.

Directors of the Jerusalem School

James Muilenburg, prominent Old Testament scholar, was typical of the directors of the Jerusalem School after World War II. Most were Old Testament biblical specialists, and several participated in archaeological field work, despite their lack of specialized training. Learning the techniques of digging "on the job," they often produced creditable results. The part-time archaeologist faces an extraordinary challenge today because the whole discipline has become so complex.

The directors and other appointees of the School in the postwar period found their experience in Jerusalem enriching and challenging, inevitably affecting their professional lives. The field trips, for example,

[1]*BASOR* 116 (1949) 5.

especially the longer study tours to the neighboring countries, were an excellent opportunity to learn firsthand the geography and topography of the Mideast. Muilenburg's comments as he assumed the directorship of the School were typical:

> The American School of Oriental Research at Jerusalem is a center of learning and research of tremendous importance in this part of the world and its possibilities for the future, perhaps today more than at any other time during its past history, are beyond anything we have yet realized. It is a thrilling opportunity to be part of this great institution, and all the members of the School this year [1953-1954] face the year with the expectation that greater things lie ahead.[2]

ASOR Fellowship Program

Despite limited financial resources, ASOR has always taken seriously its mandate to encourage younger scholars by providing them the opportunity of firsthand experience in the Mideast through residence at ASOR's overseas institutes. Annual fellowships have enabled many junior scholars to become acquainted with the land and to have access in their research to primary sources nonexistent outside the Mideast.

Between 1948 and 1967 the political reality excluded all Jews, not only Israelis, from East Jerusalem; ASOR members of Jewish background were, therefore, during that time ineligible for fellowships assigned to the School in Jerusalem. In response to this situation, Louis M. Rabinowitz, an ASOR trustee who supported Nelson Glueck's expeditions to the Negev, in 1951 subsidized a fellowship for study in Israel, thereby providing the opportunity for Jewish ASOR members to do research in Israel. Recipients of the Rabinowitz fellowship were considered Fellows of the Jerusalem School, although their scholarly projects were directed by the Department of Antiquities and Hebrew University. Two recipients of the Rabinowitz fellowship, Helene J. Cantor of the University of Chicago and Karl Katz of the Metropolitan Museum of Art, might not otherwise have been able to study and travel in Israel.

The Dead Sea Scrolls

In the postwar era archaeology continued to develop as a scientific discipline, achieving greater precision in both method and recording. Then the most electrifying event in the history of biblical archaeology came about, by accident, as is so often the case: the discovery of the Dead Sea Scrolls in the wilderness of Judah. While the details are too familiar to be repeated, ASOR's part in this scholarly drama deserves to be recorded.

[2]*ASOR Newsletter* 3 (1953-1954).

John C. Trever, famed photographer of the Dead Sea Scrolls, points to the Isaiah Scroll (40:3) which inspired the founding of the Qumran community. In the background are artifacts from Qumran.

In the winter of 1947 the Taamireh Bedouin, a tribe of seminomadic Arabs dwelling in the area between Bethlehem and the Dead Sea, happened upon the manuscripts, which were secreted in a cave on the west coast of the Dead Sea. Almost a year later, in 1948, Father Butros Sowmy, representative of the Syrian Orthodox Metropolitan of Jerusalem, Athanasius Yeshue Samuel, brought five of the newly discovered scrolls to the Jerusalem School for evaluation. The director, Millar Burrows, who was also the president of ASOR, was making an official visit to the Baghdad School at the time and had left John C. Trever in

Three of the Dead Sea Scrolls were exhibited to the public at the Library of Congress for the first time anywhere in the world from October 23 to November 6, 1949. Left to right: Elias Sugar, pastor of the Assyrian Apostolic Church (New Jersey), Alvin Kremer, the Library's Keeper of the Collections, Athanasius Y. Samuel, Archbishop and Metropolitan of Jerusalem and Transjordan, and David Mearns, Assistant Librarian, inspect the Scroll of Isaiah. (Photo by the Library of Congress.)

charge. Trever received the Syrian Archbishop's representative, who showed him the scrolls. Examining them, he became aware of their importance and sought permission to take photographs. He then sent two of his prints of the Isaiah Scroll to W. F. Albright in the United States for his judgment. Albright responded by air letter:

> My heartiest congratulations on the greatest manuscript discovery of modern times! There is no doubt in my mind that the script is more archaic than that of the Nash Papyrus.[3] I should prefer a date around 100 B.C. . . . What an absolutely incredible find! And there can happily not be the slightest doubt in the world about the genuineness of the manuscript.[4]

[3]A pre-Christian text from Egypt containing the Decalogue and the Shema; it is dated in the Maccabean period, between 165 and 37 B.C.

[4]*Biblical Archaeologist* 11 (1948) 55.

The Dead Sea Scrolls on exhibit at the Library of Congress. Left to right: Athanasius Y. Samuel, who lent the scrolls for display, Luther Evans, librarian of Congress, William Albright, and Elias Sugar. The scrolls were placed on exhibit following a lecture by Dr. Albright on October 22, 1949. (Photo by the Library of Congress.)

Despite the controversy that later surrounded the antiquity of the scrolls, Albright's spontaneous judgment about their age and authenticity, on the basis of the script alone, has held up.

From the beginning, the names of Burrows and Trever and William H. Brownlee have been associated with the scrolls project. As president of ASOR, Burrows made the first public announcement to the world about the remarkable discovery of the Dead Sea Scrolls. When ASOR was granted permission by the Metropolitan of St. Mark's Convent in Jerusalem to publish the manuscripts,[5] Burrows, with the assistance of Trever and Brownlee, edited the Isaiah Manuscript and the Habakkuk

[5] "I was happy to grant the American Schools of Oriental Research the full rights to photograph and publish these documents in order that all scholars might have the opportunity to study them, and that their full value for our knowledge of the Bible might be gleaned." Foreword of A. Y. Samuel in *The Dead Sea Scrolls of St. Mark's Monastery*, New Haven, 1950, vol. 1.

Commentary for the trustees of ASOR. The results of their labors appeared in 1950, in a volume published by ASOR, *The Dead Sea Scrolls of St. Mark's Monastery*. In retrospect it is hard to believe that only 2,000 copies were printed, but it is not surprising that twenty years after publication the volume had gone out of print. In 1972, with the aid of a grant from the Zion Research Foundation of Boston, a new edition was issued, *Scrolls From Qumran Cave I*, edited by Frank M. Cross, David N. Freedman, and James A. Sanders. It included The Great Isaiah Scroll, The Order of the Community, and The *Pesher* ("Commentary") to Habakkuk. This magnificent edition, published jointly by ASOR's W. F. Albright Institute of Archaeological Research (formerly the Jerusalem School) and the Shrine of the Book in Jerusalem, contains photographs of the scrolls in both black-and-white and color reproduction of the photographs made by Trever in 1948.

The scholarly world owes a large debt of gratitude to John Trever, the first American to examine the scrolls, for his skillful photographing of the Qumran manuscripts. The photographs have become an indispensable scientific tool. The Dead Sea Scrolls cannot be handled directly by scholars because exposure to the atmosphere would only accelerate their deterioration. Unfortunately there has already been considerable deterioration of the scrolls from intermittent exposure to light and from the results of early handling by Bedouin, merchants, and scholars. As of now, Trever's photographs are better witnesses to the text in almost all cases than the scrolls themselves.

Eliezer Sukenik and Nahman Avigad of Hebrew University must be credited with recognizing the Qumran scrolls as authentic, reassured, no doubt, by Albright's own statement about their genuineness. Sukenik published three scrolls (Isaiah Scroll B, the War Scroll, and the Scroll of the Thanksgiving Psalms) from Cave One; he acquired them for Hebrew University from an Armenian friend who was a dealer in antiquities.[6]

Millar Burrows

Millar Burrows was internationally known and appreciated for his prompt editing of the Dead Sea manuscripts of Cave One, especially The Great Isaiah Scroll. The fifteen years of his ASOR presidency (1934-1948) spanned a time of extraordinary turmoil and violence in Palestine. During the academic year 1947-1948, when the Dead Sea Scrolls were discovered, Burrows held two ASOR offices simultaneously: the presidency of ASOR and the directorship of the Jerusalem School. Shortly after completing his term as ASOR president he resigned from the organization in order to dedicate his efforts to alleviating the dire conditions of Palestinian refugees. A conscientious man, he did not want to do anything that would compromise the political neutrality of ASOR.

[6]*The Dead Sea Scrolls of the Hebrew University*, Jerusalem, 1955.

Although Burrows was primarily a biblical scholar, he produced some excellent books in the field of archaeology. In 1941, for example, ASOR published his first-rate survey of excavations and their significance for biblical studies, entitled *What Mean These Stones?*. His two volumes on the Dead Sea Scrolls, one published in 1955 and the other in 1958, were on the best-sellers' list. These books treat in a balanced way the data and issues surrounding the monumental discovery at Qumran.

When Burrows retired from the ASOR presidency in 1948, the board of trustees commended him for dedicating himself to the "task of upbuilding the Schools and of expanding their contribution to the scholarly research in and interpretation of the culture, literature and history of the ancient Near East." The resolution continued,

> Largely through his [Burrows's] far-seeing and wise leadership and efficient administration, particularly during the difficult period of World War II, the Schools have become firmly established, have achieved preeminence in their particular fields of labor and research and have contributed mightily to the enhancement of the fame of American scholarship.[7]

The Qumran Expedition

During the period when many new caves were being discovered in the area of Qumran (some by the clandestine digging of the Bedouin), ASOR helped to explore them in an intensive search for additional manuscript finds. Between 1949 and 1956 teams led by G. Lankester Harding of the Department of Antiquities and Roland de Vaux of the Ecole Biblique examined almost 300 caves; in all, eleven yielded scrolls and inscribed fragments. William L. Reed, director of the Jerusalem School from 1951 to 1952, was participating in this expedition in March of 1952 when thirty-nine caves and crevices containing pottery and other artifacts were discovered. The most sensational find of this campaign was two rolls of copper in Cave Three. These rolls turned out to be the mysterious Copper Scroll, which contained a list of entries giving a description of treasure in metals and other items, and their location.

Harding and de Vaux also excavated the ruins of a fortified monastery at Khirbet Qumran, a monastery which apparently housed the Essenes, a Jewish community responsible for assembling the Qumran library, the contents of which date from the third century B.C. to A.D. 68. Had it not been for the strenuous and perservering efforts of these two archaeologists, many of the Dead Sea Scrolls would perhaps not have been recovered.

G. Lankester Harding

G. Lankester Harding was a prominent archaeologist of this period. He directed the Department of Antiquities of Jordan from 1936 to 1956,

[7]*BASOR* 114 (1949) 4.

founded the Archaeological Museum in Amman and served as curator of the Palestine Archaeological Museum in Jerusalem. He learned field archaeology by digging with Flinders Petrie in southern Palestine at Tell Jemmeh, Tell el Farah, and Tell el Ajjul, all situated on Wadi Ghazzeh in the general vicinity of Gaza. He also worked with James Starkey at Tell ed Duweir (Lachish), where he was assistant director from 1932 to 1938. Harding showed himself a good friend of ASOR by facilitating several of its projects in Transjordan and cooperating with ASOR personnel.

No one had a more comprehensive knowledge of Transjordan's geography and topography and of that land's history from prehistoric times to the Islamic period than Harding; nor had anyone been more dedicated to the archaeology of Transjordan. Absent from Jordan for twenty years, when Harding returned in 1976 the Jordanian government officially recognized him for his remarkable service in recovering the country's cultural history. When he died in 1979 his remains were interred on a height in the southwest corner of his beloved Jerash—a gracious gesture by the Jordanian government that would have pleased Harding greatly.[8]

Roland de Vaux

Roland de Vaux, a Dominican priest, was one of the leading historians of the ancient Near East, a biblical scholar, and an archaeologist. Arriving in Jerusalem from his native France in 1933, he took up residence at the Ecole Biblique and spent the rest of his life in Palestine pursuing biblical research. He held many prominent positions in the scholarly community of Jerusalem: editor of the *Revue biblique*, a distinguished biblical journal (1938-1953); director of the Ecole Biblique (1945-1965); president of the board of trustees of the Palestine Archaeological Museum; chief editor of the International Project for the Publication of the Qumran Manuscripts. Possessed of an ebullient personality, his lively spirit and warm personality accompanied a profound intelligence and a wide erudition.

De Vaux's goal in life was to write a thorough and profound analysis of the history of ancient Israel, and his scholarly research always pointed in that direction. When he died unexpectedly in 1971, his lifelong ambition was only partially realized—just the first volume of the intended trilogy had appeared. The second volume, dealing with the period of the biblical judges (1200-1020 b.c.), was reconstructed by his Dominican colleagues posthumously from his notes. Even this uncompleted legacy, which has been published in English as *The Early History*

---

[8]The Jordanian government plans to repair the Jerash museum, damaged in 1970, as a memorial to Harding.

of Israel, is an impressive piece of scholarship and a fitting monument
to a great man.[9]

The Excavation at Tell el Farah (Tirzah)

Between 1946 and 1960 de Vaux directed nine seasons of excavation
at Tell el Farah, seven miles northeast of Nablus. Albright had identified
the site as Tirzah, the capital of the Northern Kingdom of Israel from
the time of Jeroboam I (922-901 B.C.) until Omri's transfer of the royal
residence to Samaria about 870 B.C. Albright's proposed identification of
the site seemed to be confirmed by de Vaux's excavations; among other
results, they revealed that the site had been abandoned in the ninth
century B.C. when Omri established a new capital city at Samaria.

Qumran Caves and the Bedouin

While the professional archaeologists were conducting their surveys
of caves in the Qumran region, the freelance Bedouin continued their
own surreptitious investigations, discovering in 1952 Cave Four. The
richest of all, it yielded fragments from about 400 manuscripts. Then, in
1956, additional manuscripts began to appear in Jerusalem; they were
traced to Cave Eleven, the final Qumran cave to be discovered and the
find-spot of the Psalms Scroll. One of the best preserved of the Dead Sea
Scrolls, it is designated as The Elizabeth Hay Bechtel Psalms Scroll
because she purchased it for the Palestine Archaeological Museum; at
that time it became the property of the Jordanian government. ASOR
obtained publication rights and entrusted the decipherment and editing
of the Psalms Scroll to James A. Sanders in 1961. Written in Hebrew the
scroll dates to the first century A.D. (from about A.D. 30-50). Cave Eleven
also contained a copy of the Book of Leviticus in the archaic Hebrew
script; David N. Freedman with the assistance of Kenneth Mathews
prepared the edition for publication. Of the eleven caves containing
manuscripts, Caves One, Four, and Eleven are considered major in
respect to their contents, while the remainder are minor. The eleven
Qumran caves have revealed scrolls or fragments of all the books of the
Hebrew Bible except Esther.

Other Dead Sea Discoveries

Additional valuable manuscripts have turned up at Wadi Murabbaat,
Khirbet Mird, Nahal Hever, and Masada, all in the region of the Dead
Sea. In addition, there have been discoveries at Wadi ed Daliyeh, nine
miles north of Jericho. Like the Qumran caves, several of these remote

---

[9]De Vaux's detailed history, which steers a middle course between the more radical
views of Martin Noth and the more conservative position of John Bright, is a worthy
companion to their standard texts on the history of Israel.

sites were first uncovered by the Bedouin; afterward ASOR played a role in the recovery and publication of some of these manuscripts.

Elizabeth Hay Bechtel

No account of the Dead Sea Scrolls project would be complete without tribute to Elizabeth Hay Bechtel, the ASOR trustee who used personal resources for the purchase of several Qumran manuscripts from the Bedouin, especially the materials from Cave Four, the Psalms Scroll of Cave Eleven, and the Daliyeh Papyri, so that they could be made available to scholars. Mrs. Bechtel also established in 1978 the Ancient Biblical Manuscript Center for Preservation and Research at the School of Theology in Claremont (California). As the title suggests, the Center collects and preserves ancient manuscripts by the most advanced photographic methods. Its main but not exclusive interest is manuscripts having to do with the Bible; its goal is to make them accessible to the present generation of scholars and to guarantee their preservation for posterity. The center is also the secure repository for copy negatives of the Dead Sea Scrolls. Because of ASOR's interest in every aspect of manuscript study and its concern for the preservation of Western civilization's cultural heritage, it works closely with the Claremont Manuscript Center.

In the words of Kenneth W. Clark, who distinguished himself in safeguarding ancient manuscripts:

> Manuscripts and other artifacts go hand in hand. The former often speak where the latter are inarticulate. Indeed, the manuscript often guides the archaeologist to the discovery of those sites and objects which will illustrate and illuminate the text. Because many an ancient text has been printed, it is easy to fall under the delusion that the text itself is no part of archaeology. We need only the reminder that every ancient document demands a critical text which, in turn, requires that manuscript copies be uncovered and thoroughly explored. It is well to recognize that these manuscripts are *desiderata* of archaeology.[10]

Carl H. Kraeling

Carl H. Kraeling succeeded Millar Burrows as ASOR president and served in that post for five years (1949-1954). Kraeling began his academic career at Yale, where he taught New Testament studies and established the Department of Near Eastern Languages and Literature. He then accepted an appointment to the University of Chicago, where he directed the Oriental Institute. In addition to serving as annual professor at the American School in Jerusalem (1934-1935), he excavated at Gerasa (Jerash) in Jordan and at the ancient city of Dura ("the fortress"), which

[10]*BASOR* 122 (1951) 8.

the Greeks called Europos, on the middle Euphrates in Syria. He made important contributions to the final publication of these two monumental sites; his thorough study of the synagogue at Dura-Europos is a model of its kind.[11]

Commenting on Kraeling's dual appointments as director of the Oriental Institute (1950-1960) and president of ASOR (1949-1954), Albright stated:

> He [Kraeling] was the only man seriously considered for both posts because of his rare combination of qualities and his remarkable ability to take a neutral position on political and other critical issues. It is not too much to say that he saved both institutions from *debacle*.[12]

One can only conjecture about the meaning of Albright's last comment. Academe is filled with single-minded scholars, who at times are a mixed blessing; their expertise is indispensable, their tenacity insufferable. Situations sometimes require a Solomonic diplomat if an institution is to survive. To take political sides in the Mideast, for example, is the shortest route to destroying a scholarly organization like ASOR. All would agree with Albright that Kraeling was a good diplomat; he was also a capable administrator and an excellent scholar.

The Qumran Manuscripts

During his term as president of ASOR, Kraeling supported the Dead Sea Scrolls project by securing funds to establish the "scrollery." This was the large workroom in the Palestine Archaeological Museum where specialists sorted and pieced together the manuscript fragments prior to editing them. Kraeling also raised money to support the publication of the scrolls.

To provide for the ongoing task of editing and publishing the Qumran manuscripts, an international and interconfessional team of scholars was appointed, including several ASOR members. Frank M. Cross of Harvard University and Patrick W. Skehan of the Catholic University of America were assigned responsibility for publication of the biblical material of Cave Four; they did their preliminary work on these texts as ASOR appointees in residence at the Jerusalem School.[13]

---

[11]Dura-Europos was founded by the Seleucids about 300 B.C. as a fortress to protect the trade routes and as a form of military control of the region. It came to an end in A.D. 256.

[12]*BASOR* 198 (1970) 6.

[13]The international team included R. de Vaux, J. T. Milik, J. Strugnell, P. Skehan, F. M. Cross, J. Starcky, J. M. Allegro, D. Barthélemy, and M. Baillet. Several volumes of Qumran texts have been produced, but the pace has been slow, with many long-awaited editions yet to appear. Questions raised by the discovery of the Dead Sea Scrolls about, for example, the transmission of the biblical text, the nature of the Qumran community, and the relationship of the scrolls to the New Testament can be answered only when all the evidence has been published.

Clark's Microfilm Project

Through the scholarly efforts of Kenneth W. Clark of Duke University, annual professor at the Jerusalem School from 1949 to 1950, ASOR made a permanent contribution to the study of New Testament manuscripts.[14] A leading textual critic and an authority on early Christian manuscripts, Clark served as general editor of a monumental microfilm project, which he conducted both in the Sinai and in Jerusalem as annual professor. At that time a new set of variant readings for the Greek New Testament was being compiled, requiring additional textual witnesses to complete it. The American Foundation for the Study of Man sponsored the Sinai portion of the project, with the cooperation of ASOR and the Library of Congress. Wallace Wade of the Library of Congress was chief photographer, and ASOR-affiliated scholars Howard C. Kee, Lucetta Mowry, and C. Umhau Wolf assisted Clark. The results of this vast undertaking continue to be available for study at the Library of Congress in Washington, D.C.

The monastery of St. Catherine at the foot of Mount Sinai, one of the world's oldest fortress-monasteries, served as headquarters for the project. St. Catherine's has been famous as a treasury of rare manuscripts since the mid-nineteenth century. At that time (1859), Konstantin von Tischendorf, a New Testament critic from Leipzig, Germany, visited the library of the monastery and discovered the historic *Codex Sinaiticus*.[15] This Greek manuscript of the fourth century A.D. contains portions of the Old Testament and the entire New Testament and is one of the two most ancient texts of the Greek Bible.

In Clark's project, a staff of twenty photographed more than 2,000 Greek manuscripts during a seven-month period; they worked seven hours a day, six days a week. Altogether, about 3,000 manuscripts in twelve languages were microfilmed at St. Catherine's; the achievement earned for Clark the title "The Tischendorf of the Twentieth Century." While work was in progress, Clark received requests from scholars around the world to photograph specific texts, and he honored every one. Clark described the procedure in these words:

[14]ASOR has always recognized the importance of literary remains and its obligation to assist with their transcription and interpretation. Accordingly, there is an ASOR standing committee for ancient manuscripts, presently composed of trustees with a lively interest in this area of scholarship: Elizabeth H. Bechtel, James H. Charlesworth, Frank M. Cross, David N. Freedman, James A. Sanders, and Joy Ungerleider-Mayerson.

[15]James H. Charlesworth, colleague of the late Professor Clark, has reported the 1975 discovery at St. Catherine monastery of a large collection of manuscripts dating to the first millennium A.D. (fourth to the ninth centuries); it includes at least eight pages from the *Codex Sinaiticus*. Until these new documents can be photographed and studied, one can only speculate about their significance, but they will certainly help to clarify ancient biblical texts as well as the history of the Greek script.

Imagine in our large workroom a table in one corner where three people are processing Greek manuscripts. On the other side of the room at another table two people are preparing Arabic manuscripts. In another place, an editor examines Syriac Books. At two microfilm cameras, operators are filming codices, while at the third the firmans are being run. . . . Enough manuscripts for all these people, for four hours of work, must be listed and drawn from the library shelves promptly each morning, and carried literally by the bushel basket to the workroom. All these manuscripts must be returned at noon, and at two o'clock a similar supply for the afternoon must be made immediately available. Such a daily procedure was rigidly followed in order to make the most of our time.[16]

To complete the Jerusalem portion of the project, Clark and his associates worked in the libraries of the Greek Orthodox and the Armenian Patriarchates, where they microfilmed over 150 manuscripts written in Greek, Armenian, Georgian, Syriac, and Arabic. Clark's microfilming was of great service to the International New Testament Project's preparation of text critical footnotes for the canonical books of the New Testament. During his tenure as annual professor at the School in Jerusalem Clark amply demonstrated that "manuscripts belong to archaeology" (to borrow the title of his article honoring W. F. Albright on his sixtieth birthday).

The Excavation at Dhiban (Dibon)

Transjordan was the scene of several excavations after World War II, especially under American and British auspices. Between 1950 and 1956 successive directors of the Jerusalem School conducted four campaigns at biblical Dibon (modern Dhiban), the capital of ancient Moab, located about forty miles south of Amman.

The site of Dibon had not been excavated before 1950; prior to that time there had simply been a surface examination of the mound. It was well known, however, as the find-spot of the famous Moabite Stone, the black basalt stele with an inscription commemorating the victories of Mesha, king of Moab, over Israel about 850 b.c. The discovery of this stone in 1868 by F. A. Klein, a French missionary priest from Alsace, had been a fresh stimulus to explorers of the nineteenth century.

Fred V. Winnett of the University of Toronto, who inaugurated the project at Dibon in the 1950s, is better known for assiduously copying hundreds of Greek, Safaitic, and Kufic inscriptions in the region of northeastern Transjordan.[17] Then William L. Reed (who had been

---

[16]*BASOR* 123 (1951) 21-22.

[17]Winnett and Harding made several expeditions into the desert of northeastern Jordan, where they discovered more than 4,000 inscriptions, mostly Safaitic, dating from 100 b.c. to a.d. 300. In 1959, on one of these expeditions, W. G. Oxtoby, an ASOR appointee, collected several hundred of the Safaitic inscriptions for his Yale dissertation. Later, in 1980, Vincent Clark, another ASOR appointee, gathered a corpus of the same inscriptions from the area northeast of Azrak.

The Dhiban excavations and tent camp.
(Photo by W. L. Reed.)

associated with the Dead Sea Scrolls project), A. Douglas Tushingham of the Jericho excavations, and William M. Morton took their turns overseeing the Dibon excavations, while at the same time serving as directors of the School in Jerusalem. The frequent staff turnover, combined with the complex stratigraphy of the site, made the initial results somewhat disappointing. However, as the dig progressed the staff, benefiting from experience gained at Jericho under Kathleen Kenyon, vastly improved their method of excavating Dibon. In fact, this was the first American dig to profit from the Wheeler-Kenyon techniques in the field. The American excavations established that Dibon was settled from the Early Bronze Age through the Byzantine and Arab periods, with gaps in the Middle and Late Bronze Ages.[18]

Kenyon's Excavation at Jericho (Tell es Sultan)

The most important dig in this postwar period was Kathleen Kenyon's expedition to Tell es Sultan (Old Testament Jericho).[19] This

[18]Winnett and Reed published their results jointly in ASOR *Annual* 36-37 (1961), while Tushingham's final report appeared in *Annual* 40 (1972). In 1978 Morton returned to the site for further investigation of an Iron Age structure that may have been a temple, a palace, or a public building. Because of the significance of this site and some inconclusive results, Dibon warrants several additional seasons of excavation.

[19]It was actually the third expedition to this site. The first was by Sellin and Watzinger from 1907 to 1909; the second was conducted under Garstang between 1930 and 1936.

Kathleen Kenyon at Qalandia Airport, Jerusalem, in 1952 during the excavations at Jericho. (Photo by M. M. Tushingham.)

was not Kenyon's first experience in Palestine; she had already dug with Crowfoot at Samaria in the thirties. Kenyon directed the Jericho excavations from 1952 to 1958 on behalf of the British School of Archaeology in Jerusalem, with A. Douglas Tushingham of ASOR as associate director. Although Jericho was primarily a British project, from time to time ASOR shared the sponsorship. In that way, several ASOR archaeologists had the opportunity to learn firsthand Kenyon's field method, which they later applied on their own excavations. In fact, during the second half of the present century, practically every dig in Palestine adopted the Wheeler-Kenyon method or a modification of it.

The Wheeler-Kenyon Method

Kenyon's greatest contribution to Palestinian archaeology was her stratigraphic technique in excavation called the Wheeler-Kenyon method. Mortimer Wheeler, distinguished and controversial British archaeologist and Kenyon's teacher, developed a system known as debris analysis while digging at the Romano-British town of Verulamium (England) in the 1930s. Kenyon assisted him and helped to improve this archaeological method. The Wheeler-Kenyon method is often contrasted with the Reisner-Fisher technique; in fact, they are more similar than dissimilar, the latter system anticipating the former by two decades. While the procedure of each is basically the same, the Wheeler-Kenyon method permits greater precision. The first complete statement of the Kenyon method, *Beginning in Archaeology*, appeared in 1952, the year Kenyon undertook the excavation of Jericho.

In the course of excavating Jericho Kenyon ran a deep trench, but not in the crude way as excavators had done before World War I. Her procedure was characterized by stratigraphic control and careful recording, as she dug the site in stratified layers, within five-meter squares. When this grid method of excavation is used, sections automatically occur on the four sides of the five-meter square. The section is the vertical surface that is exposed in the course of excavating squares plotted on a grid. This section of earth which is left standing is known as a baulk. Kenyon paid special attention to the drawing of sections; she did many of them herself, but in consultation with the area supervisor. While greatest emphasis was placed on the sections, the pottery was not neglected; there was daily pottery analysis at Jericho, though not quite the same as Ernest Wright's systematic pottery-reading sessions at Shechem. Kenyon's meticulous technique guarantees excellent control, but it also provides only a limited exposure of the site. There is the danger that its great detail can make publication of final results very difficult.

Although Wright surpassed Kenyon in typological analysis of pottery and in historical method, he readily acknowledged her accomplishments at Samaria and Jericho, when he said:

> I have no hesitation in affirming that the Kenyon work at Samaria is one of the most remarkable achievements in the history of Palestinian excavation. The publication of *Samaria III*, when considered together with the extraordinary work done at Jericho between 1952 and 1958, makes her one of the leading field archaeologists of our generation.[20]

Kenyon's Results at Jericho

Despite the fact that two excavation teams had already dug at Tell es Sultan (Jericho) in the twentieth century, Kenyon carried out extensive work at the site. Limitations in field technique had led earlier excavators to ascribe erroneous dates to some of the remains; notably, Garstang mistook two successive walls of the Early Bronze Age (3300-2000 B.C.) for a double-wall of the Late Bronze Age (1550-1200 B.C.), which he identified as the fortification destroyed by Joshua.

According to Tushingham, the main purpose of Kenyon's first campaign in 1952 was ". . . to obtain further evidence to settle once for all the disputed question of the date of the fall of the Late Bronze city, that is, the date of Joshua's conquest." Much of the confusion associated with the excavation of Jericho arose from the attempt to reconcile the archaeological record with the biblical account of Joshua's destruction of the city.

As Kenyon pointed out, the denudation of the mound by previous excavators, combined with the natural erosion of the mudbrick, has made it difficult to speak precisely about the events of the Late Bronze Age, particularly thirteenth-century Jericho. Many scholars assign the entry of the Israelites into Canaan to the thirteenth century B.C., but Kenyon's excavations reveal that Jericho was practically a deserted village in that period. She concluded from her investigation of Jericho that the village was destroyed in Late Bronze II A (about 1400 B.C.), too early to support a thirteenth-century conquest of Canaan.

During her campaigns at Jericho in the 1950s, Kenyon uncovered evidence that the earliest remains at the site date to the Mesolithic (Palestinian Natufian) era (about 8000 B.C.), while the oldest permanent occupation began in the prepottery Neolithic period (about 7000 B.C.). Kenyon's excavations at Jericho are far more significant for what they reveal about prehistoric civilization than for their failure to support the conquest tradition of the Bible.

---

[20]*BASOR* 155 (1959) 17.

Herodian Jericho

Herod the Great, king of Judea under the Romans (37-4 B.C.), founded Jericho of the New Testament (identified with Tulul Abu el Alayiq), which is situated on both sides of the Wadi Qelt about a mile southwest of Tell es Sultan (Old Testament Jericho). At this site Herod built his first palace—a winter palace—an elaborate complex beautified by a sunken garden and a pool, as well as a citadel and amphitheatre. Appointees of the Jerusalem School conducted extensive excavations at Herodian Jericho, though it had been dug earlier by Warren, Watzinger, and others.

With the joint sponsorship of ASOR and the Pittsburgh-Xenia Theological Seminary, James A. Kelso directed the 1950 season; he was assisted by Dimitri C. Baramki, who had been associated with the Palestine Department of Antiquities during the British mandate. The following year, James B. Pritchard, A. Henry Detweiler, and Fred V. Winnett excavated at the site. In the process they unearthed Herod's palace, though Pritchard initially identified it as a gymnasium.[21]

Biblical Gilgal

While the dig at Herodian Jericho was in progress, James Kelso engaged in a satellite project at nearby Khirbet en Nitleh, one of several possibilities for biblical Gilgal, the site made famous by Joshua's encampment after crossing the Jordan. The excavation revealed that a church that had been erected on the site underwent destruction and rebuilding several times between the fourth and ninth centuries.

The name Gilgal, meaning "circle of stones," is associated in the Bible with several towns in Palestine; it has piqued the curiosity of geographers since the time of Edward Robinson. For the Gilgal in the region of Jericho (from the Book of Joshua [4:19], where Gilgal is said to be on the east border of Jericho), archaeologists suggest two likely possibilities; one is Kelso's Khirbet en Nitleh, about three miles southeast of Old Testament Jericho, and the other is Khirbet Mefjir, about one mile north of ancient Jericho. In 1954 James Muilenburg, resident director of the Jerusalem School, made a small sounding in the immediate vicinity of Mefjir where he uncovered Iron Age occupation (1200-600 B.C.). On the basis of his reconnoitering in the Jericho area, Muilenburg favored Mefjir as the site of biblical Gilgal.[22]

[21]In the 1970s Ehud Netzer conducted a salvage operation at the site under the auspices of Hebrew University and was able to correct some of the mistaken identifications of the earlier excavations. Some ASOR appointees in residence at the Albright Institute (formerly the Jerusalem School) took part in this campaign in order to protect the interests of ASOR, under whose auspices the previous operation had been conducted.

[22]The quest of Gilgal has continued to be a concern to ASOR scholars. In 1967 Boyce M. Bennett, a Fellow at the Jerusalem School, conducted a surface exploration in the

Excavations at Bethel

James Kelso returned to Bethel in 1954, 1957, and 1960 to continue the excavations he and Albright had conducted at the site some twenty years earlier. As before, ASOR and the Pittsburgh-Xenia Theological Seminary served as joint sponsors. Bethel's long history of settlement, extending from the third millennium B.C. to the Byzantine era, makes it one of the most frequently mentioned place-names of the Old Testament. About 920 B.C. Jeroboam I of Northern Israel established sanctuaries at Bethel and Dan, cities in the extreme south and north of his kingdom, both with a long history as centers of worship. The present Israeli excavator of Dan, Avraham Biran, has located the remains of a tenth-century shrine or high place at this site, but Kelso found no trace of a royal sanctuary at Bethel dating to the time of Jeroboam I. In a preliminary report, Kelso mentioned a Canaanite high place found at Bethel "which was used as early as 2500 B.C." and made reference to "the blood of the sacrificial animals still staining the white limestone."

In a well-known essay, "On Right and Wrong Uses of Archaeology," Roland de Vaux criticized Kelso for unwarranted use of archaeological evidence to illustrate the biblical narrative. He complained:

> Bethel was destroyed in the course of the thirteenth century, but this does not authorize J. L. Kelso to write, "The last Bronze Age city was destroyed by Joshua's troops"; because a) the date of the destruction has not been securely fixed; b) the capture of Bethel is not mentioned in the book of *Joshua*; c) its conquest by the house of Joseph was, according to the book of *Judges*, the result of treason and not of military attack; nor does the text say that the city was then destroyed.[23]

Excavations at Dothan

Tell Dothan, thirteen miles north of Shechem, preserves the ruins of biblical Dothan, a city associated with the stories of Joseph and the prophet Elisha. From 1953 to 1964 Joseph P. Free of Wheaton College excavated at Tell Dothan and recovered evidence of settlement extending

region of Jericho in an attempt to pinpoint Gilgal. However, his results were inconclusive, leaving the location of Gilgal unsettled. Bennett excluded Khirbet en Nitleh as a possibility because it lacked remains earlier than Byzantine; he likewise dismissed Khirbet el Mefjir, which bore the remains of an Arab palace of the Umayyad period. In the course of his survey Bennett encountered an antiquity site known in Arabic as Suwwanet eth Thaniya in the Jordan Valley, north of Jericho. George M. Landes, annual professor at the Jerusalem School in 1967-1968, directed a rescue operation at this site when it was being threatened by new road construction. His salvage revealed occupation in the Late Chalcolithic period (3750-3300 B.C.), in the Iron Age II B (late seventh, early sixth century B.C.), and in Early Roman (first century A.D.), but it furnished nothing definitive about the location of Gilgal.

[23] J. A. Sanders, ed., *Near Eastern Archaeology in the Twentieth Century: Essays in Honor of Nelson Glueck*, Garden City, 1970, p. 77.

from the end of the Chalcolithic period to the Mamluk era (A.D. 1250-1516), although not continuously. At present the publication of excavation results is fragmentary, but it is hoped that Robert E. Cooley, the director and editor-in-chief of the Dothan publication project, will correct the deficiency.

In 1959 Cooley excavated an unusually rich tomb at the site; in addition to some 288 bodies, it yielded 3,200 ceramic and metal vessels dating from about 1400 to 1100 B.C. As annual professor at ASOR's Albright Institute in 1980, Cooley studied these pottery vessels preparatory to publication. As well as illustrating the prosperity of the city of Dothan, the contents of this tomb will shed light on the political, cultural, and religious history of Palestine in the Late Bronze-Iron Age I.

The Baghdad School

World War II disrupted the work of field archaeologists in Syria-Palestine and brought American undertakings in Iraq to a standstill. It did not prevent the Iraqis from carrying out their own Mesopotamian projects, however.

Albrecht Goetze

In 1947 Albrecht Goetze assumed the directorship of the Baghdad School and continued in that post until 1956. Born in Leipzig, Germany, Goetze was compelled by the Nazis to leave his homeland in 1934. Relinquishing his professorship at Marburg, he joined the faculty of Yale University and became an American citizen in 1940. It should be noted that Goetze was not a Jew, but a Gentile and was forced to leave Germany because he was an anti-Nazi, who defended Jews in the University and in his academic world. There were very few such people who were driven out of Germany or left for reasons of conscience.

Both Assyriologist and archaeologist, Goetze served for a time as the epigraphist at Nippur. This religious and cultural center of Sumer was the site of the first American dig in the Mideast at the end of the nineteenth century. Archaeologists from the University of Pennsylvania Museum and the University of Chicago resumed the excavation of Nippur after World War II, with ASOR joining in from time to time. The renewed expedition concentrated on the temple of Inanna, which was built by King Shulgi about 2000 B.C. Goddess of love and war, Inanna was also the consort of Enlil, the deity of Nippur and the head of the Sumerian pantheon.

The new phase of excavations at Nippur, begun after World War II, continued for twenty-five years; in addition to Goetze, several other ASOR appointees associated with the Baghdad School participated as members of the dig staff, including Thorkild Jacobsen of the University of Chicago (later of Harvard University) and Vaughn E. Crawford of New York's Metropolitan Museum of Art.

The Journal of Cuneiform Studies

While serving ASOR in several capacities, Goetze made his most lasting contribution to the field of ancient Near Eastern studies by founding and editing ASOR's *Journal of Cuneiform Studies* (*JCS*), a scholarly review of the literature, languages, and cultures of ancient Mesopotamia and neighboring lands. He launched this journal in 1947 and continued as its editor until his death in 1971. Two other leading Assyriologists, Thorkild Jacobsen and Abraham J. Sachs of Brown University, assisted Goetze with the *JCS*. This official publication of the Baghdad School was one of the first journals devoted exclusively to the literary remains of the cuneiform civilizations. When the *JCS* was established, Ephraim Speiser was prompted to make these comments about the undertaking:

> It is equally gratifying to make formal acknowledgement at this time of the founding of the *Journal of Cuneiform Studies* under the sponsorship of our Schools. The need for such a journal could scarcely be overstated. Before the War Europe had a monopoly on such periodicals as were devoted mainly to the study of the various ancient lands which utilized cuneiform writing as their common cultural denominator. As a result of the specialization we now enjoy a greater insight than would have been possible otherwise, not only into the life and role of Sumer, Babylonia, and Assyria, but also into the legacy of the Elamites and the Hittites, the Hurrians and the Urartians, as well as the rich literature of Ugarit. Much of that fruitful activity was curtailed by the War, and some of it was cut off altogether. For various reasons it became our responsibility to maintain the volume and the quality of this important effort.[24]

The journal continues to serve Assyriologists and other scholars under the editorship of Erle V. Leichty of the University of Pennsylvania, with the assistance of Hans G. Güterbock, Jerrold S. Cooper, and Maria deJ. Ellis.

George Cameron

George G. Cameron of the Near Eastern Department, the University of Michigan, was annual professor at the Baghdad School from 1948 to 1949. During that year his research centered on the inscription of Darius I the Great, Achaemenid king of Persia (522-486 B.C.); it was cut into the face of Mount Bisitun (Behistun) in the Kermanshah region of western Iran to commemorate Darius's victory in suppressing a revolt led by the usurper Gaumata. Carved into a crag which towers 500 feet above the

[24]*BASOR* 104 (1946) 6.

level of the plain, this trilingual inscription in cuneiform characters was composed in Old Persian, Elamite, and Babylonian and has important significance for the study of the cuneiform script.

In 1835 Henry C. Rawlinson, an officer of the British army, made copies and squeezes of the inscription at the risk of his life. Cameron climbed this precipitous cliff in 1943 and 1948 to take new photographs and to study those portions of the text that had until that time been inaccessible. In addition to making a permanent record in latex of the inscription, he clarified some uncertain readings in the text. The government of Iran acknowledged Cameron's heroic effort in 1949 by conferring upon him the decoration of the Persian Order of Homayoun. ASOR and the University of Michigan, cosponsors of the project, shared in the honor.

Surface Surveys in Mesopotamia

Despite the central importance of Mesopotamia to ASOR's scholarly concerns, the organization has not worked so intensively in Iraq as in Syria-Palestine because of limited financial resources and lack of a permanent ASOR research center in Baghdad. On the other hand, ASOR has sponsored or participated in several topographic surveys which have helped in understanding the cultural development of Mesopotamia.

While affiliated with the Baghdad School, Jacobsen and Crawford conducted a survey of the ancient mounds in southern Mesopotamia in an attempt to reconstruct the topography of the area. According to Jacobsen who was annual professor at the Baghdad School in the academic year 1953-1954:

> The goal was to determine—within limits imposed by time and funds available—the major structural lines of the settlement in Sumer and in Sumerian times, to identify the probable course of rivers and important canals underlying and shaping the structure, and to establish whenever possible the position and identity of the more important ancient political and economic centers. In every particular our study on the ground was to go hand in hand with information derived from the ancient written sources themselves.[25]

Bruce Howe of Harvard's Peabody Museum, who was annual professor at the Baghdad School from 1954 to 1955, worked with Robert J. Braidwood of the Oriental Institute in northeastern Iraq in search of the remains of early village life. Braidwood is well known for his prehistoric studies in Iraq, Iran, and Turkey, especially his Iraq-Jarmo project in northern Mesopotamia. Qalat Jarmo, a prehistoric site east of Kirkuk in northeastern Iraq, contains evidence of a settled agricultural way of life as far back as 7000 B.C. Braidwood was a pioneer in prehistoric archae-

[25]*ASOR Newsletter* 6 (1953-1954).

ology and the first to make use of an interdisciplinary team of specialists in studying the environmental background of ancient life in the area. Although some of his conclusions have been superseded, his work is still significant.

In the mid-fifties ASOR and the Oriental Institute jointly sponsored the Iraq Surface Survey, which focused on the southern sector of the country. Robert McC. Adams, anthropologist of the University of Chicago and director of its Oriental Institute, supervised this project; he was assisted by Vaughn Crawford, who served as epigraphist. They concentrated on sites inhabited in antiquity (villages, towns, and cities) and on the rivers and canals associated with these sites. Their survey extended between the Tigris and the Euphrates from Baghdad at the north and Nippur at the south. In a mere fifty days, 800 tells were explored and mapped—a rate of sixteen mounds a day. Overall, they investigated between 1,500 and 1,800 tells, as Crawford reported:

> It has been a busy five months. We have spared no effort to visit as many ancient tells as possible. The number of such mounds is no longer clear in my mind. The last I knew it had reached some 1,500. Perhaps 1,800 would not be far wrong for the final count. From all this mass we actually gave numbers to 180 sites and made sherd collections from almost all of them. Of the 180 tells about 90 belong to the Old Babylonian and older periods on back to Ubaid (4000-3500 B.C.). At least 75 of the 90 are mounds which do not appear on any antiquities map. These have, so to speak, been rediscovered.[26]

Archaeologists place increasing value on systematic surface surveys throughout the geographical regions of a country (in contrast to a one-site emphasis) as a means of tracing the development of a culture. In addition to casting light on the cultural history, the survey of Adams and Crawford, with its focus on the ancient canal systems, also contributed indirectly to modern water conservation in Iraq, thereby improving the quality of present-day life in that country.

Israeli Archaeology

The establishment of the Jewish state in 1948 stimulated extraordinary archaeological activity among Israelis. Motivated by national pride and an intense desire to learn as much as possible about their cultural heritage, they have been working intensively; today there are more than 200 professional Israeli archaeologists, not to mention the countless amateur archaeologists. Profoundly influenced by W. F. Albright, the Israelis built on the achievements of Jewish pioneers and others and have developed their own approach to field archaeology in a series of large-scale excavations. The term "Israeli School" is sometimes

[26]*ASOR Newsletter* 11 (1956-1957).

used as a designation of this phenomenon, but in view of the divergence in procedure and technique among Israeli archaeologists, the term can be considered inaccurate. While the archaeological tradition among Israelis dates to the long-term excavations of the thirties in Palestine, Israeli archaeology has developed more through practice than theory.

Israeli archaeologists tend to excavate large sites with monumental architecture and, unlike American colleagues who have been reexcavating previously dug tells, prefer to dig major pristine tells when available. But there are exceptions on both sides, especially when the Americans and Israelis join forces in a dig. In the course of their excavations the Israelis pay close attention to the restoration of homogeneous groups of pottery as they construct a ceramic corpus for all the archaeological sites within Israel and beyond. The Israelis have the great advantage of being on the scene year-round, so that their research is an extension of their digging, and vice-versa.

From the time of Kenyon's excavations at Jericho in the fifties, American and British archaeologists have been emphasizing the stratigraphic method, with special attention to debris analysis, baulks, and section drawings. Isolated by the partitioning of Palestine in 1948, the Israelis were not able to study the features of Kenyon's dig firsthand. They continued, therefore, to uncover large areas in order to analyze architectural units, while paying less attention to the use of baulks for defining earth layers, until the seventies.[27]

Israel's Archaeological Program

To regulate a rapidly evolving national archaeological program, the Israel Department of Antiquities was established in July 1948. Shemuel Yeivin served as director from its founding until 1961. Yeivin was associated with excavations at Luxor, Beth-shan, Seleucia (Iraq), and especially at Tell esh Sheikh Ahmed Areini (Tel Erani), where he directed the work during six successive seasons (1956-1961).[28] Immanuel Ben Dor, who had dug with ASOR at Bethel and had participated in the Beth-shan and Jericho excavations, in addition to working in Egypt, Mesopotamia, and Turkey, was the first deputy director of the Israel

---

[27]Today Israeli archaeologists dig large areas to expose the architectural units but also pay attention to the vertical sections in order to establish the chronology of the site. Any technique that provides only limited exposure would be inadequate at large sites under excavation by Israelis. No one method should be established as standard, as all have different advantages. A combination of several techniques may be best, especially if adapted to the needs of a particular site.

[28]Tell el Areini, located five miles northwest of Lachish, has often been identified with Gath of the Philistines, but such an identification is not possible. Gath was an important city, yet the remains at this site indicate that the Iron Age settlement here was very small. While this mound remains unidentified, Tell es Safi is most probably Gath as Bliss maintained when he dug the site at the turn of the century.

Department of Antiquities, filling that post from 1948 to 1954; then he left Israel to join the faculty of Emory University. Yeivin was succeeded by American-trained Avraham Biran, a student of Albright at Johns Hopkins and excavator of Tell Dan, who has maintained close ties with ASOR and its Jerusalem School (the Albright Institute). At present Avraham Eitan directs the Israel Department of Antiquities; during his tenure the laws regulating antiquities in Israel have undergone revision. ASOR has enjoyed a warm relationship with these directors.

When Israel became an independent state, the Jewish Palestine Exploration Society (which had been founded in 1914 on the model of other national archaeological institutes) became known as the Israel Exploration Society. It has been conducting an impressive program of excavations and publications ever since, thanks especially to Joseph Aviram, honorary secretary of the Israel Exploration Society and the principal coordinator of its scholarly activities. Without exaggeration he has' been the steering wheel of the whole operation for many years, the moving force and the great arranger for the society and its journal. In 1984, the seventieth anniversary of the Israel Exploration Society, an international scholarly celebration will be held to honor the occasion; the focus of the congress will be biblical archaeology.

Benjamin Mazar

Benjamin Mazar, the distinguished biblical historian who has become the dean of Israeli archaeologists, in 1948 began excavating at Tell Qasile, a small site situated on the Yarkon River near Tel Aviv. In the course of digging he distinguished twelve strata, ranging from Iron Age I to the Arab period. The site is especially important for the later excavations that took place there.[29]

Yohanan Aharoni

Yohanan Aharoni was one of the leading archaeologists of Israel from the time of the establishment of the state until his premature death in 1976. A student of Mazar, to whom he dedicated his comprehensive study on historical geography entitled *The Land of the Bible*,[30] Aharoni distinguished himself in field archaeology, historical geography, and biblical studies.

---

[29]In 1971 Amihai Mazar, nephew of the original excavator, resumed the digging at Qasile and uncovered three Philistine temples, built successively on the same spot over a period of three centuries. With the oldest dating to the twelfth century B.C., this Philistine temple complex was the first of its kind ever to be excavated. Like the work at the Philistine city of Ashdod on the Mediterranean seacoast, the Qasile project is of prime importance for the light it sheds on the curious cultic practices of the Philistines.

[30]Revised and enlarged by archaeologist Anson F. Rainey of Tel Aviv University in 1979.

As an early venture, Aharoni in 1954 began a multiseason, joint Israeli-Italian project at Tell Ramat Rahel, just south of Jerusalem, probably to be identified with biblical Beth-haccherem ("house of the vineyard"); the name may be derived from the private dwellings that surround the royal fortress. This site, occupied from the Iron II period to the Early Arab era (seventh century), is important because here archaeologists excavated for the first time a palace of a Judean king; he may have been Manasseh (687-642 B.C.).

Other Prominent Israeli Archaeologists

Immanuel Dunayevsky was the leading field architect in Israeli archaeology; he also served as a surveyor and a draftsman. As a professor at Hebrew University in Jerusalem, he trained many of the present-day Israeli archaeologists and exercised enormous influence on the development of field method for the archaeology of Israel.

Moshe Stekelis, dean of Israeli prehistorians, was also outstanding in the history of Israeli archaeology. A professor at Hebrew University, he helped to inaugurate Paleolithic archaeology in the Mideast; his name is associated with several prehistoric sites in Palestine. In 1941 ASOR awarded him a grant to excavate the Abu Usba caves on Mount Carmel. He also worked at several other sites, including the Judean Desert Caves and the Lower Pleistocene site of Ubeidiya, immediately south of the Sea of Galilee. He took a keen interest in the curious megalithic structures standing on both sides of the Jordan River, especially the dolmens, which consist of several upright supports and a flat roofing slab. It has been suggested that these prehistoric monuments were burial chambers, but the last word about their function has not yet been said.

Jean Perrot

Jean Perrot, chief of the French Archaeological Mission in Israel, has made an important contribution to Palestinian prehistory. In the 1950s he excavated several prehistoric settlements near Beer-sheba: Beer Matar, Beer Safad, Horvat Batar, and Bir Ibrahim. These settlements, with evidence of subterranean dwellings, date to the second half of the fourth millennium. Perrot also explored the prehistoric settlement at the present-day village of Abu Ghosh, nine miles southwest of Jerusalem. In addition, he excavated a Neolithic site on the shore of Ashkelon, as well as the Chalcolithic tombs at Azor, three miles from Jaffa.

CHAPTER VI
AN ERA OF EXPANSION: 1956-1967

Although it is precarious to mix archaeology and politics in the Mideast, it is almost impossible to keep them apart. Like war, politics touch every aspect of life. The history of archaeological research in the Mideast must be written with reference to the politics of the region, no matter how much one tries to separate them. Political events often deter scholarly research, as the Dead Sea Scrolls project illustrates. The accurate decipherment of these extraordinary manuscripts required the joint efforts of all competent epigraphists, regardless of religious or national backgrounds. But the partitioning of Palestine and the consequent division of Jerusalem into the Arab east and the Jewish west prevented ideal scholarly collaboration from taking place. There were scrolls to be studied, compared, and deciphered on both sides of the Mandelbaum Gate,[1] but scholars could pass through with only the greatest difficulty.

In 1956 history repeated itself in the Mideast, when the Suez War shattered the fragile peace. In that year the Egyptian Gamal Abdel Nasser, president of the United Arab Republic, nationalized the Suez Canal, after the United States and Britain withdrew their offer to finance the first stage of the Aswan High Dam project. Israeli troops invaded the Sinai Peninsula, while France and Britain attacked Egyptian airfields. Yielding to pressure from the United States and the Soviet Union, France and Britain backed off; the brief Suez War came to an end without a formal peace agreement between Egypt and Israel. Inevitably, this conflict put an even greater strain on international relations, a strain also felt in the scholarly world.

Directors of the Jerusalem School from 1956 to 1961

Robert C. Dentan of the General Theological Seminary in New York directed the Jerusalem School from 1956 to 1957, an unsettled year interrupted by the forced evacuation of the School staff. For a month in the autumn of 1956 some appointees took refuge in Beirut, while others found residence in Athens. During their absence from Jerusalem two faithful Arabs, Omar Jibrin, cook and majordomo of the School, and Yusuf Saad, secretary of the Palestine Archaeological Museum, risked their own safety by staying in residence to protect ASOR's buildings and

---

[1]The link between Israeli and Jordanian Jerusalem from 1948 to 1967. At the end of the Six-Day War, the Mandelbaum Gate was dismantled and the eastern and western sections of Jerusalem were reunited.

property. Despite the imposition of martial law, the remainder of that academic year proceeded normally, if uncertainly.

The director from 1957 to 1958 was H. Neil Richardson, who spent a good part of the year engaged in archaeological field work. He participated in the excavations at Tell Balatah (Shechem) and Tell es Sultan (Jericho), was archaeological adviser to the Beth-zur dig and, with Robert W. Funk, made a sounding at Pella.

Fred V. Winnett of the University of Toronto served as director of the Jerusalem School during the academic year 1958-1959, a position that he had held ten years earlier. The year started on a tense note when a civil war broke out in Lebanon and a revolt in Iraq. During his tenure Winnett continued his interest in pre-Islamic Arabic; he directed two expeditions to northeastern Jordan in search of inscriptions. Marvin Pope and Oleg Grabar also served as annual directors in this period. Pope lectured on Ugaritic at the School; Grabar surveyed several Islamic sites in Transjordan and Syria.

Yigael Yadin at Hazor

Yigael Yadin, a leading Israeli archaeologist and the son of Eliezer Sukenik, is well known as former chief of the general staff of the Israeli Defense Forces (1949-1952). Born in Jerusalem in 1917 and educated at Hebrew University in Jerusalem, he followed in the footsteps of his father by pursuing an archaeological career. On two occasions he had to set aside temporarily his archaeological interests—once to become chief of staff of the Defense Forces and later to serve as deputy prime minister of the State of Israel in the Begin government.

Yadin directed several important excavations: Masada (the imposing fortress on the west side of the Dead Sea), Megiddo, and the Judean Desert Caves. His most significant project, however, was Hazor, where he directed the first full-scale Israeli excavation, between 1955 and 1958, on behalf of Hebrew University. Tell el Qedah, strategically situated about nine miles north of the Sea of Galilee, is the site of Hazor. Mentioned in both biblical and extrabiblical records, Hazor was the largest city in Palestine during biblical times. Although Yadin conducted the first systematic excavation at this site, John Garstang of the British School of Archaeology had made soundings there in 1928. Prior to Yadin's dig, practically nothing was known about the region of Galilee. In the course of excavating Yadin identified twenty-one strata on the tell, representing occupation that extended across 2,500 years.[2]

Yadin attributed the destruction by fire of the Late Bronze Age city of Hazor in the latter part of the thirteenth century (stratum XIII) to the conquest of Joshua. Excavators of sites such as Jericho and Ai, which are

---

[2]In 1968 when Yadin conducted a fifth season of excavation at Hazor, he discovered a gigantic underground water system similar to Megiddo's. Relating it to stratum VIII, Yadin dated it to the dynasty of Omri in the ninth century B.C.

reported to have been sacked during the Israelite occupation of Palestine, find it difficult to reconcile their investigations of these cities with the traditional understanding of the Israelite conquest. Yadin, however, has found his evidence at Hazor compatible with the conquest tradition in the biblical account.

Yadin's military experience was clearly reflected in his extremely well-organized dig. The staff functioned as a team, with each member responsible for one of the fields under excavation.[3] Up to that time all responsibility on a dig had resided with the director, who usually delegated little authority. Kathleen Kenyon, for example, maintained almost total control over her excavations, hardly shared responsibility, and did almost everything herself, including the section drawings (the latter in consultation with the area or square supervisors). This style placed an extraordinary burden on the director and was almost too much even for the formidable Kenyon. The team approach which is much more reasonable and efficient became the rule on most digs after Hazor.

Before undertaking his own excavation at Shechem, G. Ernest Wright visited Yadin at Hazor. He was impressed with the organization of the dig and the application of the team approach and later acknowledged his indebtedness to Yadin:

> In 1956 it was my privilege to visit the Rothschild-Hebrew University excavation at Hazor. . . . Its staff was composed of forty-five people—the largest ever assembled in one Syro-Palestine expedition—and its procedures were beautifully organized. I learned much from it, though I found myself wishing that Miss Kenyon's methods were more seriously taken. In any event, I was most impressed, and adapted certain things for use at Shechem. . . .[4]

Wright adopted the organization and recording model that he observed at Hazor, although he also credited Reisner with some of this influence. Yadin had applied Albright's practice of analyzing pottery on a regular basis in the course of the dig. Wright, too, inherited this procedure from Albright and utilized it with great care at Shechem.

G. Ernest Wright and the Shechem Excavation

The year 1956 signalled the beginning of a great era in American archaeology in the Mideast. G. Ernest Wright, who had already served in

---

[3]Yadin's senior staff consisted of the following Israelis, all of whom became prominent archaeologists in Israel: Yohanan Aharoni, Ruth Amiran, Moshe and Trude Dothan, Immanuel Dunayevsky, and Claire Epstein. Jean Perrot of the French Archaeological Mission also played a key role on the Hazor dig.

[4]G. Ernest Wright, *Shechem: The Biography of a Biblical City*, New York, 1965, p. 52. Wright's popular volume on Shechem deals with the history of the site and its excavation. It is the most complete report available today but is being revised and updated by Edward F. Campbell in light of work done after 1965.

Ernest Wright reading pottery with some of his staff at Shechem. Left to right: Edward Campbell, John Holladay, Nancy Lapp, Ernest Wright, and Paul Lapp. (Photo by J. McCracken.)

several roles for ASOR, began to emerge as a prominent figure among Syro-Palestinian archaeologists. At that time he led a major expedition to Tell Balatah, the site of biblical Shechem in central Palestine, with the support of Drew University, McCormick Theological Seminary, and ASOR.

In retrospect, Wright's work at Shechem (which spanned many years) was a watershed in the archaeology of Syria-Palestine. Wright conceived of Shechem as a training ground for Americans in the period after World War II. He wanted younger archaeologists to learn how to dig according to the Reisner-Fisher technique, with the refinements that Kathleen Kenyon had developed at Samaria and Jericho. Shechem was the first large-scale American dig to apply these methods; at the same time, Wright instituted other practices as well. He stressed the importance of teamwork among the staff, not only in theory, but also in practice. He paid close attention to pottery analysis, making certain that the potsherds were promptly and properly studied and recorded. He also made the members of the core staff responsible for publishing the areas dug under their direction.

Yadin correctly observed that Wright had created a new school of field archaeology at Shechem. Almost every later excavation, regardless

Ovid Sellers on his eightieth birthday during the 1964 season at Shechem. Oliver Unwin, the intrepid surveyor for the Tell er Ras part of the Shechem project, was unable to come down the mountain for the birthday party, so he sent a "card," a slab of limestone. (Photo by Lee Ellenberger.)

of sponsorship, reflected the influence of the Shechem project. In fact, the Shechem excavations, either directly or indirectly, spawned several digs. The Gezer project was certainly an outgrowth of Shechem; Gezer, in turn, produced subsequent excavations such as Hesi, Shema, Idalion, and Lahav. It may be difficult to measure, but Taanach, Ai, and Heshbon certainly owed much to Shechem.

The ancient city of Shechem, strategically situated at the pass between Mount Gerizim and Mount Ebal, was an important political and religious center dating back to the third millennium B.C. In view of Shechem's prominent role in biblical history, it seemed appropriate that Ernest Wright should direct a long-term excavation at this site. Like Sellin, his predecessor at Shechem, Wright was both an archaeologist and a biblical scholar. After a twenty-year absence from the field, Wright arrived at Balatah, the modern Arab village adjacent to Shechem, in the summer of 1956 at the urging of his colleague at McCormick Theological Seminary, Frank M. Cross. Wright began by conducting a three-week exploratory dig, assisted by Bernhard W. Anderson and Robert J. Bull of the Drew University faculty.

Reexcavating the tell was to be a challenging task; German archaeologists who had worked there at various times between 1913 and 1934 had done only meager recording and had misdated several of the architectural features of the ancient city. Furthermore, Wright did not have access to their published results—unfortunately Sellin's files, excavation reports, and several small objects recovered from the site had been destroyed by fire when the Americans bombed Berlin in 1943. There was some continuity with the earlier German campaigns, however: Hans H. Steckeweh, an architect who had directed the 1934 season, joined Wright's staff in 1957. In 1934 Steckeweh and Wright had worked under Albright at Bethel, where they learned the techniques of archaeological fieldwork.

Schooled in the methods developed by Reisner, Albright, and Kenyon, Wright adapted them to suit the peculiarities of Tell Balatah. He combined stratigraphic digging and daily ceramic analysis with a detailed recording system, which included maps, architectural plans, and abundant photographs. As an *aide-memoire* for the publication of the final report, the area supervisors kept a diary of their procedures in the form of a progress report. The supervisors also paid special attention to the vertical sections or baulks in order to control the stratigraphy; these sections were drawn to scale on a regular basis. The registrar also systematically described in written form all objects and other finds unearthed in the course of digging. Finally, the chief photographer, Lee C. Ellenberger, made his own pictorial record of every phase of the project.

The excavators at Shechem uncovered twenty-four strata of occupation, the oldest dating to the Chalcolithic period (about 4000 B.C.). The frequent references to Shechem in the Bible indicate that this city played a central role in the history of the Israelites. In addition to Shechem's place in the patriarchal narratives of the Book of Genesis, other Old Testament books, especially Joshua, contain references to the city. Biblical allusions to Shechem, as well as the succession of temples discovered at this site by the excavators, attest to its importance as a religious center. By combining literary evidence with the results of digging, scholars are clarifying the complex history of these sanctuaries at Shechem.

Lawrence Toombs and Edward Campbell

During the record-long dig at Shechem (1956-1973), numerous staff members participated in the project; several later became directors of their own excavations. Two deserve special mention for their contribution to the Shechem project: Lawrence E. Toombs and Edward F. Campbell—the right and left hands of the director, Ernest Wright.

Toombs had learned his skills under Kenyon's tutelage at Jericho and brought them to bear on Shechem. He described the field method used at Shechem in an appendix to Wright's volume on Tell Balatah, *Shechem: The Biography of a Biblical City.* After the War of 1967 Toombs played a leading role in excavations located in Israel—at Tell el Hesi and Caesarea Maritima. When illness prevented Wright from being in the field at Tell Balatah, Toombs and Campbell shared directorial responsibility. Following Wright's unexpected death in 1974, Campbell took steps to bring the Shechem excavations to final publication; up to that time only preliminary reports had appeared.

Tell er Ras

Tell er Ras, the northernmost peak of Mount Gerizim, was the site of another important temple in the Shechem area. Tell er Ras provides a spectacular view of the plain below. It would have been visible to Jesus and the Samaritan woman in the Gospel of John as they met and conversed at Jacob's well in the immediate vicinity of Shechem, the main city of the Samaritans. Designated as field XII of the overall Shechem project, Tell er Ras was excavated as a satellite of Tell Balatah between 1964 and 1966; Robert J. Bull, a member of the original Shechem team, served as director. The War of 1967 brought his work to a standstill, although he returned to Tell er Ras in 1968 to clarify some earlier interpretations in preparation for publication of his report.

Bull's soundings in 1964 revealed Roman and Hellenistic remains at Tell er Ras. During the 1966 campaign he excavated the stairway and terraces on the north slope of the mountain; in that season he also discovered the foundations of a Greek-style temple. On the basis of numismatic and literary evidence, Bull concluded that the temple, dedicated to Zeus Hypsistos, had been erected by Emperor Hadrian in the second century A.D. In fact, second-century coins minted at the neighboring city of Neapolis (modern Nablus) depict this temple. Bull believes that the Roman Zeus temple was constructed over the Samaritan sanctuary, an earlier edifice dating from 335-330 B.C., which the Hasmonean ruler John Hyrcanus destroyed in 128 B.C. Bull is satisfied that the archaeological results generally concur with the account of the Jewish historian Josephus, who is the source of the tradition that Hyrcanus razed the Samaritan temple.

In addition to the temple sequence, in 1966 the excavators of Tell er Ras unearthed six plaster-lined, vaulted cisterns, constructed in the third century A.D. When normality returns to the disputed West Bank, excavation must be resumed at the imposing site of Tell er Ras to clarify the temple structures, only partially studied to date, as well as the historical context of the cisterns and other features of the excavation.

The Expedition to Sardis

ASOR was involved in another long-term excavation project: at Sardis in Turkey, the famous Lydian and Roman city located in western Asia Minor about fifty miles east of Smyrna (modern Izmir). In 1958 a joint expedition from Harvard and Cornell universities, in cooperation with ASOR, began a new phase of digging at Sardis under the direction of George M. A. Hanfmann of Harvard, assisted by architect A. Henry Detweiler of Cornell, who was president of ASOR at the time.[5] Excavation and restoration at the site are continuing in the eighties.

One of the main objectives of Hanfmann's undertaking at Sardis was to record the monuments that had been standing exposed to the elements for centuries. In addition, the Harvard-Cornell expedition carried out the partial restoration of the Roman gymnasium and the monumental synagogue, which forms part of the gymnasium complex. Hanfmann's campaigns have also illuminated the historical periods at Sardis from Lydian through Hellenistic, Roman, early Christian, Byzantine, and Ottoman. Most of the preliminary reports on the results of the Sardis project have been published in *BASOR*.

A. Henry Detweiler

A. Henry Detweiler played a leading role not only in the Sardis excavations but also in the activities of ASOR generally. Trained as an

---

[5]Earlier expeditions at Sardis worked under other auspices. Howard Crosby Butler of Princeton University excavated the temple of Artemis from 1910 to 1914, when World War I interrupted the project. T. Leslie Shear, professor at Columbia and Princeton and well known for his excavation of the Athenian Agora, dug at Sardis from 1921 to 1922, when his work was brought to a halt by the Graeco-Turkish War. Butler, who served as an ASOR trustee from 1921 to 1922, also conducted important surveys in Syria and northern Transjordan in the early years of the present century.

archaeological architect, he spent most of his academic life at Cornell, where he was both professor and dean. He gained his field experience as a member of several ASOR-affiliated digs in Palestine and Mesopotamia. From 1930 to 1931 he excavated with Speiser at Tell Billa and Tepe Gawra; the following year he joined the staff of Tell Beit Mirsim, where Albright was developing and refining the ceramic index for Palestine. He also participated in the excavations at Gerasa (Jerash) in Transjordan and at Dura-Europos on the middle Euphrates, two spectacular sites with a special attraction for Detweiler because of their impressive architectural remains. Always a close friend of the Crowfoots of the British School of Archaeology in Jerusalem, Detweiler also dug with them at Sebastiyeh (Samaria) in 1935. As well as his work in the Mideast, Detweiler carried on architectural research in northern Italy. Drawing on field experience gained from these projects, Detweiler wrote *A Manual of Archaeological Surveying*, which ASOR published in 1948; it continues to be a useful guide for archaeologists.

In addition to functioning as an archaeological architect on ASOR field projects, Detweiler served in several of ASOR's key administrative posts. He was acting director of the Jerusalem School in 1949 and director during the academic year 1953-1954 (although James Muilenburg served as the resident director that year). From 1955 to 1965, a period of expansion, Detweiler was ASOR's president; then, upon retirement from that position he became a life trustee. Detweiler's dedication to ASOR earned him, at the time of his death in 1970, this well-deserved tribute from Albright, "To few men have the American Schools of Oriental Research been so much indebted as to Henry Detweiler." In his lifetime he distinguished himself as a skilled architect and an excellent administrator.

The W. F. Albright Fellowship

At the end of 1959 Paul F. Bloomhardt of Wittenberg University, Springfield, Ohio, proposed that a fellowship be established to honor W. F. Albright for his services to ASOR and his overall contribution to ancient Near Eastern studies. Bloomhardt made the initial contribution to the Albright fund, and other friends were invited to do likewise. Consequently the trustees of ASOR established in 1961 the W. F. Albright Fellowship for study anywhere in the Mideast; junior scholars have availed themselves of this fellowship for study both in Israel and Jordan.

James Pritchard

James B. Pritchard, associated for a long time with the University of Pennsylvania Museum, was prominent among the officers and trustees of ASOR. He also directed three important excavations—el Jib, the site of biblical Gibeon; Tell es Saidiyeh, often identified with Zarethan; finally Sarafand, the site of ancient Zarephath (Sarepta in Greek).

The Gibeon (el Jib) Excavation

Located six miles northwest of Jerusalem, Gibeon appears frequently in the Bible; the first reference is contained in the Book of Joshua, where the people of Gibeon secured by ruse a covenant of peace from Joshua and the invading Israelites. In 1838 Edward Robinson, struck by the similarity between el Jib, the name of the Arab village, and biblical Gibeon, equated the two; his identification was confirmed over a hundred years later by the discovery at the site of thirty-one storage jar handles inscribed with the name "Gibeon." These jar handles of the wine industry are sixth century B.C., judged paleographically by Frank Cross and ceramically by Ernest Wright.

Pritchard undertook the first major excavation of Gibeon between 1956 and 1962. During five seasons of digging, he made several important discoveries, notably the spectacular water system, with its huge round pool and spiral staircase, carved from solid rock and dating to the tenth century B.C. Like Jerusalem, Hazor, Megiddo, and Gezer, Gibeon had its technique for providing water completely within the bounds of the city wall. Such a system was especially important when the city was under enemy attack. Pritchard also gained an understanding of the wine industry of Gibeon; uncovering sixty-three wine cellars at Gibeon, Pritchard estimated that the city could store about 25,000 gallons of wine. It was during the eighth and seventh centuries B.C., according to the excavator, that Gibeon flourished because of its lucrative wine industry.

The Expedition to Tell es Saidiyeh

In 1964 Pritchard began his investigation of Tell es Saidiyeh, which Nelson Glueck had tentatively identified as biblical Zarethan. An impressive site, it is a double mound situated midway between the Lake of Tiberias and the Dead Sea, a mile to the east of the Jordan River. Pritchard chose to excavate this site because so little was known about the Jordan Valley. Dr. Awni Dajani, director of the Jordanian Department of Antiquities at the time, enabled Pritchard and other American archaeologists to excavate in Jordan. After four seasons the Six-Day War of 1967 brought Pritchard's work at Tell es Saidiyeh to a halt. Fortunately, he had already made several important discoveries, including a cemetery dating from the thirteenth to the eleventh century B.C. One of the spectacular burials was that of an apparent noblewoman (Tomb 101); her skeleton was adorned with jewelry of silver, gold, and carnelian and surrounded with bronze vessels.

The presence of bronze objects at Tell es Saidiyeh calls to mind a verse in the biblical Book of Kings, which mentions the casting of bronze vessels in the vicinity of Zarethan and Succoth for use in the temple (1 Kings 7:46). It is significant that nearby Tell Deir Alla contains evidence of a bronze-smelting industry. Following the suggestion of Glueck, some would identify this site with biblical Succoth, but the current Dutch excavator of Deir Alla, Henk J. Franken, does not agree, preferring instead to locate Succoth at Tell el Ahsas, just west of Tell Deir Alla. Franken points out that both Ahsas (Arabic) and Succoth (Hebrew) mean "booths."

Pritchard also unearthed what appears to be a stairway from the Iron Age on the north side of Tell es Saidiyeh; it extends from the summit to a spring at the bottom of the mound. (Archaeologist James A. Sauer would interpret this installation as a watercourse or the like, but not a stairway.) The expedition also concentrated on the domestic quarter, located on the upper mound, where eighth-century B.C. mudbrick houses were excavated.

John E. Huesman, annual professor at the Jerusalem School from 1966 to 1967, directed the 1967 campaign at Tell es Saidiyeh, the final season of digging. Pritchard had aspirations of returning to the site to finish the project after the war, but he abandoned that plan. Digging must resume someday because the site is so promising and the work so unfinished.[6]

The Expedition to Beth-zur

After an interval of twenty-six years, Ovid R. Sellers returned to Beth-zur in 1957 to conduct a second campaign, with the sponsorship of ASOR and McCormick Theological Seminary. His serving that year as professor of archaeology at the Jerusalem School allowed him to re-examine some problems that had arisen during an earlier phase of his dig at Beth-zur. There had been question, for example, about the defense system of the city, so further investigation was in order.

Briefly, excavation established that occupation of the site extended from the third millennium to at least 100 B.C., though not continuously. Beth-zur, a frontier fortress between Judea and Idumea, reached its peak in the Hellenistic period, when the city was fortified several times during the Maccabean wars fought between the Syrians and the Jews. In 165 B.C. Judas Maccabeus defeated Lysias, the Syrian regent, at Beth-zur; after the victory Judas rebuilt the city wall, chiefly as protection against the

---

[6]After his excavation at Tell es Saidiyeh in Jordan was aborted, Pritchard began in 1969 a new dig at Sarafand in Lebanon. At the time Lebanon was peaceful, but war also disrupted that expedition later.

incursions of the Idumeans. When the Syrians regained control, they strengthened the defenses of the city. Peace was finally restored at the end of the Greek period, between 140-100 B.C. It was thought that the city was abandoned about 100 B.C., but the redating of the "John Hyrcanus I" coins to John Hyrcanus II puts the date of the end of Beth-zur at least in the seventies B.C.

Several ASOR appointees in residence at the School in 1957 assisted with the excavation: H. Neil Richardson, director of the School, served as archaeological adviser; Robert L. Funk, John L. McKenzie, and Paul and Nancy Lapp participated in the dig and helped to prepare the final report for publication.

The Expedition to Tuleilat el Ghassul

The series of low mounds a few miles northeast of the Dead Sea, known as Tuleilat el Ghassul, were once again the subject of excavation, as a sequel to the campaigns of Alexis Mallon (1929 to 1934) and Robert Koeppel (1936 and 1938). Robert North, professor of archaeology at the Pontifical Biblical Institute in Rome, began a new phase of digging at Ghassul in 1960; J. Basil Hennessy, presently at the University of Sydney, continued the work in 1967 and 1975. Mallon had been attracted to Ghassul originally by the abundance of flints and ceramics lying on the surface, and it was his work at the site which stimulated so much later interest. Today Ghassul is best known for the unique, multicolored, geometric designs of its mural paintings; at least they are its most characteristic feature. The eight-pointed Star of Ghassul is one example of this distinctive art form.

Separating the various stratigraphic layers at this site has proved to be a difficult undertaking for all the excavators. North, who was assisted by Louis F. Hartman, annual professor at the Jerusalem School in 1960, came to the conclusion that there was "a recognizable succession of some four occupation levels" over the surface of Ghassul. The complexity of this site requires future campaigns to clarify its stratigraphy and pottery typology; Ghassul has much more light to shed on Chalcolithic culture.

Joseph Callaway and the Excavations at Ai

Joseph A. Callaway, one of ASOR's leading archaeologists, had the benefit of digging with Ernest Wright at Shechem and with Kathleen Kenyon at Jerusalem. Between 1964 and 1972 Callaway led his own expedition to et Tell (biblical Ai), with the sponsorship of ASOR, the Southern Baptist Theological Seminary, where he was a professor, and several other supporting institutions. Callaway's was the most meticulous dig in the Kenyon tradition. His intent was to complete the project begun by Judith Marquet-Krause in 1933 but interrupted by her untimely death in 1936 after only three seasons of digging. After Garstang's soundings at the site in 1928 and Marquet-Krause's work there, Callaway's

Director Joseph A. Callaway making a section drawing at Ai.

expedition was the third phase of excavation at et Tell. For the most part Callaway's findings confirmed the interpretations of Marquet-Krause.

From the results of his own survey of the area, Albright suggested in 1924 that et Tell was the site of biblical Ai (Hebrew always with the article, *ha'ai,* "the ruin"). Some scholars challenge this identification, but Callaway accepts it for lack of a satisfactory alternative. The proposed site of Ai was occupied in the Early Bronze Age from about 3100 to 2350 B.C., according to the excavator; then it was destroyed and abandoned. After a gap of at least 1100 years, it was resettled for a short time in the Iron I period (about 1220 to 1050 B.C.) before being abandoned permanently. Marquet-Krause and Callaway's finding no evidence of Late Bronze Age remains makes it difficult to reconcile the traditional date of the conquest in the Late Bronze Age (thirteenth century),

Joseph A. Callaway and Roland de Vaux discussing a problem of stratigraphy at Ai.

Joshua's capture of Ai as recounted in the Book of Joshua, and the archaeological evidence. Marquet-Krause considered the biblical account to be legendary and without historical foundation. Callaway accepts the basic historicity of the Book of Joshua but suggests that the reconstruction of the conquest of Palestine, which so far as Ai is concerned may have been embellished by the biblical author, needs to be modified.

Excavations in Jerusalem

Jerusalem is the most fascinating site in Palestine and perhaps the most excavated city in the world. The first systematic excavations were conducted there by the Palestine Exploration Fund from 1867 to 1870 under the direction of Charles Warren, who investigated the walls of the city and the Temple Mount by means of shafts and tunnels. Among other archaeologists who worked to make sense of the complex history of Jerusalem are familiar names: Clermont-Ganneau, Bliss, Dickie, Macalister, and Crowfoot.

Kathleen Kenyon

A new phase of Jerusalem excavations began in 1961, when Kathleen Kenyon, assisted by Roland de Vaux, dug at the site of the City of David, a very small part of modern Jerusalem, to test the conclusions of earlier archaeologists. Concentrating on the Ophel ("mound"), the steep slope on the southeastern spur of the Old City, she attempted to determine the boundaries of the original Jebusite city. Kenyon excavated in a long, narrow trench from the crest of the hill to Gihon Spring. Her large-scale project, which yielded valuable information about the Bronze Age, the Canaanite period, and the Israelite occupation of Jerusalem in the Iron Age, came to an abrupt end with the outbreak of the Six-Day War in June 1967. Kenyon produced a nontechnical report entitled *Digging Up Jerusalem* (1974) but died before finishing her final report for publication. The Jerusalem dig was Kathleen Kenyon's last field project; it was an important undertaking but lacked the excitement of Jericho.[7]

Kenyon spent her final years—little more than a decade—in England preparing her excavation reports for publication. However, like many of her archaeological colleagues, she died with the bulk of her material unpublished. *Jericho*, volume 3, edited by T. A. Holland, has now appeared (1981); responsibility for publication of the Jerusalem dig has been assigned to A. Douglas Tushingham of the Royal Ontario Museum.

In the closing months of her life Kathleen Kenyon was presented a Festschrift, *Archaeology in the Levant*, as an expression of appreciation and affection. This collection of essays, extending from the Neolithic to the Islamic period, reflects a diversity in subject matter commensurate with her own broad interests. When Dame Kathleen Mary Kenyon died in 1978, she had earned a place beside William Foxwell Albright and Roland de Vaux; she lacked their historical sense and language skills but surpassed them as an excavator. History will regard her as a distinguished Syro-Palestinian archaeologist.

Paul Lapp

Paul W. Lapp, a promising Syro-Palestinian archaeologist, arrived in the Mideast during the period of ASOR expansion; he joined the dig at Tell Balatah in 1957. His field work at this site and elsewhere attested to his unusual competence as a stratigrapher and a ceramicist. After studying with Albright at Johns Hopkins University and with Wright at Harvard, Lapp produced an excellent dissertation entitled *Palestinian Ceramic Chronology, 200 B.C. to A.D. 70* (1961). This work quickly became an invaluable handbook of Palestinian pottery for the Late Hellenistic and Early Roman periods, which up to this time had been a dark age. Based on well-stratified sites, Lapp's detailed study presented

---

[7]In 1978 Yigal Shiloh of Hebrew University began to reexcavate the City of David. Acknowledging the correctness of many of Kenyon's interpretations, Shiloh believes that some of her dates will have to be revised in the light of new evidence. Shiloh planned to dig for several seasons, but ultraorthodox Jews, charging him with the desecration of "holy ground," halted the project at least temporarily.

the most complete ceramic corpus possible for its time and was a significant breakthrough in the archaeology of Syria-Palestine.

Anyone who served on the staff of a Lapp dig will remember how enthusiastically he shared his vast knowledge of ceramics, as he read the potsherds at the end of each day's work. His early death cut short his work on final publication, already well advanced in some cases, but his preliminary reports are a valuable source of information for his colleagues.

In addition to developing pottery typology, Lapp made improvements in the method of recording excavations. For example, the daily top plan, which he implemented in 1961 at Araq el Emir, was Lapp's innovation. It is a schematic diagram of an area under excavation, drawn to scale. As well as serving as a record of the daily progress of a dig, it complements the section drawings. The combination of the daily top plan and section drawings assures both horizontal and vertical control in digging and recording.

Besides leading several archaeological expeditions Lapp held prominent professional posts within ASOR. During the academic year 1960-1961 he was annual professor at the School in Jerusalem; from 1961 to 1965 he served as the School's long-term director, as Albright and Glueck had done before him. From 1965 to 1968 Lapp was professor of ancient Near Eastern history and archaeology at the Jerusalem School. While serving in that capacity, he toured ASOR-affiliated academic institutions in the United States, presenting illustrated lectures on current developments in the archaeology of the Mideast. Albright and Glueck had performed the same service during their tenure as directors of the School in order to generate interest and support for ASOR.

Lapp also acted as senior adviser to the United States Agency for International Development (USAID) for its program on the West Bank and in Jordan. The program was concerned with the conservation and preparation of historic sites (Qumran, Jerash, Amman, Kerak, Samaria, Jericho, and Petra) for tourism. Other ASOR appointees—William L. Reed, Prescott H. Williams, and Rudolph H. Dornemann—have also served as advisers to the USAID, informally assisting with studies related to cultural resources and environmental impact. In 1980 ASOR was registered with the USAID and now cooperates with this agency in a more formal way.

Lapp made a great contribution to ASOR as director of the Jerusalem School, especially through his example of serious archaeological scholarship. An intense worker, he seldom took time from his research for social activity. During his directorship several well-qualified annual professors were in residence and were able to share some of the director's responsibilities and contribute to the scholarly atmosphere of the School. In addition to their own research, they assisted with the planning and execution of the School's field trips, which are a vital educational feature of the academic program each year.

Annual Professors under Lapp

James A. Sanders (1961-1962) of Colgate-Rochester Divinity School spent the year preparing the publication of *The Psalms Scroll of Qumran Cave XI*, which appeared in 1965. R. B. Y. Scott (1962-1963) of Princeton University had a strong interest in metrology and dedicated his research to weights and measures. Bernhard W. Anderson (1963-1964) of Drew University chose as his project the restudy of the conquest traditions. According to Lapp's *Newsletter*, Anderson "led what was undoubtedly the most ambitious and research-oriented local field trip program of recent years, visiting the sites of the conquest narratives." Edward F. Campbell (1964-1965) of McCormick Theological Seminary devoted the year to the preparation of Shechem field reports.

Lapp's Expedition to Araq el Emir

During his short career Lapp led archaeological expeditions to seven sites on the West Bank and in Jordan. While it would be difficult to rank these digs in their order of importance, Araq el Emir is certainly one of the more impressive. Located in the Wadi es Sir midway between the Jordan River and the city of Amman, Araq el Emir was discovered in 1817 by Charles Irby and James Mangles, officers in the Royal Navy. In 1904 the survey team of Howard Crosby Butler provided a detailed description of the site. Lapp originally chose to dig at Araq el Emir in hopes of unearthing evidence that would shed light on the Persian and Hellenistic periods, especially the pottery of these periods. However, the results were somewhat disappointing—there was a lack of Persian and Early Hellenistic remains. So far as the Late Hellenistic period is concerned, Lapp discovered Hellenistic potsherds clearly belonging to the first half of the second century B.C.; they are important for dating the megalithic Qasr el Abd ("fortress of the servant").

In 1961 Lapp made his first sounding at Araq el Emir in an attempt to determine the stratigraphical history of the site and to date the construction of the monumental building known as the Qasr el Abd. A second campaign in the autumn of 1961 was followed by a final season in 1962. The most exciting find of the third season was a feline, sculptured on a megalith of mottled red-and-white dolomite; the mouth of this animal functioned as a water spout.

On the basis of a few stratified Hellenistic sherds, Lapp identified the Qasr as a Hellenistic-style temple, dating to the early second century B.C. and connected with the Tobiad family. Tobiah, who may have been governor of Ammon in Transjordan, was an opponent of Nehemiah, the Jewish governor who rebuilt the walls of Jerusalem (about 445-437 B.C.). The erection of the Qasr is associated with the Tobiad Hyrcanus, who died about 175 B.C.

Like Lapp, Butler identified the monumental structure as a temple, but the evidence for this attribution remains inconclusive. Beyond

Paul Lapp, director of the Araq el Emir dig, stands on the southwest corner of the Qasr during the 1962 season.

Feline sculptured on mottled red and white dolomite block inserted in lowest dressed course of Qasr at Araq el Emir. (This sculptured animal serves as the logo of the American Center of Oriental Research [ACOR], Amman.) (Photo by Paul Lapp.)

Josephus, there is no literary support for this position. The only basis for considering the Qasr a temple is architectural typology: the stairway, terrace, and tower of the Qasr are architectural features commensurate with a temple. If the temple interpretation is correct, Araq el Emir would have served as a religious center for Jews disenchanted with the Jerusalem temple.[8]

An earthquake in A.D. 365 had destroyed much of the megalithic building, which was later rebuilt in the Byzantine period. Arguing from the geographical location of Araq el Emir and from the presence of Iron

---

[8]"Although it is tempting to identify the second century Qasr el Abd as a temple, the evidence is lacking. Those who maintain that the structure is a temple must find motivation for its construction in the political circumstances in Judea during the time of Hyrcanus. As had been suggested, there is no evidence for a conflict of a religious nature between Hyrcanus and the Jerusalem high priesthood. And, although the history of the Tobiad family as meddlers in affairs of the Judean state, together with the change in political overlordship of Judea in Hyrcanus's time, provide a plausible setting for the building of an alternative temple, the archaeological data do not conclusively support a temple interpretation." Debra Chase, "A Review of the Fifth Century Temple at Elephantine and the Second Century Temple (?) at Araq el Emir," (unpublished paper, Harvard University).

Age I remains at the site, Lapp and others suggested that Araq el Emir be identified with biblical Ramath-Mizpeh.[9]

The Tell er Rumeith Excavation

In the spring of 1962 Lapp made soundings at Tell er Rumeith, a small mound situated east of the Jordan in Gilead, near the modern Syrian border. He decided to work in the highland region of Gilead, whose archaeological history was little known, in order to learn more about the Iron Age sequence of Syrian pottery. During an earlier survey of the region, Nelson Glueck had identified Tell er Rumeith as the site of Ramoth-gilead, mentioned several times in the Old Testament. This site is well known as the place where King Ahab of northern Israel (about 869-850 B.C.) was fatally wounded in a battle fought against Syria, in an attempt to recover the city.

In addition to Tell er Rumeith, there are at least two other sites which may have been Ramoth-gilead—Ramtha on the Syrian border and the imposing Tell el Husn southeast of Irbid. German topographers Dalman and Noth favored the latter and Albright concurred, but until this site is excavated, the identification is moot. Lapp did not feel that his excavations at Tell er Rumeith settled the question. He held, however, that the weight of the evidence would favor this mound as the location of Ramoth-gilead. He argued:

> The continuity of the name, the congruence of occupational history with that of the literary record, and its geographical position fit such an identification. The smallness of the site is probably the strongest argument against identification. . . . But this objection must be coupled with evidence for a larger site in the area with equally impressive claims if it is to replace Tell er-Rumeith as the most viable candidate for Ramoth-gilead.[10]

James A. Sauer disagrees with Lapp's conclusion on the basis of his surveys in Jordan and his firsthand knowledge of the Tell er Rumeith

---

[9]Since 1976 the Institut Français d'Archéologie du Proche Orient (represented by Ernest Will, director; J. M. Dentzer, field archaeologist; and François Larché, architect) has been making an architectural study of the Qasr in preparation for the reconstruction of this monumental building; in 1980 the restoration began. During the new phase of work at the site, another feline fountain was uncovered on the west side of the building. Also discovered were winged eagles, which decorated the corners of a frieze high on the walls. In the process of study and restoration, the French architectural team confirmed Lapp's conjecture that the Qasr was never completed, nor was it ever used in the Hellenistic period. Without doubt, Araq el Emir will be one of the principal tourist sites of Jordan when restoration is completed.

In 1976 Robin M. Brown, an ASOR appointee, served as field director of a project to clarify the dating of the various phases of the Qasr. These soundings, which were made in cooperation with the French architectural project, confirmed Lapp's Late Hellenistic dates.

[10]ASOR Newsletter 6 (1967-1968).

pottery. It may be that if Lapp were living today, he too would be looking for a more plausible location for Ramoth-gilead.

During the 1967 season Howard M. Jamieson of Pittsburgh Theological Seminary served with Lapp as codirector at Tell er Rumeith. This final campaign demonstrated that the site had been a small fortress, occupied for about two centuries before being destroyed by Tiglath-pileser III, king of Assyria, about 733 B.C.

Lapp's description of the 1967 campaign at Tell er Rumeith, a dig altogether characteristic of its director, provides insight into the man and his work. Several ASOR appointees residing at the School that year were eager to experience field archaeology firsthand; they constituted the staff of the Tell er Rumeith expedition. Living conditions at the tent camp were adequate but austere, while the physical work was strenuous but satisfying. Above all, Lapp made the dig a genuine learning experience.

> The days and weeks spent at Tell er-Rumeith were busy ones. The day began shortly after six o'clock when there would be a great rush to the water storage tank to fill a basin with cold water for the morning ablutions. Breakfast was served shortly thereafter, and it consisted of hot cereal, eggs, bread, and coffee. This was more than adequate preparation for a full day's work. The workers began to arrive from Ramtha during our breakfast period, which meant that they were well ahead of the seven o'clock roll-call. The first few hours on the mound were chilly and windy, but by the time of the coffee break at 9:45, the sun had warmed the tell to a comfortable degree. The fifteen minute respite sustained us until noon when work stopped for 45 minutes. After lunch we excavated for three more hours till 4 o'clock when the laborers began to return to Ramtha and we fortified ourselves with tea and bread. Invariably most of the field supervisors then returned to their plots to draw the top plan or help one another with section drawings. Darkness would force us to leave the mound and return to our camp by six o'clock. It was then almost time for supper. After a half hour elapsed in the mess tent we were ready to begin the pottery reading. We had worked out a system so each knew when he was due at the pottery tent, and in that way there was no delay. The remainder of the evening was given to preparation of the field books. Pressure lamps are not conducive to the kind of precision that is required for keeping records so one has to be careful to double-check each entry. The field book up to date, it was then almost eleven o'clock and time to retire for the night. From that moment on no human sound broke the stillness of the night in the plain of Gilead. Every moment of sleep counted in order to be ready to face the rigors of the next day's work.[11]

The Caves of Wadi ed Daliyeh

In the spring of 1962 the Taamireh Bedouin, famous for the discovery of the Dead Sea Scrolls, unearthed twenty-seven papyri (and

[11]*ASOR Newsletter* 6 (1967-1968).

small fragments of perhaps a hundred papyri) in a limestone cave of Wadi ed Daliyeh, a remote and rugged site about nine miles north of Jericho. While making soundings there in January 1963 to verify the original location of these papyrus scrolls, Paul Lapp's team was hampered by swarms of screeching bats within the labyrinthian caves and by the guano dust, which hindered breathing. Outfitted with masks, goggles, and lamps, the excavators, under Lapp's direction, investigated four caves and recovered abundant pottery and fragmentary papyri. Consisting of commercial and legal materials, the Wadi ed Daliyeh documents, written in Aramaic, date from about 375 to 335 B.C. These important finds cast light on the fourth century B.C., an era not well known to historians of Palestine. Lapp's explorations at Wadi ed Daliyeh illuminated both the paleography and the ceramic chronology of that period.

ASOR trustee Elizabeth Hay Bechtel purchased the Wadi ed Daliyeh documents, known also as the Samaria Papyri, for the Palestine Archaeological Museum. At that time the Jordanian Department of Antiquities entrusted the decipherment and publication of this collection to Frank Moore Cross of Harvard. According to Cross, the fragmentary papyri from Wadi ed Daliyeh are the oldest legal papyri of Palestinian origin yet found. He has also reported that these documents are closer to Neo-Assyrian and Babylonian patterns than the Elephantine papyri, but much is uniquely West Semitic.

In addition to the papyri in the Daliyeh cave, the team uncovered about 300 skeletons, grisly mementos of foul play. The rings, beads, and other personal effects found with the bones suggest the affluence of the victims. Cross hypothesized that they were hapless Samaritans who rebelled against Alexander the Great and escaped from Samaria in 331 B.C. when his troops captured and destroyed the city. According to Cross's conjecture, while these Samaritans were taking temporary refuge in the Daliyeh cave, Alexander's Macedonian troops discovered their hiding place and suffocated them by lighting a huge fire at the mouth of the cave.

The Tell el Ful Expedition

Albright's first dig in 1922-1923 was at Tell el Ful, identified as ancient Gibeah, the provincial capital of Saul. He returned to the site for a final season of digging in 1933. In 1927, between these two campaigns, a violent earthquake had "caused the collapse of all insecure sections of masonry (on the summit). While regrettable," observed Albright, "this destruction made renewed excavation in the interior of the fortress possible."[12]

---

[12]*BASOR* 52 (1933) 6.

In the spring of 1964, under the aegis of ASOR and the Pittsburgh Theological Seminary, Paul Lapp, assisted by James L. Kelso, undertook a six-week salvage campaign at Tell el Ful. Lapp hoped to clarify some of Albright's conclusions that had occasioned scholarly skepticism.[13] Once Kenyon's correction of Garstang's dating of "Joshua's walls" at Jericho had cast doubt on the interpretations of earlier digs, scholars began to question Albright's dates for "Saul's fort," believing that the fort should be dated to the Hellenistic period.

Lapp's campaign at Gibeah resulted in some modification of Albright's conclusions. The opinion that Saul's fort was a casemate or double-walled construction can no longer be maintained; the casement wall is to be dated to the late seventh century B.C., when the city was rebuilt. Lapp's investigation confirmed, on the other hand, Albright's identifiction of the fortess as Saul's. As Lapp commented:

> While it is therefore not categorically proved that the fortress belonged to Saul, the identification rests on evidence about as strong as archaeology is ever able to provide—especially in light of the comparably strong case for the identification of Tell el-Ful with Gibeah of Saul. In fact, no rival hypothesis of any substance has been proposed, and the evidence upon which Albright based his identification of 1922-1923 stands confirmed.[14]

According to Lapp's ceramic analysis, the five occupation layers at Tell el Ful extended from about 1200 B.C. to the Hellenistic period, specifically the last two-thirds of the second century B.C. In other words, contrary to Albright's dating, the site flourished in the Maccabean period. Lapp was otherwise favorably impressed with Albright's excavation of Tell el Ful, especially when compared with the techniques of other archaeologists working in Palestine in the 1920s and 1930s. When Lapp finished at Tell el Ful, he felt confident that his efforts, combined with those of Albright, had fulfilled ASOR's responsibilities vis-à-vis the excavation at Gibeah of Saul.

The fact that Pittsburgh Theological Seminary cooperated with Lapp in excavating at Tell el Ful was not surprising. This seminary and its parent institutions (Xenia Theological Seminary and Western Theological Seminary) have established a record for supporting ASOR-affiliated projects. Other institutional members of ASOR's corporation have participated in ASOR's archaeological projects but none to the degree of the Pittsburgh Theological Seminary and its forebears. Pittsburgh's sponsorship of the 1964 campaign at Tell el Ful coincided with

---

[13]Lapp was also prompted to dig at Tell el Ful because the ancient ruins were scheduled to be demolished to make way for the construction of a new West Bank palace for King Hussein of Jordan. In spite of the appropriateness of the site for a king, the Six-Day War of 1967 interrupted the building of the palace.

[14]*ASOR Newsletter* 6 (1963-1964).

the fortieth anniversary of the joint ASOR-Xenia expedition to Moab and the Dead Sea.

Melvin G. Kyle and James L. Kelso were principally responsible for the Pittsburgh Seminary's involvement in archaeology. As a fitting tribute to these two scholars who so diligently supported the archaeology of Palestine, the Kyle-Kelso Excavation Foundation was established, with Robert A. Coughenour as manager, to promote additional excavations in the Holy Land. In 1975 the archaeological museum at Pittsburgh Theological Seminary was renamed the James L. Kelso Bible Lands Museum, in recognition of Kelso's enduring contribution. It is appropriate that Nancy Lapp, an active field archaeologist, serves as curator of this museum.

The Tell Taannek Expedition

Although Ernst Sellin had directed three campaigns of digging from 1902 to 1904 at Tell Taannek, the site of biblical Taanach, his inexact methods of excavating and recording made it difficult to reconstruct the cultural history of Taanach. However, the discovery of an archive containing twelve Akkadian cuneiform tablets, dating about 1450 B.C., and a Canaanite incense stand of the tenth century B.C. is evidence that Sellin's work at Taanach had some positive results. When Sellin finished this dig, he was convinced that all the important discoveries had come to light. Paul Lapp, director of a new undertaking at Taanach between 1963 and 1968, almost sixty years after the completion of Sellin's project, was in a better position than anyone to assess the work of his predecessor. He commented:

> The tell suffered surprisingly little depredation after the German excavations, and Sellin's plans can still be checked in many cases. Despite what from present-day standards would be considered shocking excavation technique and woefully inadequate recording of discoveries, especially of the second and third campaigns, it should be noted that his prompt and in many respects perceptive reports command respect in comparison with most excavation reports from the Mediterranean world in the early 1900's—especially coming from one who never claimed to be a technically trained archaeologist.[15]

Lapp's expedition to Taanach was jointly sponsored by ASOR and Concordia Seminary of St. Louis; he concentrated, for the most part, on the southwest quadrant of the mound during three seasons in the field. The staff consisted principally of Lutheran biblical scholars affiliated with the seminary, some of whom gained field experience on Wright's

[15]*ASOR Newsletter* 11 (1962-1963).

Paul Lapp reading pottery at Taanach.

Paul Lapp (extreme right) explaining his Taanach dig to Awni Dajani (on Lapp's right) and other members of the Department of Antiquities of Jordan before the Six-Day War of 1967. Albert Glock, field director, is dialoguing with Lapp.

Shechem dig during the 1962 season. They chose Taanach as their excavation site because of its prominent role in the Bible, beginning with the Book of Joshua.

In the course of excavating, Lapp dated the earliest occupation of Taanach to the Early Bronze Age (about 2700-2400 B.C.), a conclusion that coincided with Albright's but contradicted Sellin's, who had associated the first occupation of the site with the fifteenth to the fourteenth centuries. Lapp also succeeded in locating the city's defense walls, which Sellin had not found, despite his long trenches across the mound. Excavation under Lapp helped to clarify the function of the fortifications, installations, and local cult of Taanach. Interestingly, the Lapp project came close to matching Sellin's in terms of notable discoveries— Lapp found an Akkadian cuneiform tablet of the same period as Sellin's archive (about 1450 B.C.) and a Canaanite cuneiform tablet of the early twelfth century; in addition, a decorative, tenth-century B.C. cult stand, lying near the find-spot of Sellin's cult stand, turned up.

Preparation of the final reports is progressing. After the unexpected death of Paul Lapp in 1970, Albert E. Glock, a staff member of the Taanach expedition, assumed responsibility for the publication of the

Cult stand from the tenth century B.C. found by Paul Lapp at Taanach.

Taanach dig. Under his direction the pottery and other artifacts are being analyzed in accordance with the latest scientific techniques preparatory to publication. Walter E. Rast, a member of the Taanach core staff, prepared for publication the ceramic sequences of the Iron Age strata uncovered at the site in the sixties; ASOR published this volume, *Taanach I: Studies in Iron Age Pottery*, in 1978.

The Bab edh Dhra Excavation

In 1924 when Albright and Kyle led an expedition to Moab and the Dead Sea, Alexis Mallon, who was a member of the party, discovered the site of Bab edh Dhra on the southeast shore of the Dead Sea, just east of the Lisan Peninsula. Excavation has revealed that the settlement known as Bab edh Dhra consisted of a town of mudbrick domestic structures surrounded by a defense wall dating to 2700 B.C. A mammoth cemetery with more than 20,000 tombs was located in the adjacent area. The town was occupied from 3100 to 2300 B.C., while the massive burial ground came into use as early as 3200 B.C. and continued to serve as a cemetery for over a thousand years. Archaeologists estimated that there may have been as many as 500,000 individual burials at the site. The newer figures are much less though still supportive of a large burial ground.

When Early Bronze Age pottery vessels, obtained by illegal digging at Bab edh Dhra, appeared for sale in Jerusalem antiquities shops, Paul Lapp decided to undertake an excavation at the site. He directed three seasons of digging at Bab edh Dhra between 1965 and 1967; he devoted two seasons to excavating the shaft tombs used for secondary burials and the charnel houses where primary burial was practiced and one season to digging the town proper.[16]

The Dhahr Mirzbaneh Cemetery

In September 1963 Lapp investigated the Dhahr Mirzbaneh cemetery, which is situated near the modern village of Mughayir, about two miles west of Wadi ed Daliyeh. The project (which was similar to that at Bab edh Dhra, though on a much smaller scale) concentrated on excavating and recording the contents of about thirty shaft tombs dating to the Middle Bronze Age I (about 2050-1900 B.C.). Lapp also discovered a Middle Bronze I cave at Wadi ed Daliyeh; it yielded several large Middle Bronze I jars.

Lapp was not the first ASOR scholar to explore this desolate area, known as Ain es Samiyeh. In 1907 while serving as director of the Jerusalem School, David G. Lyon had made several visits to this remote region. Like Lapp, he had been attracted to Samieh by the large amounts of pottery from this site appearing in Jerusalem. As in the case of Bab edh Dhra, grave robbers had been at work. In the director's report Lyon stated:

[16]Both Albright and Lapp felt there might be a connection between Bab edh Dhra and the "cities of the plain" (Sodom, Gomorrah, Admah, Zeboiim, and Zoar) mentioned in the Book of Genesis. Walter E. Rast and R. Thomas Schaub, who undertook a new phase of work at this famous site in 1975, are curious about the possibility and plan to pursue it after the other four Early Bronze sites near the Dead Sea—Numeira, Safi, Feifa, and Khanazir—have been scientifically investigated.

Suffice it here to say that Samieh is probably the most important necropolis yet found in Palestine. In addition to numerous later graves of well-known types, more than a hundred shaft tombs had been plundered. . . . From these tombs have come large quantities of pottery and many bronze objects . . . which are estimated, by comparison with similar material from the lower strata at Tell el-Hesy, Gezer, Taanach, and Mutesellim, to be of Canaanite origin, and not later than 1500 b.c.

Albright had also paid a visit to Samieh, riding in on horseback in 1922 while on a School field trip. He suggested that the area had been a sanctuary.

The burials in the Dhahr Mirzbaneh cemetery have raised questions that can be answered only when some literary evidence comes to light. What community, for instance, buried its dead in such a remote area? What cultic practices accompanied the burials? De Vaux, Albright, and Kenyon identified the shaft tomb builders as Amorites, one of the pre-Israelite tribes in Canaan. Amiran, Lapp, and others made their conjectures, too, but uncertainty remains. On the basis of his salvage excavations at two other Middle Bronze Age I sites, Jebel Qaaqir and Khirbet Kirmil, Dever made a study of the material from the Middle Bronze Age I tombs in the area of Ain es Samiyeh in the Judean hills. Speculating about an isolated cemetery in such a remote region, Dever suggested it may have been "the tribal burying-ground of semi-nomadic pastoralists moving on a seasonal circuit."

Tragedy in Cyprus

Having spent most of his time in the Mideast excavating in the Arab lands, Lapp developed a close relationship with the Arabs and became a strong supporter of their cause. After the Six-Day War in 1967, as the political climate changed, Lapp chose to excavate in Cyprus instead of in the Israeli-occupied West Bank. Meanwhile in 1968 he returned to the United States and joined the faculty of the Pittsburgh Theological Seminary as professor of Old Testament and archaeology.

In 1970 Lapp went to Cyprus to direct an excavation at ancient Idalion, near the modern town of Dhali and not far from Nicosia. However, his promising career came to an abrupt end when he drowned in a swimming accident off the coast of Kyrenia in northern Cyprus. He was only thirty-nine years old.[17]

Palestinian archaeology is fortunate that Lapp's widow, Nancy, a trained archaeologist, is diligently overseeing the publication of his field projects, with the assistance of several who had served on Paul Lapp's excavation teams. Paul and Nancy had been an effective couple, sharing

---

[17]After the shock of Lapp's death, G. Ernest Wright, president of ASOR, rallied an excavation team and undertook the excavation of Idalion.

administrative responsibility at the Jerusalem School and working together on digs.

When Paul Lapp died, Delbert R. Hillers of Johns Hopkins University and a member of the Taanach staff described him as "the outstanding Palestinian archaeologist of his generation," especially in pottery typology. Few would dispute the accuracy of Hillers's observation. Although some of his colleagues found him abrasive on occasion, Paul Lapp was a resolute man of candor and integrity who won the respect of all who knew him.

Expedition to Gezer

Under the auspices of the Palestine Exploration Fund, Tell Jezer, the location of ancient Gezer, was excavated by the Irish archaeologist R. A. S. Macalister between 1902 and 1909 and by the British archaeologist Alan Rowe in 1934. Hebrew Union College in Jerusalem and the Harvard Semitic Museum jointly sponsored the third expedition to this site, a project that began in 1964 and continued for a decade. Macalister's undertaking suffered from his working almost alone, helped only by one Egyptian foreman who supervised the gang of workers. Functioning as his own administrator, architect, and recorder, Macalister inevitably missed much. For example, he was able to identify only nine strata of occupation on the mound, whereas the more recent excavators have identified twenty-six separate strata ranging from Chalcolithic to post-Byzantine.

In 1964 G. Ernest Wright decided to lead an expedition to Gezer. A study of this site had been suggested to him in 1937 as a dissertation topic, but he did not pursue it at that time. During the academic year 1964-1965 while Wright was serving as the visiting archaeological director of the Hebrew Union College in Jerusalem, William G. Dever and H. Darrell Lance, two of his Harvard graduate students who had accompanied him to Jerusalem, were in search of an archaeological field project. Wright suggested Gezer to them as a site needing reexcavation. For the first season Wright served as field director; he then relinquished the post to Dever, who became director, with Lance as associate director. Under their joint leadership the first phase of the new excavations at Gezer continued through 1971.[18]

Gezer was an ASOR project only indirectly; its core staff had learned the techniques of digging as apprentices at ASOR's Shechem excavations, where Wright, Toombs, Campbell, and other ASOR archaeologists were the instructors. The new generation of Gezer archaeologists applied

---

[18]During the next two seasons (1972 and 1973) Joe D. Seger, one of Wright's students, directed another phase of digging at Gezer. Nelson Glueck and Ernest Wright, the official advisers to the project, visited Gezer each season to discuss strategy with the staff and to address the volunteers.

Yigael Yadin, Ernest Wright, and Nelson Glueck visiting the "mess hall" of the Gezer excavations.

what they had learned at Shechem; they also improved upon the Shechem techniques.

Among American projects in the Mideast, Gezer was one of the first to initiate new approaches to field archaeology. Thanks in good measure to Gezer, Syro-Palestinian excavations began to include specialists in environmental studies and in the social and the natural sciences, who have regularly participated in prehistoric digs. When geologist Reuben Bullard was invited to join the Gezer core staff, he was the first of a variety of such specialists, including physical and cultural anthropologists, paleoethnobotanists, and zoologists, who eventually became an integral part of almost all digs in the Mideast. Today, interdisciplinary archaeology is the rule in the ASOR world.

Hundreds of dig volunteers will always remember the late sixties and early seventies when Gezer was their training ground. Previously in the Mideast local laborers had been hired to move dirt on a dig; at Gezer volunteers recruited from the United States and elsewhere not only performed the tasks of unskilled laborers, but they also assumed the more technical responsibilities. Through in-service training on the tell volunteers gained limited proficiency in all aspects of digging. Lectures and seminars at the site expanded the educational dimension of the excavation project to the point that the dig became a genuine field school qualified to grant academic credit. Many American universities now accept academic credit from students who have spent their summers on such excavations.[19]

The volunteer system, utilized at Gezer and adopted later by several other digs, owes much to the pioneering efforts of Yigael Yadin at Masada. He recruited students and other volunteers worldwide to participate in the excavation and restoration of that spectacular mountaintop fortress. The American version of the volunteer program is producing the archaeologists of the future; several have already advanced to staff positions on digs in Israel, Jordan, and elsewhere, while others are now directing their own excavations.

Gezer was the first site in Palestine to be excavated on a large scale, through Macalister's digging sixty percent of the thiry-acre mound to bedrock. Dever's work at Gezer was small in comparison; he dug less than two percent of the tell. The efforts of the two excavators differed, of course, in quality, as well as in method; Dever's dig was far superior.

Occupation at Gezer extended from Late Chalcolithic to the Roman and Byzantine periods, but not continuously; in Early Bronze III-IV and Middle Bronze I (about 2500-1900 B.C.) the site was abandoned. In Middle Bronze II (about 1900-1550 B.C.) Gezer reached its height as a

---

[19]Today, all of ASOR's large-scale digs conduct field schools. The program of lectures, the training sessions, and the field trips to other sites, combined with basic training in excavation technique and close supervision by specialists, constitute an impressive educational experience for volunteers.

Canaanite city state; it was a period of prosperity and new construction. From this period date both the massive defense wall encircling the city and Macalister's "high place," consisting of ten pillars or standing stones, which Dever designated an "open-air sanctuary."

One of the exciting discoveries of the Israelite era at Gezer was the Solomonic four-entryway gate in field III, like those at Hazor and Megiddo. Macalister had mistaken this gate structure for a Maccabean castle, since Gezer figured prominently in the Maccabean wars. Yadin recognized its true identity with the help of a verse in the First Book of Kings (9:15), which refers to Solomon's building Hazor, Megiddo, Gezer, and the wall of Jerusalem.

The great water system of Gezer cannot be definitively dated because the stratigraphic evidence is lacking; Macalister suggested the Middle Bronze Age, Dever the Late Bronze, and Yadin Iron II. Whatever its date, the hydraulic technology of ancient Palestine is impressive in its workmanship.

The Baghdad School

While ASOR was quickening the pace of archaeological activity in Syria-Palestine during the fifties and sixties, field work in Mesopotamia (an area almost coextensive with the present Republic of Iraq) progressed slowly, for two reasons already stated. The Baghdad School, not having the luxury of its own facilities, was obliged to borrow space from the United States consulate and from the Iraq National Museum. Secondly, the School received only limited funding from ASOR, an amount that was small in comparison with the subsidy for the Jerusalem School. Despite its handicaps, the Baghdad School has made a notable contribution to the cultural history of Mesopotamia through excavations and, especially, through systematic surface surveys.

In fact, the American emphasis on surveys anticipated a new approach to archaeological investigation, an approach that studies a region as a whole instead of concentrating on individual sites. The regional-survey concept is an effective way to understand the occupational history, the settlement patterns, and the interrelation of settlements in a given zone, as well as to answer socioeconomic questions.

Archaeological work has continued in Iraq, despite the political instability and internal dissension that have been rife since independent statehood was declared in 1932. The revolution of 1958 put an end to monarchy and proclaimed the country a republic; during 1963 to 1968 numerous military coups took place, leading to the Arab Baath Socialist Party's revolution of 1968. While emphasizing nationalism and socialism, the present government has raised cultural standards as well. Archaeology has continued to develop through excavation, restoration and preservation of antiquities and historical buildings, development of regional museums, salvage in the Hamrin Dam basin (which will be inundated when the dam is completed), restoration of Babylon and Ashur (threatened by the rising water table), and the protection of antiquities. The 20,000 archaeological sites in Iraq present the Directorate General of Antiquities with a monumental challenge. The picture is bright, however; not only are native Iraqis actively engaged in the archaeology of their country, but they are interested in modern methods and are less concerned than formerly with searching for texts, monuments, and museum pieces.

Field Projects

Vaughn E. Crawford of the Metropolitan Museum of Art succeeded Albrecht Goetze as director of the Baghdad School in 1956. Crawford's name is associated with several field projects in Iraq, particularly the excavations at Tell el Hiba, situated in the southeastern part of the country. In his 1953 survey, Jacobsen identified this site as Lagash (modern Telloh), one of the most important capital cities in ancient Sumer. Donald P. Hansen of New York University's Institute of Fine Arts also participated in the Lagash excavations.

In 1959 ASOR made its first field foray into Iran. Robert J. Braidwood, anthropologist of the Oriental Institute, served as director of the Iranian Prehistoric Project in Khuzistan, assisted by Bruce Howe of Harvard's Peabody Museum, annual professor of the Baghdad School from 1959 to 1960. This undertaking, which was a joint venture with the Institute of Archaeology of the University of Tehran, included the survey of more than 230 mounds and the excavation of two sites, Warwasid and Tepe Asiab. Samuel N. Kramer, chairman of the Baghdad committee, reported:

> The Baghdad School is participating this year in the extensive and many-sided prehistoric survey in Iranian Khuzistan. The purpose of the expedition to this area, which is practically *terra incognita* from the point of view of the origin and growth of village-farming communities, is to explore and excavate along the flanks of the Zagros Mountains in order to learn how, when, and where food production was first achieved in this area, and to correlate the results with those obtained from excavating the earliest agricultural settlements in the arc of hills running from Palestine, through Syria and Lebanon, Southern Turkey, and especially Iraqi-Kurdistan.[20]

Robert Adams of the University of Chicago, annual professor at the Baghdad School from 1966 to 1967, continued the survey begun earlier by Jacobsen, concentrating this time in the Warka region of southern Iraq. While mapping and recording, Adams gave special attention to ancient settlement patterns. The results of Adams's comprehensive study

[20]*ASOR Newsletter* 4 (1959-1960).

of Mesopotamia have been published in an important volume, *Land Behind Baghdad* (1965), which is a history of settlement on the Diyala Plains.[21] His survey of the ancient canal systems in Mesopotamia not only adds to the knowledge of antiquity but is proving helpful to the Iraqis, who are rebuilding the irrigation systems of their country to benefit the modern economy.

Israeli Excavations

From the time Jewish archaeologists began to excavate in Palestine, they were closely related to the American School in Jerusalem, and this alliance has endured. Even though the political situation made it impossible for ASOR appointees and their Jewish colleagues to collaborate between 1948 and 1967 (separated as they were by the Mandelbaum Gate), they shared a mutual concern for research on both sides of the line. Archaeology as a scientific discipline can develop only to the extent that scholars collaborate continuously, regardless of national backgrounds. This ideal is yet to be achieved, but there are some encouraging signs within the discipline itself. Today's comprehensive, regional approach to field archaeology, for example, replacing exclusive concentration on isolated sites, aims at such a synthesis.

The Avdat Excavation

The Israelis conducted several major excavations in the late fifties and sixties, such as the dig at Avdat from 1958 to 1960 led by Michael Avi-Yonah and Avraham Negev of the Hebrew University. Avi-Yonah was an authority on the archaeology and art history of ancient Palestine during the Roman and Byzantine periods; Negev is a specialist in the Nabateans. This site was especially meaningful to the two excavators because it was a Nabatean-Byzantine city. In antiquity it was called Eboda (probably from the name of a Nabatean king); it is located at Khirbet Abdah (which preserves the name Eboda) in the central Negev of modern Israel, about forty miles south of Beer-sheba. The city was strategically located at the intersection of caravan routes running from Petra and Elath to Gaza. A well-known commercial center, Eboda was occupied from the fourth century B.C. to the time of the Arab conquest. The reign of the Nabatean King Aretas IV (9 B.C. - A.D. 40) marked the high point of Eboda's history, as the splendid temple built during that period attests.

The significance of the site prompted the State of Israel to restore Khirbet Abdah as a historic monument; today it is a popular stop

---

[21]Adams's most recent book, *Heartland of Cities* (1981), based on his surveys of "ancient settlement and land use in the central floodplain of the Euphrates," is an important study of settlement patterns in Mesopotamia, taking into account the interaction between environmental factors and social institutions.

between Beer-sheba and Elath. In addition to Eboda, two other Nabatean cities are to be found in the Negev, Mampsis (Mamshit) and Subeita (Shivta). These Nabatean "ghost towns" have also been excavated and partly restored.

Judean Desert Caves

The chance discovery of the Dead Sea Scrolls provided strong incentive for a more extensive exploration of other caves in the region. During 1960 and 1961 Joseph Aviram of Hebrew University's Institute of Archaeology worked with the Israel Exploration Society to organize a full-scale expedition to the ten-mile area between En-gedi and Masada on the west side of the Dead Sea, and as far as the Jordanian border to the east. The two principal periods of occupation encountered in the Judean Desert Caves were Chalcolithic (4200-3300 B.C.) at one end of the archaeological time scale and the Bar Kochba era (A.D. 132-135) at the other.

Exploration of the Dead Sea area was divided among four teams, each led by an Israeli archaeologist. As director of Expedition A, Nahman Avigad investigated caves in the vicinity of En-gedi. Expedition B, under the leadership of Yohanan Aharoni, worked in the caves of Nahal Seelim, where the team discovered some manuscript fragments. Pesah Bar-Adon's Expedition C concentrated on the Mishmar Valley; in the Cave of the Treasure, this group uncovered Chalcolithic remains that shed light on the life-style of the people of that period—household utensils of ceramic, metal vessels, fragments of textiles, ornaments, etc.

Under the leadership of Yigael Yadin, Expedition D discovered the Cave of the Letters, situated on the northern bank of Nahal Hever. This cave contained fifteen letters written in Aramaic, Hebrew, and Greek which had been sent from Bar Kochba, the leader of the Second Revolt against Rome, to the commander of En-gedi. An additional archive of thirty-five documents composed in Greek, Nabatean, and Aramaic contained family letters and legal documents dating from A.D. 93 to 132. Artifacts of all kinds, including metal utensils and wooden and leather objects, were found with the documents; together they provide insight into the history of the Roman period. In fact, the actual name of Bar Kochba was uncertain until the discovery of these letters. Bar Kochba ("son of the star") was a nickname; in Jewish sources he is called Bar (or Ben) Koziba.

Surveys in En-gedi

From 1949 on, the Israelis conducted several surveys in the region of En-gedi. Between 1961 and 1964 Benjamin Mazar, Trude Dothan, and Immanuel Dunayevsky carried out five seasons of excavation at Tel Goren (Tell el Jurn in Arabic). This most prominent site in the oasis of

En-gedi had been occupied from the latter years of the Judean kingdom until the Roman-Byzantine era (seventh century B.C. to sixth century A.D.).[22]

Masada

Masada, the impregnable mountain fortress of Herod the Great, rises 1300 feet above the Judean desert on the southwestern shore of the Dead Sea. It was first identified in 1838 by Robinson and Smith. This sumptuous royal citadel had been surveyed several times before Yigael Yadin, assisted by Israeli colleagues, made a full-scale excavation here between 1963 and 1965. The dig verified the accuracy of Josephus's account in *The History of the Jewish War*, which is based on eyewitness testimony of the handful of Jews who survived Masada. After the fall of Jerusalem in A.D. 70, Jewish Zealots at Masada held out against the Romans for almost two years. When Flavius Silva, the commander of the Tenth Legion, was at the point of capturing Masada, the 960 Zealots who were occupying the fortress refused to surrender. Preferring death to servitude, they executed a suicide pact. Only seven women and children survived to recount the tragic tale.

Volunteers came from around the world to assist in digging this monumental site. Part of the strategy called for the reconstruction of Masada to make it easier for tourists to visualize the rock fortress as it appeared in Roman times. The remains unearthed at Masada fall into three main periods: the Herodian (37-4 B.C.), the Revolt (A.D. 66-73), and the Byzantine (fifth-sixth century A.D.). The fortress is a monument to the courageous resistance of the Zealots, who held out at Masada against the conquering Roman legions. The site has become a national shrine in Israel and a symbol of heroism for the Jewish people.

During excavations at Masada important documents came to light, notably a fragmentary scroll containing a Hebrew version of Ben Sira (the Book of Ecclesiasticus). If Yadin is correct in dating this manuscript to the end of the second century B.C., it was copied within a hundred years of its composition (about 190 B.C.). The excavators also found fragments of the Books of Genesis, Leviticus, and Psalms, none of which can be later than A.D. 73, when Masada fell to the Romans.

The Expedition to Tell Arad

In 1962 Israeli archaeologists began digging at Tell Arad, the site of the ancient Israelite city of Arad, which is located in the eastern Negev

---

[22]In the 1970s Dan Barag of Hebrew University excavated the remains of a beautifully decorated synagogue of the Byzantine period, located northeast of Tel Goren. In addition to the discovery of the mosaic pavement adorned with five inscriptions in Hebrew and Aramaic, a seven-branched menorah cast in bronze was recovered.

about twenty miles south of Hebron. Ruth Amiran, a leading archaeologist and the ceramicist on the Hazor dig, directed the excavation of
the Early Bronze II fortified city (3000-2800 B.C.) on the lower part of
Tell Arad.[23] Yohanan Aharoni, assisted by Moshe Kochavi, was responsible for the Iron Age settlement, including the six successive Israelite
citadels dating from about the tenth to the sixth century B.C. The most
exciting discovery was the Israelite sanctuary, the first ever excavated.
Forming an integral part of the royal fortress, it was complete with
sacrificial altar, the holy of holies, and cult objects.

About 200 ostraca were also found; half were written in Aramaic
and the remainder in Hebrew. The former date to the Persian period
(about 400 B.C.), and the Hebrew ostraca pertain to the Iron Age. The
Aramaic inscriptions do not belong to the royal fortress; the Hebrew
inscriptions belong to the fortress but not to the temple for the most
part. It is not surprising that Aharoni retrieved such an important
assemblage of epigraphic material; he always insisted that pottery be
"dipped" (not scrubbed) preparatory to analysis. No doubt, overzealous
pottery washers at many other sites have inadvertently obliterated a
number of inscriptions; just how many will never be known.

As archaeologists have recovered no remains at Arad dating to the
Middle and Late Bronze Ages (about 2000-1200 B.C.), the site cannot be
identified as Canaanite Arad.[24] The work at Arad continues, however, as
Amiran presses on to learn more about the Early Bronze Age at this key
site and the relationship of Arad to other tells of the same period.

The Expedition to Tell Ashdod

Tell Ashdod, situated three miles inland on the southern coastal
plain of modern Israel, is the site of Ashdod, one of the five principal
Philistine cities. In 1962 a joint Israeli-American expedition began
digging here with the following international staff: David N. Freedman
of the Pittsburgh Theological Seminary served as director, James L.
Swauger of the Carnegie Museum in Pittsburgh was associate director,
and Moshe Dothan was designated chief archaeologist and director of
excavations. Although ASOR was not directly involved in this expedition, the two American representatives have always been closely related
to ASOR.

An important city in the Late Bronze and Iron Ages, Ashdod was
occupied from the seventeenth century B.C. to the Byzantine period.

---

[23]Amiran's *Ancient Pottery of the Holy Land* (1969) is an important and comprehensive study of pottery from the Neolithic period to the end of Iron Age II.

[24]In Canaanite times, either Arad was located at another site, perhaps Tell Malhata
(eight miles southwest of Tell Arad), or the name Arad designated the entire region rather
than the city.

According to an Akkadian document from Ugarit in Syria, three Palestinian cities—Acco, Ashkelon, and Ashdod—participated in trade with Ugarit. In Hellenistic times the name Ashdod was changed to Azotus, as it is called in the New Testament.

The Expedition to Tell Dan

One of the most attractive sites in northern Galilee is Tell Dan, the city mentioned in the classical definition of the Israelite kingdom's borders, "from Dan to Beer-sheba." Situated in the Huleh Valley at the foot of Mount Hermon, it is known in Arabic as Tell el Qadi which, like the Hebrew name, means "the mound of the judge." The literal translation was Robinson's clue to the identity of the site. The fifty-acre mound went unexcavated until 1966, when Avraham Biran (Bergman) launched an expedition at Dan; he has been digging every year since then. This project is one of the longest continuous digs in Syria-Palestine.[25]

Biran has made some fascinating discoveries concerning the history of Dan, whose occupation extended from Early Bronze II (3000-2800 B.C.) through the Byzantine period. In 1974 a horned altar made from a single limestone block was recovered; the following season, a bilingual (Greek-Aramaic) inscription of the second century B.C. appeared. Reading "the vow of Zilas to the god of Dan," it confirmed Robinson's identification of the site. The high place, or *bamah*, which Biran uncovered in the northern part of the city, may be the sanctuary that the Bible attributed to Jeroboam I, first king of Israel after the secession of the northern tribes about 920 B.C. The most spectacular discovery at Dan is the Middle Bronze (1900-1700 B.C.) arched gateway—a fully preserved mudbrick city gate with the arch intact, the earliest known in Syria-Palestine. Although such gates exist in Mesopotamia and elsewhere, the one at Tell Dan is the best preserved because, until exposed by recent excavation, it was securely buried under a Middle Bronze glacis.

G. Ernest Wright's Presidency

In 1965 ASOR's president, Henry Detweiler resigned after a decade in office. In recognition of Ernest Wright's contribution to biblical archaeology, especially at Shechem and Gezer, and of his other scholarly achievements and service to ASOR, the trustees elected him president of ASOR. Wright proved to be a vigorous leader who interested himself in every aspect of the organization. He became so closely identified with

[25]After completing his graduate studies under Albright at Johns Hopkins University, Biran was appointed Thayer Fellow at the School in Jerusalem from 1935 to 1937. He is presently serving as director of the Nelson Glueck School of Biblical Archaeology in Jerusalem, the sponsoring institution of the excavations at Tell Dan.

G. Ernest Wright. (Photo by Paul Koby [Cambridge, MA].)

ASOR that he did not always consult the board of trustees when making appointments to the various scholarly posts within ASOR. While he acted in good faith, his proprietary attitude toward the organization sometimes irritated the membership.

ASOR was growing so rapidly that no one could serve as president while being a full-time professor and do justice to either position. To ease Wright's burden, and in the interest of efficiency, the trustees in 1968 confirmed the appointment of Thomas D. Newman as administrative director; he was to oversee the day-to-day business of the administrative office in Cambridge (Massachusetts). During his tenure as president of ASOR, Wright was ably assisted by Newman. Together they reorganized ASOR by securing public funding and expanding the activities of the overseas institutes. Wright also strove to improve the quality of field projects affiliated with ASOR. Aware of the limitations of earlier excavations in both staff and method, Wright established the policy of reexcavating important sites to clarify or correct the interpretations of predecessors. With the passage of time, he also recognized the limitations of his own work at Shechem and encouraged his students to benefit from the new developments in field archaeology.

CHAPTER VII
THE MODERN PERIOD: 1967-1980 (Part 1)

Politics and ASOR

The Mideast has been a battlefield for centuries. In its eighty-year history ASOR has survived five wars in that part of the world, although each conflict has forced ASOR to adjust to a new set of circumstances. Perhaps no event has had a greater effect on the structure of ASOR than the Six-Day War of 1967.

At first glance it would seem that archaeology, by definition retrospective, would be untouched by modern politics, but that is not the case. The explanation may lie in the fact that people in the Mideast are as interested in their past as in their present, constantly seeking historical justification for the current state of affairs. Some even invoke the Bible or the Koran.

ASOR's declared policy of political neutrality has helped it to survive and even prosper amidst the political turmoil of the Mideast. Nonetheless, some appointees have understandably found it difficult not to voice strong personal convictions about politics. The official minutes of ASOR's board of trustees for December 30, 1968, record one such case. Four members of the Jerusalem School staff joined other residents of East Jerusalem in signing a notice printed in the *Jerusalem Post*, protesting an Israeli military parade through the Arab section of Jerusalem. Motivated by the desire to maintain neutrality at a sensitive moment in Arab-Israeli relations, ASOR President Wright dispatched a strong letter of consternation to the signers of the statement. Subsequently, the ASOR trustees formally disassociated themselves from "the unduly harsh tone" of the president's letter and were satisfied that the ASOR appointees in question had not intended to contravene the stated ASOR policy in such matters.

The record shows that the October War of 1973 precipitated a similar incident, but this time two appointees took the other side, protesting the Arabs' preemptive attack on Israel during the observance of Yom Kippur. An official reprimand followed. The fact that there have been only a few instances of this type is a tribute to ASOR scholars, who endeavor under stressful circumstances to maintain evenhandedness. To do otherwise could jeopardize ASOR's commitment to scholarly research throughout the Mideast and could even endanger the safety of colleagues.

The Six-Day War

During the academic year 1966-1967, it became obvious to everyone in Jerusalem, including the residents of the Jerusalem School, that full-scale war between the Israelis and the Arabs was inevitable. As the year progressed and the war clouds gathered, the atmosphere grew more tense and gunfire in the neighboring no-man's-land more frequent. Appointees of the School will recall the inconvenience of frequent curfews, which curtailed some field trips and other activities. By the morning of June 5, 1967, when shooting began in Jerusalem, all the occupants of the School except Director John H. Marks, his family, and Siegfried H. Horn of the aborted Tell Hesban expedition had left Jerusalem at the insistence of the United States consulate. As the conflict was erupting, Omar Jibrin, the devoted majordomo of the School, secured a taxi for those remaining few, and they hastily headed east to Amman and safety. Once again Omar stayed behind at the risk of his own security to guard the School property. When in the course of fighting in Jerusalem the building of the American consulate general, situated vulnerably beside the Mandelbaum Gate, came under fire, the consulate transferred its operations to the Jerusalem School; the personnel took up residence in the School temporarily.

In the brief span of six days the Egyptian army was destroyed, the Sinai Peninsula seized, the West Bank of Jordan occupied, and the Syrians expelled from the Golan Heights. Shortly thereafter, the Israelis unified Jerusalem by annexing the Jordanian sector of the city, an action that served only to increase the bitterness of the Arab population.

The Jerusalem School

Nelson Glueck was one of the first to visit the Jerusalem School after the Six-Day War; it was a homecoming for him. Before 1948 the School had been his residence for several years. His return was the occasion of a moving reunion with Omar. The long-standing friendship between the Palestinian Arab and the American Jew, which had endured in spite of geographical barriers, proved that personal relationships transcend international conflicts.

Hostilities ended, ASOR's new director, William Van Etten Casey of the College of the Holy Cross (Worcester, Massachusetts) arrived in Jerusalem from Europe at the earliest possible moment. He did not come as a stranger; he had already lived at the School as a research Fellow under Lapp's directorship. The days immediately following the war were full of fear and uncertainty. Despite the turmoil in Jerusalem, Casey quickly restored the Jerusalem School to normality and prepared for the arrival of the appointees who were to reside at the School in the academic year 1967-1968.

Omar Jibrin, majordomo of the Jerusalem School
(Albright Institute), serving dinner on Thanks-
giving Day, 1965.

Casey made no pretense at being an archaeologist, although he had
field experience under Lapp at Araq el Emir; he is a humanist with a
gift for writing, as his *Newsletters* attest. He was a close observer of the
events immediately following the war and described them in the *Newsletters*. All his readers appreciated his literary style, but some did not
share his interpretations. In his first *Newsletter* as director he paid a
well-deserved tribute to Omar for his loyalty to the School during the
1967 War by remaining on the premises to protect the property:

Those who have known Omar over the years will not be surprised at this
latest manifestation of his faithfulness and self-possession in time of crisis,
but we can glory in it again and thank him once more for another
performance above and beyond the call of duty. In his loyalty and devotion

Omar is typical of the high quality of the many Palestinians whose friendship and service have honored and prospered the School for almost seventy years.

During his initial days as director of the School Casey witnessed the demolition of the Mandelbaum Gate, which had divided the city into two hostile entities since 1948. On the occasion of the reunification of Jerusalem, Casey reflected in another of his *Newsletters*:

Athough Jerusalem always has been and apparently always will be deeply involved in politics, both secular and religious, its ultimate dimension is not political but mystical and messianic. . . . The word of the Lord still goes forth from the city of Jerusalem and it says: what was broken can be mended, what was wounded can be healed, what was divided can be reunited.

The Six-Day War's Aftermath

Between 1948 and 1967, when an "iron curtain" divided Jerusalem, no communication had taken place between the east and west sides of the city; each sector remained unaware of what was happening in the other. When the barrier was finally removed, scholarly exchange became possible once again. A whole generation of Israelis and Arabs had grown up unable to visit the archaeological sites of the other side; a reunited Jerusalem restored that opportunity anew.

As a sign of the new unity, scholars who had been forced to work in isolation from one another before 1967 made a joint field trip to Masada. Yigael Yadin, the excavator of the site, served as host to Roland de Vaux of the Ecole Biblique and to Paul Lapp and William Casey of the Jerusalem School. The visit was a communal venture reminiscent of times before 1948. Colleagueship of this kind became commonplace after the war.

Effects on Field Trips

The new international boundaries that resulted from the war restricted the scope of the School's field trips. Before 1967 it had been easy to travel to most of the Arab countries from East Jerusalem; now that was no longer possible. However, as compensation, Israel (which had been off-limits for field trips from 1948 to 1967) now welcomed visits from residents of the Jerusalem School. It was a strange reversal of the previous situation, but such vicissitudes are routine in the Mideast.

Work in the West Bank

Before the 1967 War, ASOR had been affiliated with three major excavations in the West Bank—Shechem, Ai, and Taanach. It is ASOR's

At Masada in Israel shortly after the Six-Day War of 1967, Roland de Vaux (left) of the Ecole Biblique and Paul Lapp (center) of the Jerusalem School are briefed by the excavator of Masada, Israeli archaeologist Yigael Yadin. (Photo by William Casey.)

policy to adhere to UNESCO's guidelines, which do not permit archaeologists to begin new digs in occupied territory but do allow salvage projects to go forward in order to preserve endangered antiquities. In addition, any archaeological undertaking conducted in the West Bank after the War of 1967 had to conform to Jordanian laws regulating antiquities. ASOR was careful to report its West Bank salvage projects to the Department of Antiquities of Jordan and to UNESCO headquarters in Jerusalem.

Shechem was the scene of limited salvage archaeology in the period after 1967. Edward F. Campbell continued an important area survey that he had begun in the vicinity of Shechem in 1964, a survey which included the mapping of about fifty sites. In 1968 the survey team made a careful study of Khirbet Makhneh el Fawqa, situated two miles south of Tell Balatah (Shechem). The extensive Bronze Age remains at this ruin indicate that it had been a prominent town in the valley before 1850 B.C., when Shechem came to prominence. Geologist Reuben Bullard, a member of the survey staff, was able to identify the source of the building stone used at Tell Balatah and neighboring Tell er Ras and the origin of the clay used to fashion the local pottery.

In 1969 Joe D. Seger, a veteran of the Shechem and Gezer excavations, returned to Shechem to resolve a problem of the dating of the Middle Bronze-Late Bronze transition at Tell Balatah. Then in 1973 William G. Dever, who had also dug at Shechem and Gezer, located a large tripartite building at Tell Balatah. Dating from about 1600 B.C., the building stood in the Northwest Gate area, designated field IV; it has been identified as a temple. These short-term salvage projects preserved archaeological evidence that would otherwise have been destroyed by erosion, frequent when a site is left unprotected and exposed.

Between 1969 and 1972 Joseph Callaway and Robert E. Cooley cleared an Early Iron Age (about 1200-970 B.C.) village at Khirbet Raddana. Located on the north edge of modern Bireh, it was contemporary with the Iron Age village at Ai (et Tell). This salvage project was necessitated by the construction of a new road in the vicinity.

From 1977, Albert E. Glock, a director of the Albright Institute (formerly the Jerusalem School), has been conducting a salvage excavation in the modern city of Jenin (biblical En Ganim). This project, done with the assistance of archaeological students from Bir Zeit University on the West Bank, was made necessary by modern building construction. Glock identified occupation at the site in the Early Bronze, Late Bronze, and Iron Ages.

William Dever on behalf of Hebrew Union College conducted two West Bank salvage operations west of Hebron between 1967 and 1971, at Jebel Qaaqir and Khirbet el Kom. When the excavators arrived, they found that tomb-robbers had already done some illicit digging. Jebel Qaaqir ("mountain of the cairns") is a one-period site dating to the Middle Bronze I period. A necropolis and a settlement were discovered at this site, where Dever excavated thirty-eight tombs that had been undisturbed. Bearing in mind the name of the site, visitors are not surprised to see six large stone cairns at Jebel Qaaqir.

Khirbet el Kom in the southern Judean hills showed evidence of occupation in the early Bronze Age II, in the Iron Age, and later. Excavators discovered eight ostraca on the floor of the late third-century B.C. house; inscribed in Aramaic, they provide help in dating the Aramaic script. This site is tentatively identified with Shaphir, mentioned in the Book of Micah (1:11). In 1971 John S. Holladay of the University of Toronto also conducted a brief season of excavation at this site.

The Non-Sale of the School Property

In the year preceding the Six-Day War, G. Ernest Wright, ASOR's president, had been negotiating, with the approval of ASOR's trustees, the sale of the Jerusalem School property. Expanding archaeological activity at the School and a growing demand upon its residential quarters made the need for a larger building increasingly felt. However, the war curtailed these transactions, and they were never resumed—a blessing in disguise. The present location of the School, then, is the traditional one; it is ideal in its accessibility to libraries and museums. After so many years of occupancy it has become an American landmark in Jerusalem. The question of selling the School property is occasionally raised but quickly dropped.

Changes in ASOR's Infrastructure

The War of 1967 seriously affected the infrastructure of ASOR, necessitating a total realignment of ASOR overseas institutes. From the time of its establishment in 1900, ASOR had used the Jerusalem School as its base of operations for archaeological work east and west of the Jordan River. To continue ASOR's presence on both sides of the newly erected "iron curtain" along the Jordan, adjustments had to be made in the organization's composition. G. Ernest Wright recommended to the board of trustees that the Jerusalem School and the Amman Center, which came into existence as an expedient after the war, be incorporated as autonomous institutes. Meanwhile, the parent organization (ASOR) would function in the United States to raise funds for the support of the overseas projects and to direct the publications program. The trustees approved this proposed reorganization at a meeting in December 1969, enabling ASOR-affiliated scholars to work on the political side of their choice and at the same time preserving ASOR's pluralism of interests.

ASOR and Saudi Arabia

In 1967 Fred V. Winnett and William L. Reed undertook an archaeological expedition to Hail in northwestern Saudi Arabia. Hail is an oasis situated on one of the principal pilgrimage routes from Iraq to Mecca. According to some scholars, the earliest Arab tribes traced their origins to this important commercial and agricultural center, although it lacks evidence of Nabatean occupation. On an earlier reconnaissance in 1962, Winnett and Reed had covered 1,800 miles of Northern Arabia, photographing 300 Thamudic and Nabatean inscriptions. On this second trip, sponsored jointly by ASOR and the Saudi Department of Antiquities, the two explorers visited twenty-five sites in the Hail area. Encouraged by the success of this joint undertaking in Saudi Arabia, ASOR has been investigating the possibility of engaging in additional joint projects.

Abdullah Masry, who received his graduate training in archaeology at the University of Chicago, is the first to be director general of Archaeology and Museums in Saudi Arabia. In that capacity he is playing a leading role in establishing the archaeology of Saudi Arabia on a scientific basis. While drafting the antiquities laws in 1973 and 1974, he laid plans for a comprehensive archaeological survey to span a five-year period. Meanwhile, in addition to the National Museum in Riyadh, he has overseen the development of six regional museums. Saudi Arabia now has its own archaeological journal, *Atlal*, which carries the official reports of all projects within the country.

Planning for a Research Center in Beirut

Before the outbreak of the War of 1967, ASOR announced its intention to establish a research center in Beirut in order to study firsthand the diverse cultural heritage of Lebanon. Even before that modern state was created from five Turkish districts of the Ottoman Empire in 1920, ASOR had sponsored Torrey's expedition to Sidon. Choosing to excavate in Lebanon requires no justification because of its importance in the history of the ancient Near East; Lebanon contains a rich mixture of Phoenician, Hittite, Egyptian, Greek, Roman, Byzantine, and Arab cultures. To be sure, the undug tells of Lebanon conceal a wealth of material that will eventually shed light on the history, trade, and alphabet associated with the Phoenicians, who were both sea-traders and colonizers.

Despite ASOR's good intentions, budgetary constraints and the continuing civil wars in Lebanon have so far prevented the establishment of an overseas institute in Beirut. Someday there may be an opportunity to survey, if not to excavate, in Lebanon before the most promising sites are destroyed by military encroachment. It may, however, be too late to hope; the country lies in ruins, torn apart by hostile factions.

The Excavations at Sarafand (Zarephath)

After hostilities disrupted his dig at Tell es Saidiyeh in Jordan, James B. Pritchard of the University of Pennsylvania Museum went to Lebanon in 1969 to select a site needing excavation. Lebanon's political stability at the time provided an ideal opportunity for field archaeology. Pritchard chose to dig at the modern fishing village of Sarafand, known in the Bible as Zarephath, situated on the Mediterranean coast midway between Tyre and Sidon. The site was definitively identified with the Phoenician town of Zarephath in 1971 when the excavators found a stone inscription in Greek reading "to the holy god of Sarepta" (the Greek form of Zarephath).

In the course of four seasons of digging, Pritchard's team uncovered Phoenician and Roman occupation levels. More important, they discovered a sanctuary dating to the seventh century B.C., similar to the Philistine sanctuary at Tell Qasile. It contained benches along the walls, an offering table, and a group of figurines. The residents of Zarephath worshipped the goddess Tanit, who was the equivalent of the West

Semitic Astarte. (A later ASOR excavation at Carthage unearthed ample evidence of child sacrifice in the worship of Tanit at the Tophet, a precinct for the sacrificing of children in the Phoenician colony of Carthage.) Because of the large number of pottery kilns discovered at Sarafand, Pritchard concluded that ancient Zarephath was an important Phoenician pottery-making center in the Late Bronze and Iron Ages.

As in the case of his dig at Tell es Saidiyeh in Jordan, political violence interrupted Pritchard's work at this site in Lebanon. Pritchard has had the good fortune to select exciting and productive sites to excavate; unfortunately, they have been located in unsettled areas. The history of Mideastern archaeology simply repeats itself.

A Succession of Annual Directors

Following the War of 1967 four successive annual appointees directed the activities of the School in Jerusalem. Kermit Schoonover of Southern Methodist University succeeded Casey and continued the task of restoring the School to normal life. Schoonover devoted his attention to the internal activities of the institute by encouraging the residents in their individual research projects. David N. Freedman of the San Francisco Theological Seminary became director in 1969; he immediately revitalized the School, welcoming Israeli and other scholars to use the resources of the School and to participate in its programs. He also undertook major refurbishing of the physical plant, painting and redecorating every room. Robert J. Bull of Drew University, Freedman's successor, completed this major renovation project. Bull continued to establish relationships with West Jerusalem, while maintaining old friendships with the Arab community of East Jerusalem.

Contact with West Jerusalem expanded the School's academic possibilities. Between 1948 and 1967 West Jerusalem had become an impressive university city endowed with excellent libraries and other research facilities; West Jerusalem was now an international center of learning and culture. Elsewhere in Israel, five institutions of higher learning were founded before 1967: the Weizmann Institute of Science and the Universities of Tel Aviv, Bar-Ilan, Haifa, and Ben-Gurion of the Negev. In addition, cultural institutions such as the Israel Museum in Jerusalem and the Israel Academy of Sciences and Humanities and hundreds of libraries exist throughout the country.

William G. Dever

Throughout ASOR's history, the annual directors of its institutes have administered effective academic programs, but there is no substitute for long-term appointees. The Jerusalem School was most productive when Albright, Glueck, and Lapp each served as director for several years. William G. Dever became the fourth multiyear director of the

Albright Institute of Archaeological Research (formerly the Jerusalem School) in 1971, after having served for several years as archaeological director of the Hebrew Union College Biblical and Archaeological School in Jerusalem. The experience of living first in West Jerusalem, then in East enabled Dever to cement a relationship between these two schools and gave him a comprehensive view of the archaeology of Israel and part of the Arab world. Dever was a second Glueck, as both scholars had firsthand association with Jerusalem's two American archaeological institutes. Dever's experience also enabled him to promote a regular lecture program under the joint sponsorship of the Albright Institute and Hebrew Union College. An annual series of lectures has been taking place at the Rockefeller Museum; both the scholarly and lay communities have responded enthusiastically to this joint venture.

Building on the achievements of his predecessors, Dever expanded the archaeological facilities and the field program at the Albright Institute. The installation of a photographic studio, a darkroom, and a drafting room enabled archaeologists and their staff to prepare preliminary dig reports at the Albright Institute instead of scurrying about the city for alternate facilities. Unfortunately, during Dever's tenure ASOR's strained finances made it impossible to support him at the level his archaeological talents deserved.

Like the long-term directors before him, Dever undertook extensive lecture tours for ASOR in the United States and Canada to acquaint affiliated academic institutions with current developments in the archaeology of the Mideast. These tours by ASOR directors and other appointees have effectively disseminated the results of archaeological research; they have also given ASOR needed visibility in the wider community.

The Tell Hesban Expedition

Several archaeological projects fell victim to the Six-Day War and its aftermath. The Tell Hesban expedition, scheduled to be in the field at the time the war broke out, had to be postponed until 1968. Tell Hesban is located about fifteen miles southwest of Amman in Transjordan and is probably the Heshbon mentioned by Isaiah and Jeremiah in the oracles against Moab. Tell Hesban was traditionally thought to have been the site of the Moabite city that Sihon, king of the Amorites, conquered and made his capital. He was defeated in turn by the invading Israelites when he opposed their proposed passage through his territory.

Siegfried H. Horn of Andrews University organized the Hesban excavations, which were jointly sponsored by Andrews and ASOR. In 1974 Lawrence T. Geraty, also of Andrews, assumed the directorship of the project. Horn chose this previously unexcavated site in order to answer questions about the early history of Transjordan, especially the Israelite conquest and settlement, events that continue to perplex historians.

Siegfried H. Horn, director of the Hesban excavations during the first three seasons (1968-1973). (Photo by Avery Dick.)

Excavations at Tell Hesban revealed that the occupational history of the site included twenty-six strata, extending from the Iron I period (1200 B.C.) to Mamluk times (A.D. 1500). The absence of Late Bronze remains casts doubt on the identification of the tell with the capital city of King Sihon. Archaeologists speculate that the royal city may in fact be located at nearby Tell Jalul, one of the largest sites in Transjordan, which was occupied throughout the Bronze Age and in the Iron Age. The Andrews University team, under the direction of Lawrence T. Geraty, plans to begin excavation at Tell Jalul as part of their Madaba Plains Project. At this time the ancient identification of Tell Jalul remains unknown.

Roman and Byzantine tombs were also excavated at Hesban; the bulk of the remains at this site date to the Roman period. In addition, the foundation of a basilica-type church of the Byzantine period (about A.D. 550) was unearthed. In 1978 John I. Lawlor of the Baptist Bible College of Pennsylvania directed the Hesban North Church project, uncovering material from three periods: Ayyubid/Mamluk (A.D. 1200-1450), Umayyad (A.D. 640-750), and Byzantine (A.D. 323-640).

In conjunction with the excavations at Tell Hesban, the archaeologists conducted a regional survey, which included more than 125 sites within a radius of six miles of the main tell. This undertaking was part of the overall survey of Jordan in which ASOR archaeologists have been

Lawrence Geraty, director of the Hesban excavations, taking his mentor, Ernest Wright, on a tour of the site in 1974.

Lawrence Geraty, director of the Hesban excavations, introduces his teacher, Ernest Wright, to Jordanian Department of Antiquities representatives Mahmoud Rousan, Sabri Abbadi, and others at the dinner table in camp in 1974.

actively engaged. The Hesban project has been a model of inter-disciplinary research. Its inquiry into the occupational history and the environmental setting of central Transjordan has led to an understanding of the cultural development of the region starting with the Iron Age.

The archaeology of Jordan owes an extraordinary debt of gratitude to the Hesban expedition, especially for its pioneering efforts in many areas of archaeological research. The following list of Hesban accomplishments is only a suggestion of their long-term implications for the scientific development of archaeology in the land east of the Jordan River. Hesban was the first truly interdisciplinary undertaking in Jordan on a large scale. The comprehensive environmental studies at Hesban included work on the climate, geology, soil, hydrology, phytogeography (the biogeography of plants), and zoogeography. At the same time, the Hesban dig has pioneered methods and procedures for processing large quantities of animal remains; the accumulation of what is probably the most comprehensive assemblage of animal bones from any site in Palestine has resulted.

This expedition was the first in Jordan to introduce ethnoarchaeology, the ethnographic study of material and social life in the present for the purpose of aiding integration of evidence from the past. Starting

Tell Hesban ceramic expert James Sauer reading pottery with supervisors Rose Habaybeh and Harold Mare in 1974.

in 1971, Hesban may have been the first ASOR-related field project to use the computer in a systematic way. The Hesban archaeologists deserve special recognition for having published a full preliminary report each season before returning to the field for the next season.

Through its field school Hesban has touched almost every dig in Jordan by serving as the training ground for scores of graduate students, several of whom now direct their own projects. That a number of native Jordanian archaeologists received their initial field training at Tell Hesban is noteworthy. In all these achievements the Hesban project has admirably fulfilled the objectives of ASOR as set down in ASOR's original statement of purpose and its later revision.

During the long-term excavation of Tell Hesban Roger S. Boraas of Upsala College served as the chief archaeologist. The field manual which he developed for the Tell Hesban dig has become the standard text used in nearly all American digs in Jordan, as well as those sponsored by the Department of Antiquities of Jordan.

In 1969 Boraas directed a preliminary sounding at Rujm el Malfouf, on the western side of the city of Amman, a project designed as part of an area-study program for undergraduates. This site consisted mainly of a round, stone tower and an adjoining rectangular building, part of a fortification line protecting Amman. Boraas's work confirmed Glueck's

Iron Age date (1200-600 B.C.) of this Ammonite defensive installation. Sauer suggests an Iron Age II date for these circular megalithic towers.

Excavations at Mount Gerizim

When the semblance of normality returned to the Mideast after the war, Robert G. Boling of McCormick Theological Seminary undertook a salvage project on behalf of ASOR. In 1968 he reexcavated a Bronze Age structure situated on the lower slopes of Mount Gerizim, in the area of Tananir. Gabriel Welter, who had dug in Sellin's era at Shechem, had also excavated here in 1931, but he had erroneously described the building as a Late Bronze temple destroyed by Abimelech, briefly king over Shechem. In Albright's opinion, the building in question was a patrician house of the Middle Bronze II C period (1650-1550 B.C.). The argument about whether the structure is a house or a sanctuary is still unsettled, but the dig confirmed Albright's Middle Bronze date. In the process of excavating, Boling encountered an additional building from the same period, situated one step down the slope of Gerizim.

Boling directed the Tananir salvage project while serving from 1968 to 1969 as a resident Fellow at the School in Jerusalem. Other appointees for that year were happy to assist with the field work in exchange for the experience that the project offered. Having participated in the Shechem excavations, Boling was well qualified to instruct beginners in the techniques of field archaeology.

The New ASOR Institutes

ASOR's institutes in Jerusalem and Amman were newly constituted in the spring of 1970 in response to the political reality of the Mideast. The Amman Center was officially entitled "The American Center of Oriental Research," abbreviated ACOR, with John H. Marks of Princeton University as president. The logo of the American Center of Oriental Research (ACOR) in Amman has been adapted from the unique animal fountain discovered at Araq el Emir, the site of an ASOR dig. Depicting a feline figure sculptured on a block of mottled red and white dolomite, the logo adorns the east wall of the Qasr (palace?). According to Dorothy K. Hill of the Walters Art Gallery, who worked at the site with Paul Lapp, this particular figure may represent either a lion or a leopard.

The Jerusalem School was appropriately renamed "The W. F. Albright Institute of Archaeological Research," or AIAR, with Edward F. Campbell of McCormick Theological Seminary as its president. Every word in the new title of the Jerusalem School—the W. F. Albright Institute of Archaeological Research—had been carefully chosen. Naming the School after Albright was not just a symbolic gesture, but a genuine tribute to the Jerusalem School's most distinguished director, and it pleased him greatly. The term "Archaeological Research" is to be

The W. F. Albright Institute of Archaeological Research (formerly the Jerusalem School). Munira Said, the AIAR administrative secretary, appears in her typical welcoming pose.

understood with its broadest connotation, as the study of ancient culture, not merely field excavation. Anything less would not have done justice to Albright's all-encompassing concerns. The Certificate of Incorporation of the Albright Institute states:

> The purposes for which the corporation is formed are to promote the study and teaching and extend the knowledge of the geography, history, archaeology, and languages and literatures of ancient Israel and other lands of the Near East by affording educational opportunities to faculty and students of American and Canadian colleges and universities, and to other qualified faculty and students.

The logo of the Albright Institute consists of a Judahite scaraboid, which dates to the late eighth century B.C. In Egypt the dung beetle (*scarabaeus sacer* [the Latin *scarabaeus* is related to the Greek *karabos*, literally "a beetle"]) was a symbol of continual existence and resurrection. The upper register of the scaraboid depicts a four-winged flying scarab beetle with two pairs of wings outstretched and the forelegs grasping a dung ball, which scarabs roll. The first line in the lower register reads *Hananyahu*, "Yahu [Yahweh] has been gracious"; the second line reads *'mt*: it is a nickname or truncated form like *amittai* for a longer name probably with a divine element.

WILLIAM F. ALBRIGHT INSTITUTE OF ARCHAEOLOGICAL RESEARCH

Like its predecessor the Jerusalem School, the Albright Institute continues to enjoy close relationships with the Ecole Biblique, the British and German Schools, and other institutes and individuals in East Jerusalem. In addition, the institute has much in common with the Institute of Archaeology of Hebrew University, Hebrew Union College's Nelson Glueck School of Biblical Archaeology, and the other academic institutions in Israel. The Albright Institute continues to be an ideal setting for scholarly discourse, and neutral ground for non-political discussions. Those affiliated with the local academic institutions frequently visit the Albright Institute and participate in lecture programs, seminars, and social functions. In turn, the residents of the Albright Institute have the valuable opportunity of meeting local scholars on an informal basis and discussing with them research projects of mutual interest. They also have access to library resources throughout Jerusalem.

The Amman Center

When the Amman Center was established in 1968 in response to new postwar borders, Rudolph H. Dornemann became its first director. From its inception, the Amman Center worked cooperatively with the University of Jordan and the Department of Antiquities in all phases of archaeological research, with the successive directors of the center serving as lecturers at the university and advisers to the department. While director of the Amman Center, Dornemann excavated at Jebel el Qala, the Citadel of Amman, in cooperation with the University of Jordan and the Department of Antiquities. In the course of digging on Citadel Hill (the acropolis of the ancient city known in the Bible as Rabbath Ammon) during eight weeks in 1968, the excavators unearthed evidence of occupation from the Early Bronze Age to the Byzantine period. Several more expeditions were to dig at the Citadel.

Other American scholars helped to shape the Amman Center during its formative years; Roger S. Boraas, Murray B. Nicol, Bastiaan Van Elderen, Siegfried H. Horn, Henry O. Thompson, and George E. Mendenhall made notable contributions. In 1975 James A. Sauer became the first long-term director of ACOR. Building on the foundation laid by his predecessors, he developed the institute into an excellent archaeological research center.

From the time of ACOR's establishment its directors and residents have enjoyed the gracious services of Muhammad Adawi, who had been a member of the Jerualem School's domestic staff before the 1967 War. Like his tutor Omar at the Albright Institute, Muhammad is a loyal and devoted friend of ASOR. When incorporated in 1970 ACOR was housed in a modest building near the Third Circle of the Jebel Amman area. In 1977 ACOR moved to a new two-story building near the Fifth Circle, just off the main Wadi Sir road. The more spacious quarters exacted a higher rental fee, which was met through the generous support of two friends of ACOR, Robert A. Coughenour of Western Theological Seminary and Marian H. Welker. A professional librarian, Welker had previously demonstrated her interest in ASOR by supervising the library of the Jerusalem School on a volunteer basis before the Six-Day War. In addition to being a benefactor of ACOR, Coughenour excavated two iron smelting sites in the Ajlun region of Jordan, Mugharet el Wardeh and Abu Thawab, both mentioned by Glueck in his survey of Transjordan. At these sites Coughenour recovered pottery of the Ayyubid/ Mamluk period, an era that witnessed a significant resurgence of occupation in Transjordan.

Many others have been exceedingly supportive of ACOR's efforts in Jordan. The staff of the American embassy, especially Ambassadors Thomas R. Pickering and Nicholas Veliotes, deserve special mention for their encouragement and assistance, which have helped ACOR to establish itself as a vital archaeological institute in the Arab world. Thanks to both the named and unnamed, through its scholarly activities and programs, ACOR today represents a vigorous American presence in Jordan and an encouragement to meaningful cooperation between American scholars and their Jordanian colleagues.

Political Turmoil in Jordan

ACOR's initial years were complicated by the political turmoil that racked Jordan in 1970 when the Jordanian army was locked in civil war with the commando organization, representing the resistance movement. This battle culminated in "Black September," the Palestinian designation for the Jordanian army's sweeping attack which disarmed, decimated, and finally expelled the guerrillas from the country. Siegfried Horn arrived in Amman in December 1970 to assume the directorship of

ACOR; he described the raging internecine warfare in one tragic sentence, "Amman was bleeding from a thousand wounds."

Horn, although very stable and unflappable by temperament, nevertheless had a frightening experience in the midst of the turmoil. He tells of being caught in the Amman museum on Citadel Hill when fighting erupted and having to remain in the shelter for several hours. He reported that he was once caught in crossfire in the downtown area but was able to speed to safety through deserted streets.

Henry O. Thompson

Thompson, who directed ACOR during 1971-1972, concentrated his research on the Ammonites, the Semitic people who lived in central Transjordan from about 1300 B.C., or even earlier, until 580 B.C. With the assistance of students from the University of Jordan and the staff of the Department of Antiquities, Thompson excavated Tell Siran, a small mound on the campus of the university in Amman. In the course of digging he uncovered sherds from the Mamluk, Umayyad, Byzantine, and Hellenistic periods, and the Iron Age. The most exciting find, however, was a now famous bronze, bottle-shaped object about four inches long, incised with eight lines of Ammonite—the first complete inscription in that language ever discovered—referring to a construction project by a king called Amminadab. The Tell Siran dedicatory inscription, which Frank Cross of Harvard dates to about 600 B.C., helps to fill in the Ammonite king-list of the seventh century B.C., from Pedoel to Baalis. Pedoel may have been a contemporary of Sennacherib, king of Assyria (705-681 B.C.); Baalis's reign is dated to about 580 B.C.

Bastiaan Van Elderen

Bastiaan Van Elderen, director of ACOR in 1970 and again in 1972 to 1974, concentrated on the history of the Christian church in Jordan. As part of his research he excavated Tell Swafiyeh, on the western edge of Amman, and Tell Masuh, twenty miles south of Amman. At Swafiyeh he discovered the remains of a Byzantine church dating to the sixth century and its well-preserved mosaic floor with inscription. He also uncovered at Masuh a mosaic floor belonging to a large church. Van Elderen and other excavators have established that central Jordan is rich in mosaics and in the remnants of Byzantine churches built when Christianity won its battle against paganism. Both the churches and the mosaics will undergo serious study over the next decade.

ACOR Facilities and Functions

With each passing year ACOR has become an increasingly valuable research center in Jordan, serving not only Americans but also Canadians, Australians, Spanish, French, and other nationals. In addition to sponsoring archaeological field projects, ACOR must serve a variety of research needs of American and other scholars. To be an effective research center, ACOR has been building up its library, which is open twenty-four hours a day to all scholars. The basic archaeological reference works from the late G. Ernest Wright's library, acquired through a generous gift from the Zion Research Foundation, form the nucleus of the ACOR library. The Zion Research Foundation continues to make funds available for the acquisition of new books for ACOR.

ACOR's hostel can accommodate a dozen residents. Each year this small group has succeeded in forming a community of scholars who enjoy camaraderie and the opportunity to discuss their various research projects. ACOR is quickly outgrowing its physical plant but has resisted the temptation to move periodically into larger quarters lest its scholarly program be disrupted. Long-term commitment to archaeological research in the Arab world requires a permanent facility in an Arab country, and Amman appears to be the proper location for such an institute. As an indication of ASOR's commitment, a major building campaign is underway to make such facility a reality; the Jordanian government will provide the land. Ideally a permanent research center in Jordan could also service ASOR's work in Syria, Saudi Arabia, Bahrain, and other neighboring Arab countries where ASOR may be invited to excavate.

The Department of Antiquities in Jordan

ASOR/ACOR has always enjoyed a solid working relationship with the Jordanian Department of Antiquities. The department was established in 1924 as an adjunct to the Department of Antiquities of Palestine, headquartered in Jerusalem; later it became the separate department for Transjordan and ultimately the Department of Antiquities of Jordan.

During the British mandate the Department of Antiquities was overseen first by George Horsfield (1924-1936) and afterward by G. Lankester Harding (1936-1956). In addition to establishing the *Annual of the Department of Antiquities of Jordan*, Harding also founded the Jordan Archaeological Museum in Amman. Completed in 1951, the museum is located on the ancient Citadel of Amman; it incorporates the Roman, Byzantine, and Arab remains of the Citadel. Since the amazing growth of archaeological activity in Jordan has made the museum inadequate, a new museum is in the planning stage.

Several Jordanian directors of the Department of Antiquities, especially Awni Dajani and Yaqoub Oweis, who served for long terms, and the present director, Adnan Hadidi, have encouraged Americans to work in Jordan and have been supportive of American efforts. The Department of Antiquities often supplies labor and equipment to facilitate excavation and survey. The department on its own or in conjunction with foreign archaeologists conducts surveys, salvage projects, and excavations; it also undertakes the preservation and restoration of monumental sites. Jerash, Petra, Umm Qais (ancient Gadara), and Araq el Emir are being restored through the efforts of the Department of Antiquities with the assistance of foreign archaeological missions.

Higher Education in Jordan

During the past twenty years the Kingdom of Jordan made steady progress in the field of higher education. The University of Jordan, established in Amman in 1962, has an enrollment of more than 10,000 students. Programs in archaeology and Near Eastern history have kept pace with the growth of the university; a master's program in archaeology was inaugurated in 1973 and a separate department of archaeology was formed in 1977. The ACOR director and other appointees regularly offer courses in Near Eastern studies and serve as advisers to the students of archaeology as ways of strengthening the relationship between the university and ACOR.

A second institution of higher education, Yarmuk University, was founded in 1976 on a temporary campus in the northern city of Irbid; it too has developed a department of archaeology. A third university is being planned for the Kerak region, to be known as Mutah University; nearby Mutah is the site where the first battle between the Moslem and Byzantine forces occurred in the seventh century A.D.

The Friends of Archaeology

Interest in the archaeology of Jordan is not solely the prerogative of university professors and students; a large number of nonprofessionals are also avidly engaged in the enterprise. To satisfy their curiosity, the Department of Antiquities in 1962 founded an organization known as the Friends of Archaeology, which has an international membership of about 200 people. ACOR contributes to the Friends' program by sponsoring lectures and leading field trips throughout Jordan. While director of ACOR, James Sauer regularly gave lectures on the pottery of Jordan, supplemented by visits to sites related to the ceramic material under discussion.

Other Archaeological Institutes in Jordan

In addition to its connections with the Department of Antiquities, the University of Jordan, and Yarmuk University, ACOR enjoys a collegial relationship with other national archaeological institutes in Jordan. The British School of Archaeology in Jerusalem began sponsoring projects in Transjordan with its establishment after World War I. Then in 1979 the British Institute at Amman for Archaeology and History was founded, and Crystal M. Bennett became its first director. Located near the University of Jordan, the British Institute serves as the base of operations for several projects under British, Australian, and other national auspices. Bennett has led expeditions to important sites in Jordan, especially in the territory of Edom in southern Jordan; two such sites are the Edomite capital of Bozrah, identified with present-day Buseirah, and Tawilan, a modern village near Elji on the eastern outskirts of Petra, which, according to some, is the site of biblical Teman.

The German Evangelical Institute in Jerusalem supports a branch in Amman directed by Ute Lux; it serves as a base of operations for German and Danish field projects. At the time of this writing the German Institute is excavating at Umm Qais, a city of the Decapolis overlooking the southern shores of Lake Tiberias and identified with biblical Gadara. When the restoration of Umm Qais is completed, in the opinion of some observers it will rival Pompeii. In addition to overseeing the Umm Qais project with the assistance of Ernst Krueger and others, Ute Lux has been dedicating her efforts to the excavation and publication of the numerous mosaics found in Jordan.

The French Institute of Archaeology in the Near East, with headquarters in Beirut, also works in Amman under the direction of Ernest Will. In addition to its project at Petra, the French Institute has been concentrating on the reconstruction of the Qasr at Araq el Emir. Other national teams are conducting various kinds of research and field projects in Jordan; the Dutch are working at Tell Deir Alla, the Spanish at Quseir Amrah and the Amman Citadel, and the Belgians at Lahun. Since they do not yet have their own research centers and hostels in Jordan, such teams regularly use the facilities of ACOR and other national institutes.

The First International Conference

For several decades scholars from the international and local communities have been recovering the rich cultural heritage of Jordan through various forms of research and field projects. In order to coordinate these efforts and to share the results of research, the First International Conference on the History and Archaeology of Jordan was held at Oxford University in March 1980, under the patronage of His Royal Highness Crown Prince Hassan. During a six-day period, scholars from twenty-six countries gathered at Christ Church to present papers on the archaeological history of Jordan from the Paleolithic to the Ottoman period. The program was so successful that the Crown Prince plans to convene future conferences every three years in order to explore specific archaeological periods in depth.[1] An international advisory council,

---

[1] A second conference is scheduled to be held in 1983, when the scholarly presentations will center on the geographical and historical aspects of the environment of Jordan.

A view of the reconstructed west wall of the Qasr at Araq el Emir. (Photo by François Larché, architect of the restoration project.)

which includes several ASOR scholars, has also been formed to assist in planning the future of archaeology in Jordan.[2]

Funding for Work in Jordan

Scholarly enterprises are dependent upon financial support, and the undertakings of ASOR are no exception. No matter how scientifically worthwhile a project may be, without funding it will be given up. An annual subsidy from the United States government has eased ASOR's financial burden in Jordan; the government has in the past rarely supported or given funds to institutions such as ASOR. In the United States there is a long tradition of government noninterference with private especially academic institutions. However, this situation has a positive side: American research centers abroad have gained in the confidence of the local authorities who are otherwise suspicious of missions sponsored by foreign governments, as is the case with most European nations.

[2]David McCreery and Linda Jacobs of ACOR assisted with the formulation of a five-year plan to be implemented by the Department of Antiquities. Their plan provides in a systematic way for the protection and preservation of archaeological sites; it also envisions intensive surveys in those areas of Jordan that are still *terrae incognitae*.

James A. Sauer

As at the Albright Institute in Jerusalem, the American Center in Amman functions more effectively when there is a long-term director; James A. Sauer was the first to fill this important post. During his six-year tenure he earned for ACOR a leading role in the archaeological community of Jordan. Sauer is one of ASOR's most promising archaeologists. His reputation as a ceramicist was established with the publication of his study of Tell Hesban's pottery typology, which extends from the Roman period to about A.D. 500. Concerning this work, Sauer's teacher, G. Ernest Wright observed that it was the first publication of well-stratified, tightly controlled strata, dealing with archaeologists' greatest dark age, the post-New Testament era.

Sauer also figured prominently in the survey of the East Jordan Valley, a project jointly sponsored by the Department of Antiquities, the University of Jordan, and ACOR.[3] Sauer's firsthand knowledge of the land of Jordan and its archaeology qualifies him to write the archaeological history of Transjordan. By sharing his expertise as a lecturer at the University of Jordan, he has exerted a formative influence on Jordanian students pursuing studies in archaeology. By giving generously of his time to date the pottery collected on several ACOR surveys, Sauer has been a valuable resource for several American archaeologists working in Jordan.

In a review of ASOR's history, certain parallels between Albright and Sauer come to mind. In the 1920s and 1930s few in Palestine were trained in field archaeology before Albright appeared on the scene, but today Israel boasts over 200 trained archaeologists. Similarly in Jordan, the number of archaeologists is steadily increasing, thanks in part to Sauer's influence. Like the Jerusalem School of Albright's time, ACOR is now serving as a catalyst for the development of archaeology in Jordan.

Excavations in Israel

When Ernest Wright in 1956 directed his first campaign at Tell Balatah, he began to emerge as a prominent figure in the archaeology of Syria-Palestine. He exerted considerable influence on the development of field archaeology through the members of his Balatah staff and his

---

[3]The survey of the East Jordan Valley, begun in 1975 by Sauer and Jordanian archaeologists Moawiyah Ibrahim and Khair Yassine, embraced the entire region extending from the Yarmuk River in the north to the Dead Sea. It has yielded evidence of occupation from almost all the archaeological periods. In the survey process, which included photographing and mapping the sites and collecting artifacts, the team compared this region with others in Jordan and beyond. They were also able to identify many new sites for the archaeological record. The results of this survey will be helpful to the government as it makes plans for the economic development of the Jordan Valley.

Renewed excavations at Tell el Hesi in 1970 under ASOR auspices.

Harvard students, especially as they began to assume responsibility for their own projects, such as Gezer, Taanach, Hesban, Hesi, Shema, and Lahav. Benefiting from the guidance of Wright, they improved upon earlier techniques of digging and recording and also adopted the interdisciplinary approach to archaeology.

The Tell el Hesi Expedition

With Wright's planning and encouragement, the Tell el Hesi expedition took to the field in 1970. Located midway between Ashdod and Beer-sheba, Hesi is the thirty-seven acre mound crowned with a seven-acre acropolis where Flinders Petrie worked eighty years earlier. Despite the good work of Petrie and later Bliss in laying the foundations for stratigraphy and typology, the twin principles of modern archaeology, they left several questions about Tell Hesi unanswered.

Hesi's occupational history extended from the Early Bronze Age to the Roman period. The Petrie-Bliss dating of the Late Bronze Age and subsequent periods was quite accurate, but their chronology for the earlier periods was too low. Their identification of the site as Lachish, following Conder's conjecture, has been disproved by Albright. Albright's suggestion to equate Hesi with ancient Eglon, a Canaanite royal city that fell to the Israelites at the time of the conquest, is at best plausible. Noth conjectured that Tell Aitun, situated on a natural route between

Lawrence Stager excavating the elusive mudbrick in field three at Tell el Hesi in 1971. (Photo by Theodore Rosen.)

Lachish and Hebron, was the site of Eglon. However, in the absence of epigraphic evidence, the identification of Tell el Hesi remains uncertain.

John E. Worrell launched the long-term, interdisciplinary project at Tell el Hesi in 1970, under the auspices of ASOR. He continued as director until the 1977 season, when D. Glenn Rose of Phillips University succeeded him. At the end of the 1981 season the Hesi staff and volunteers were dealt a severe blow when Glenn Rose died suddenly at the Albright Institute, as he was beginning his term as annual professor.

From Hesi's first season Lawrence E. Toombs, a leading stratigrapher and veteran of the Shechem excavations, has been serving as chief archaeologist on the dig. On the Gezer model, the Hesi expedition involves its volunteers in every phase of the work and also conducts an excellent field school.

The Hesi dig is clarifying some previously unknown eras in Palestinian history, most notably the little-understood Persian period. The work of several seasons on the Hesi acropolis has revealed that it was a large grain storage area in Persian times. Lawrence E. Stager, who served on the Hesi staff, explains the subterranean pits at Hesi and neighboring sites during the Persian period as storage facilities in seasons of bountiful harvest.

Hesi is one of the largest Early Bronze sites in Palestine. As the excavators dig the lower city at Hesi, where they have uncovered the massive defensive wall and glacis of the Early Bronze Age III (2800-2400 B.C.), they are illuminating an important era in the history of Syria-Palestine. This period is of unusual interest today in view of the 1974 discovery in Syria by Italian archaeologists of the royal archive at Tell Mardikh, the site of ancient Ebla. The previously unknown Kingdom of Ebla, situated in northern Syria, dates from about 2400 B.C. ASOR archaeologists, as well as others, are coordinating sites currently under excavation that have Early Bronze Age levels, in an attempt to complete a comprehensive picture of the third millennium B.C.

The building project, consisting of a huge platform of walls and intermittent fill, undertaken on the acropolis of Hesi during the Iron II period may have been more impressive than the Early Bronze Age city's defensive system, which was constructed 1500 years earlier. Apparently in response to a military threat, the Iron Age engineers raised the level of the acropolis about twenty feet to provide the late Israelite city with a double-walled defensive system. Toombs dates this construction to the ninth century B.C., perhaps in the time of King Jehoshaphat (873-849 B.C.), although his long reign was peaceful and prosperous.

Despite the physical inconveniences especially the persistent flies associated with digging at Tell el Hesi, the staff have succeeded in engendering an admirable group spirit among the volunteers. Many have become avid alumni and alumnae, sustaining an active interest in Hesi, thanks largely to the Hesi newsletter, "Trowel and Patish," edited by J. Kenneth Eakins of Golden Gate Baptist Theological Seminary. The Hesi project also deserves recognition for the quality of its interdisciplinary staff; from the beginning of the dig, the several specialists have regularly been present at the site, collecting their materials and processing them for publication.

The Campaigns at Tell Jemmeh

Developments in archaeological method have often required that sites dug earlier, when techniques were less refined, be reexcavated, as at Megiddo, Jericho, Shechem and Gezer. In the twenties and thirties, Petrie concentrated on the northwestern Negev, excavating three sites there, Tell el Farah (Sharuhen), Tell el Ajjul, and Tell Jemmeh. From 1970 to 1978 Gus W. Van Beek, a Smithsonian archaeologist long affiliated with ASOR, directed a new project at Tell Jemmeh, located about six miles south of Gaza, under the auspices of the Smithsonian Institution. Petrie had identified the tell as Gerar, a city mentioned in the biblical narratives about the patriarchs, but today scholars are inclined to equate Jemmeh with the Canaanite city-state of Yurza, following the suggestion of Benjamin Mazar. Yurza appears in the Egyptian lists and the Tell el Amarna letters. Gerar is more likely to be located at Tell Abu Hureirah, which lies fifteen miles northwest of Beer-sheba.[4]

Separated from Tell el Hesi by about twenty miles, Tell Jemmeh is similar to it, especially regarding the Persian period, when both sites were large grain storage areas. The most striking discovery at Jemmeh was a well-preserved building with barrel vaults; constructed of mud-brick, it is the only example of its kind thus far found in Israel. According to Van Beek, this structure may have served as the residence of the Assyrian military governor of that district after Esarhaddon, king of Assyria and Babylonia (680-669 B.C.), conquered Arsa (Yurza) in 679 B.C. Before his conquest of Egypt in 671 B.C., Esarhaddon probably used the site of Tell Jemmeh as a staging ground for his campaigns against Egypt.

The Archaeology of Judaism and Early Christianity

It is not surprising that archaeologists sometimes choose sites to dig because their history coincides with personal interests. On this basis, Israelis may prefer the Iron Age for the light it casts on their national history while Arabs may opt for later periods because of their concern for Islamic culture. In reconstructing the cultural process of the ancient Near East, however, all periods are important, and none is to be neglected. Those archaeological periods that are not well known deserve attention, such as early Judaism, the beginnings of Christianity, and classical Graeco-Roman antiquity. Keenly aware of this need Ernest Wright encouraged archaeologists to undertake the excavation of sites that could illumine these relatively obscure eras.

The Excavation at Pella

Pella in Transjordan took its name from Pella of Macedonia, the birthplace of Alexander the Great. A city of the Decapolis, a loose federation of ten cities formed after the Roman conquest of Palestine in 63 B.C., Pella served as a refuge for Christians fleeing Jerusalem at the beginning of the Jewish revolt against Rome in A.D. 66. In the course of his journey of 1852, Edward Robinson had rediscovered Pella by correctly identifying the Arabic name Fahl as the equivalent of Pella. (The modern place-name is Tabaqat Fahl or "Terrace of Pella" [tabaqah literally "layer"], derived from the broad plateau in the environs.) Occupation of this site extended almost continuously from the third millennium to the late medieval period, although Pella was never

---

[4]Tell Abu Hureirah (Tel Haror) is scheduled to be excavated in 1982 by Eliezer D. Oren of Ben-Gurion University of the Negev as part of the biblical "Land of Gerar" project. Tell Abu Hureirah, the largest Bronze and Iron Age site in the northern Negev, has never been excavated.

rebuilt after the earthquake of A.D. 747. Its long history notwithstanding, Pella is best known as a Graeco-Roman city.

In 1958 H. Neil Richardson and Robert W. Funk, two ASOR appointees in residence at the Jerusalem School, made a sounding at Khirbet Fahl, the site of ancient Pella, on the eastern edge of the Jordan Valley. Robert H. Smith of the College of Wooster, with ASOR's cooperation, began a full-scale excavation of Pella just before the 1967 War; Robert J. Bull and Howard C. Kee were staff members. Bull concentrated on the West Church complex, which dated to the late fifth and early sixth centuries, while Kee excavated the East Cemetery. Only a few weeks after the team began digging, war brought the project to an abrupt halt; work was not resumed for a dozen years, by which time guerrilla activity had destroyed much of the area. The unexpected termination of the project was especially disappointing because of the meticulous preparations Smith had made during the preceding year in order to get the dig into the field. His large volume on Pella, published in 1973, details every aspect of the project, including the results obtained in the abbreviated first season.

The excavation of Pella resumed in 1979, this time as a joint project sponsored by the College of Wooster and the University of Sydney, in affiliation with ASOR. The two teams dig each year in tandem; J. Basil Hennessy, former head of the British School of Archaeology in Jerusalem, directs the work of the Australians on the eastern side of the mound while Smith oversees the American undertaking on the west side. Since the intense summer heat of the Jordan Valley makes digging impossible, the Australian team is in the field in the winter and the Americans in the spring. In their effort to reconstruct the social history of Pella, the archaeologists are supported by several specialists in the natural and social sciences, specifically geology, zoology, botany, and anthropology.

The American excavations at Pella have been widespread, including the adjacent areas as well as the mound itself. The American team paid a good deal of attention to the Civic Complex, located near the city's spring, where they have encountered ruins dating to the Roman and Byzantine periods. The Early Roman construction consisted of a small theatre complete with orchestra and stage, a temple, and a forum. In the Byzantine era a large church was built in the Civic Complex. With the assistance of the Department of Antiquities, the excavators have cleared the colonnades of the church's atrium and reset them in their original positions.

The cemetery area, located on the northern slope of the adjacent Tell el Husn, yielded two Canaanite tombs of the seventeenth-sixteenth centuries B.C. Elsewhere, the excavators uncovered a vaulted cistern associated with the West Church; it had a capacity of 72,000 gallons and dates to the late sixth or early seventh century A.D. As water is plentiful in the area of Pella, the existence of such a large cistern is unusual; a satisfactory explanation for its presence will have to await further excavation of the site.

The skeletal remains of camels and one human indicate that part of the temple in the Civic Complex may have served as a caravanserai in the Umayyad period (A.D. 661-750), just before the devastation of Pella by the earthquake of A.D. 747. In the first half of the eighth century the West Church and the church in the Civic Complex were also used for this purpose. As an integral part of its archaeological program the Department of Antiquities is eager to restore several of the sites devastated by earthquake. About 31 B.C. an earthquake destroyed Hesban and Qumran; Araq el Emir met a similar fate about A.D. 365. The earthquake of A.D. 747 demolished Jerash and Umm Qais, in addition to Pella.

The excavators at Pella have been greatly assisted by the permanent field headquarters constructed with the help of the Department of Antiquities. Once the dig has been completed, this facility will be converted into a museum for the display of artifacts unearthed at Pella. It will be one of several local museums planned for the country and modelled after Madaba's folklore museum, which was dedicated in 1979.

Excavation of Synagogues

Two German archaeologists, Heinrich Kohl and Carl Watzinger, pioneered in the exploration of synagogues during the early part of the present century. Even before the establishment of the State of Israel, Jewish scholars took an interest in the ancient synagogues of Palestine. A leader in this field, Eliezer L. Sukenik was involved in the excavation of several synagogues: Beth Alpha at the foot of the Gilboa mountains, Hammat Gader in the Yarmuk Valley, Shaalbim in the Aijalon Valley, and Japhia in Lower Galilee. Nahman Avigad of Hebrew University was associated with Sukenik in synagogue research. One of Israel's leading synagogue experts is Gideon Foerster, also of Hebrew University in Jerusalem.

In 1921 the Ecole Biblique, under the direction of L. H. Vincent, excavated the synagogue at Naarah, a site identified with the Arab village of Ain Duq, northeast of Jericho. The synagogue's remains had been discovered accidentally in 1918, during World War I, when a Turkish shell exploded in the vicinity. Excavation of similar synagogue structures suggests the assignment of a sixth-century date to the building at Naarah.

Capernaum

In 1838 Robinson first identified Tell Hum as the site of Capernaum, one of the most important cities in the Gospels. Located on the northwest shore of the Sea of Galilee, this property is owned by the Franciscans, who purchased it in 1894. They have been excavating and restoring the site and its famous synagogue since 1922; the most recent campaign occurred between 1968 and 1972. Wilson dug there initially in 1856, followed by Kitchener in 1881. Kohl and Watzinger, who worked at Capernaum in 1905, concluded that the remains of the synagogue could not date earlier than the third century A.D.

The date of the Capernaum synagogue has been the subject of a debate between the Franciscan excavators and Israeli archaelogists. On the basis of coins found beneath the pavement of the synagogue, Franciscan archaeologists Virgilio Corbo and Stanislao Loffreda claim that the synagogue dates from the last dacade of the fourth to the mid-fifth century A.D. Speaking for the Israelis, Foerster prefers a third-century date; he argues from historical evidence and architectural parallels. Avi-Yonah also had serious problems with the late chronology but conceded that the final word would have to wait for further developments in synagogal research.

Some of the ignorance about the types and dating of synagogues and their architectural development may be dispelled soon, as the ruins of more than a hundred synagogues have been discovered in Palestine; in the Diaspora the remains are even more abundant. ASOR is contributing to this research through its association with several excavations of synagogue sites in Upper Galilee as part of its overall concern for what Ernest Wright called "the archaeology of Early Judaism" (roughly, the second century B.C. to the fourth century A.D.), a relatively neglected era in Palestinian archaeology. As a by-product, this synagogue research will help to reconstruct life during the Talmudic period (A.D. 200-500) in Upper Galilee.[5]

Khirbet Shema

From 1970 to 1972 Duke University sponsored the excavation of Khirbet Shema, with ASOR affiliation. This site, whose name means "the ruin of Shammai," is located near the foot of Mount Meiron in Upper Galilee; it had previously gone unexplored. Eric M. Meyers of Duke directed the project, with Robert J. Bull of Drew University serving as the senior archaeological adviser during the first season.[6] As the name of the site suggests, popular tradition identified the great mausoleum on location as the tomb of Shammai, who flourished in the

[5]The digging in Galilee has been mainly in the Roman and Byzantine periods, and much information about Jewish life in the villages and small towns of that region has been gleaned, in particular about the synagogues which dotted the hills of Galilee during the fourth and following centuries.

[6]A. Thomas Kraabel and Dean Moe were also prominent members of the 1970 staff. As the excavation of synagogues continued under the auspices of Duke University and ASOR, the primary responsibility for fieldwork and publication devolved upon Eric M. Meyers, James F. Strange, and Carol L. Meyers.

first century A.D. A member of the Pharisees, Shammai was known for the rigidity of his religious views; he and Rabbi Hillel were the leading Jewish sages in Palestine in their day. In view of the connection of Shema with Shammai, it is not surprising that Hasidic Jews, accustomed to making pilgrimages to this shrine, were so unhappy with the excavations that they attempted to disrupt the archaeological work.

The excavators cleared an important public building at Shema; it turned out to be the first broadhouse synagogue uncovered in Galilee.[7] Meyers believes that the remains of the first synagogue date to the late third century A.D. and that a second synagogue built on the ruins of the first was completed by the mid-fourth century, then destroyed by earthquake in 419. The scientific significance of this project lies in the fact that the synagogue at Khirbet Shema was the first to be dated through excavation, that is, on the basis of sealed pottery and coins found beneath the synagogue floor. The later chronology of synagogues favored by Meyers and his team has caused others to reassess the late second-century dates previously applied to Galilean synagogues.

Meiron

Meyers and his associates were not content to excavate at only one synagogue site but adopted a regional approach, which brought them to several additional ruins. Their second excavation was at Meiron, a northern Palestinian Jewish center, across the valley from Khirbet Shema and northwest of Safed.[8] Orthodox Jews make an annual, joyous pilgrimage to Meiron to visit the tomb of Rabbi Simeon ben Yohai, a second-century rabbinic teacher.

The Meiron synagogue had been cleared by Wilson in 1868, but the first excavation in the area of the synagogue was undertaken in 1971 as part of the comprehensive Shema project; work then continued at Meiron through 1975. Two-thirds of the facade of the majestic synagogue still stand to the height of the lintels; hardly anything else survived, with the exception of some column bases. In contrast to the Khirbet Shema synagogue, Meiron's was a standard basilica-type: rectangular in shape with two rows of columns running the length of the room and dividing the structure into a nave and two side aisles. On the basis of sealed remains, the archaeologists date this synagogue to the late third century A.D. A coin from the reign of Marcus Aurelius Probus, Roman emperor (A.D. 276-282), helped to refine the chronology. The synagogue stood in the vicinity of one of the largest towns in Galilee during the Roman-Byzantine era; it was inhabited between A.D. 135 and 360, then abandoned.

---

[7]A broadhouse synagogue has its focal point situated on the long rather than the short wall. Traditionally the short wall was the sacred wall.

[8]Safed, the capital of Upper Galilee, is one of the four holy cities of Judaism (Jerusalem, Hebron, Tiberias, and Safed).

Gush Halav

From 1977 to 1978 the Meyers team excavated Gush Halav (Giscala), the present-day Christian village of el Jish (in Arabic), located five miles northwest of Safed. Two synagogues were discovered, one buried underneath the village church, the other standing on the slopes above the Gush Halav brook. The archaeologists concentrated on the latter synagogue, excavating it for the first time, although Kohl and Watzinger had surveyed it in 1905. Eric Meyers is inclined to date this basilical synagogue about A.D. 250; he has also noted that occupation continued at Gush Halav into the sixth century, a century and a half beyond the destruction of Shema and almost two centuries after the abandonment of Meiron.

Khirbet en Nabratein

In 1980 Meyers and his colleagues moved to Khirbet en Nabratein (Nevorraya), just a short distance southeast of Gush Halav. The synagogue and associated village date to the Late Roman-Early Byzantine period. The archaeologists intend to map the synagogue area and to clarify the history of the synagogue. In the process they will excavate some of the private buildings in the village and, as at other sites, will reconstruct parts of the synagogue.

In 1905 Kohl and Watzinger surveyed the synagogue at Nabratein; they later published their plan of the structure. The present excavators have distinguished three phases of the synagogue building: Middle Roman (about A.D. 150-250), Late Roman (A.D. 250-360), and Byzantine (sixth century). The current work of excavation and reconstruction at Nabratein reached its climax when the archaeologists recovered a portion of the aedicula, the Torah shrine,[9] dating to the third century A.D. It is described by the excavators as a pediment featuring rampant lions. This unique piece, of white limestone, was the uppermost part of the niche that served as the repository for the Torah scrolls in the synagogue.

Galilee and the Golan Heights

In addition to concentrating on individual synagogue sites in Upper Galilee, Meyers and his colleagues (including, this time, Dennis E. Groh and several other members of the faculty of Garrett-Evangelical Theological Seminary) conducted in 1973 and 1976 a surface survey of the ancient sites in Upper and Lower Galilee and the Golan Heights, as a way of recovering the material culture of Syria-Palestine in the Roman and Byzantine periods. This combination of regional survey and site excavation has shed abundant light on several aspects of Jewish life in

---

[9]Known also as the Holy Ark (*aron haqodesh*), it is the holiest part of the synagogue after the scrolls themselves.

Galilee before the Arab conquest in A.D. 634; it has also stimulated Israelis to a renewed interest in synagogal research.

When the Romans destroyed the Second Temple in A.D. 70, Galilee became the center of Jewish life and scholarship in Palestine. That situation prevailed until the accession in A.D. 527 of the Byzantine emperor Justinian the Great, who repressed and persecuted the Jews. With the Arab conquest, Galilee became a deprived region and the Jewish presence came to an end. This broad historical outline is clear from archaeology, but more research needs to be undertaken if the details are to be completed.

Caesarea

Caesarea Maritima, the magnificent ancient city situated on the Mediterranean coast halfway between Tel Aviv and Haifa, was built by Herod the Great between 22 and 10 B.C., in honor of his patron Caesar Augustus. This 8,000-acre site, one of the largest commercial centers of the ancient Near East, served as the capital of Syria-Palestine for over 600 years. An important center of early Christianity, Caesarea was the place where Paul was imprisoned for two years before successfully invoking his right as a Roman citizen to appeal to the emperor. There was a substantial Jewish community at Caesarea, living in tension with the Gentiles who were in the majority.

During the 1950s and 1960s, Italians and Israelis excavated at Caesarea, before the long-term project of the Americans. The Italian Archaeological Mission, directed by Antonio Frova, concentrated on the Roman theatre. Among the Israelis, Avraham Negev excavated the Crusader city and Michael Avi-Yonah the Jewish quarter. At the request of the Israel Department of Antiquities and under ASOR auspices, Robert J. Bull undertook a salvage operation at Caesarea in 1971. The project was necessitated by the encroachments of the local kibbutz, which was cultivating a banana plantation and a citrus grove on the ancient site. An added threat to ancient Caesarea was the construction of a resort with a hotel, amusement park, and marina.

Bull has made some valuable discoveries through his architectural survey and excavation of the site. By recovering the original city plan, he has been able to identify the *cardo maximus*, the main north-south road from the theatre in the south section of the city to the forum east of the harbor, and the *decumani*, the side streets. Along the seafront Bull has also uncovered a series of vaulted warehouses, each measuring ninety feet in length.

During the 1973 season, the first Mithraeum ever discovered in Roman Palestine was unearthed in one of the barrel-vault warehouses in the vicinity of the Caesarea harbor. Roman soldiers had used this sanctuary, dating from the late third and early fourth centuries A.D., for the worship of Mithra, an ancient Persian warrior-deity of light and truth, with whom the soldiers had become acquainted during their

A Mithraic medallion from Caesarea Maritima. Excavator Robert Bull describes this artifact, found in 1973, as a small, circular medallion on which is depicted in bas-relief Mithra slaying the bull; it is carved in white crystalline marble. (Photo by James D'Angelo.)

forays in the East. The cult of Mithraism was prominent in the Roman Empire and for a time rivaled Christianity; without overstating the case, there were similarities between them. Fostered by the emperors, Roman Mithraism has been defined as a religion of loyalty toward the king, often practiced by those seeking royal favor.

CHAPTER VIII
THE MODERN PERIOD: 1967-1980 (Part 2)

The 1973 Conflict

The year 1973 witnessed another full-scale war in the Mideast when Egypt and Syria reacted to the Israeli continued occupation of their territories. On October 6, the Jewish holy day of Yom Kippur and the Muslim anniversary of the battle for the conquest of Mecca by the prophet Muhammad, Egypt attacked Israel across the Suez Canal, and the Syrians followed suit from the Golan Heights. Initially, the fighting raged on the Syrian and Egyptian fronts, the Israelis suffering heavy casualties. Ordinary life was badly disrupted until the cease-fire was signed, even for the residents of the Albright Institute, who were asked to take sides on the political issue. Fortunately, William Dever was director at the time, and his firsthand experience with the Six-Day War of 1967 enabled him to maintain the institute smoothly. ASOR appointees overseas have learned to live with the often unsettled conditions of the Mideast and to carry out their scholarly mission despite political vicissitudes.

Further Excavations in Israel

Tell Halif

In 1975 Joe D. Seger of the University of Nebraska at Omaha, assisted by Dan P. Cole, Mary Elizabeth Shutler, and Karen E. Seger, made plans to survey and excavate in the vicinity of Kibbutz Lahav, located in the western foothills of Mount Hebron in Israel. The project focused on Tell Halif, also known as Tell el Khuweilfeh, about fourteen miles north of Beer-sheba. ASOR/AIAR and the Nelson Glueck School of Biblical Archaeology (Hebrew Union College) joined the Joe Allon Center for Regional and Folklore Studies in sponsoring this interdisciplinary undertaking. Like Caesarea, Tell Halif was a salvage operation. The local Kibbutz Lahav was in the process of expanding up the tell; had the site not been excavated immediately, any hope of reconstructing its cultural history would have been lost.

Tell Halif showed evidence of occupation extending from the Chalcolithic period to modern times. Soon after the digging began in 1976, it became clear that this mound bore resemblances to Tell el Hesi at the Early Bronze, Iron II, and Persian levels. This realization prompted suggestions that the two digs might be coordinated to provide a comprehensive view of the northern Negev and its settlement patterns in those periods. The next step would be a comparison with the results at other Early Bronze sites, such as Bab edh Dhra in Jordan and Tell Mardikh in Syria, in an attempt to sketch the panorama in Syria-Palestine during that age. As a transnational organization ASOR is fortunately able to excavate in several Mideast countries across modern boundaries and so to manage such coordination.

Karen Seger supplemented the work of the excavators with her ethnographic study of the Bedouin settlement and the village people of the Lahav region, who have been present there since the beginning of this century. In an effort to complete the picture, the team systematically collected and analyzed the implements and other remains that had been placed in local caves and cisterns by these inhabitants.

The identification of Tell Halif has been a problem. During the 1977 season, the excavators uncovered an unusual ceramic vessel of the Late Iron Age, decorated with a single raised pomegranate (*rimmon* in Hebrew). According to the Book of Joshua, there was a town in southern Judah called Rimmon or Ain Rimmon; this reference and the discovery of the pomegranate have suggested to some that Halif may be the site of Rimmon.[1] Others are inclined to connect Halif with biblical Ziklag, the well-known Philistine city that Achish, king of Philistine Gath, gave to the outlaw David in his flight from Saul.

However, Eliezer D. Oren of Ben-Gurion University of the Negev, who excavated Tell esh Sheriah (Tell Sera) in the northwestern Negev midway between Gaza and Beer-sheba, is convinced from archaeological evidence that his site is biblical Ziklag. The mound contains evidence of occupation extending from the Late Canaanite period to the Roman-Byzantine, including a settlement in the Philistine period, as Ziklag would require. Although some Philistine pottery has been unearthed at Halif, it is a less convincing location for Ziklag in terms of historical geography because Halif is situated in the midst of Judean territory. In the opinion of Anson Rainey and others, Halif would have been an inappropriate base for David, who was attacking the Negev of Judah.

Tell Anafa

From 1968 to 1973 Saul S. Weinberg of the University of Missouri directed the initial campaigns at Tell Anafa, the site of a wealthy Hellenistic town in Upper Galilee, which lies at the foot of the Golan

---

[1] The identification of Tell Halif with Rimmon is strengthened by the fact that Hurvat Rimmon has been discovered close to Tell Halif. This site was first settled at the end of the second century B.C., and it contained a synagogue built at the end of the third century A.D. Eusebius speaks of Erimmon (En-rimmon) as a large Jewish village in the southern part of Judea.

Heights. The site contains evidence of occupation from the Early Bronze Age through the Late Hellenistic and Roman periods. Remains such as molded glass vessels, fine red wares, and elaborately decorated buildings indicate that the residents of this Greek settlement, which formed part of the Seleucid Empire, enjoyed a high standard of living. The fact that Anafa was located near the ancient crossroads, which ran both east-west and north-south, contributed to the lucrative trade of the town. The red ware that the site has produced in enormous quantities is called *terra sigillata* and dates to the mid-second century B.C.

In 1978 Sharon C. Herbert of the University of Michigan, who had worked with Weinberg during the earlier phase of digging, returned to Anafa in order to clarify the stratigraphy of the site in the Persian, Hellenistic, and Roman periods. Inasmuch as the transition from Hellenistic to Roman is still not well known in Syria-Palestine, the excavations at Anafa are contributing valuable information on that subject and adding to scholarly understanding of Herod's reorganization of Upper Galilee. In addition, the Anafa project is helping to clarify the trade patterns in the Near East during the Hellenistic period, as well as the architectural techniques in vogue during that same period. This second expedition to Anafa, undertaken in affiliation with ASOR, has paved the way for publication of the final report of the excavation in answering questions raised earlier by the stratigraphic complexity of the site.

Iraq after the War of 1967

Since the Arab-Israeli War of 1967, ASOR's presence in Iraq has been minimal, despite the abiding interest of ASOR scholars in the archaeology of Mesopotamia. The unfavorable political climate is largely responsible for ASOR's diminution of activity in Iraq; at the outset of the war Iraq severed diplomatic relations with the United States. Between 1925 and 1963 ASOR had been affiliated with almost forty seasons of archaeological work (excavation and survey) at twenty-one sites in ancient Mesopotamia; ASOR's last field project was in 1963.

During the academic year 1968-1969, Robert Adams, well known to the Iraqi archaeological community, was resident director of the Baghdad School, with John A. Brinkman of the University of Chicago and Thorkild Jacobsen of Harvard as annual professors. Adams devoted his efforts to a survey of the Nippur area, continuing the reconnaissance and soundings that he had initiated earlier.

From 1968 the activities of the Baghdad School were diminished considerably after the coup d'état by the Arab Baath Socialist Party, with its strong emphasis on nationalism. At that point ASOR formed a Committee on Mesopotamian Civilization, to be concerned with research within Iraq, but also beyond Iraq's borders, although most of ancient Mesopotamia is coextensive with the present Republic of Iraq. In 1969 the annual professorship of the Baghdad School was changed in name to a fellowship, enabling the recipient to use the stipend for the study of Mesopotamian civilization, including philology, archaeology, and art history, in Lebanon, Syria, Turkey, Iraq, Iran, or any other country where pertinent research material would be available. Meanwhile, the recipients of this fellowship have been able to pursue their research on a fairly regular basis in Iraq itself.[2]

In 1978 the State Antiquities Organization, Ministry of Culture and Arts of the Republic of Iraq, invited ASOR to participate in an international symposium dealing with restoration and preservation of the ancient city of Babylon, Ashur (the capital city of Assyria), and the Jebel Hamrin (Hamrin Mountains) region of Upper Iraq. ASOR representatives attended the two-week sessions held at the Iraqi National Museum in Baghdad. In addition, the representatives paid official visits to principal archaeological sites throughout the country. At the end of the symposium, ASOR pledged to the Ministry of Culture and Arts its renewed cooperation in the recovery of the history and culture of Iraq.

Since 1975 a series of government-sponsored salvage operations has been revitalizing Mesopotamian archaeology. As this new era opens in Mesopotamian archaeology, ASOR may have the opportunity to revive its once substantial involvement in the archaeology of Iraq. John A. Brinkman, chairman of ASOR's Baghdad Committee, has challenged the trustees to consider seriously the new opportunities for archaeological work in Iraq. If ASOR does not soon reclaim its traditional role in Mesopotamian archaeology, another organization eventually will. If ASOR overcomes its financial constraints and Iraq's political situation, which is exacerbated by the Iran-Iraq War, improves, ASOR would again be able to make a substantial contribution to Mesopotamian archaeology.

Excavations in Cyprus

As ASOR was prevented by prolonged civil war in Lebanon from pursuing the history of the Phoenicians on the mainland, it turned toward two of the principal colonies of ancient Phoenicia—Cyprus and Carthage—to learn more about these extraordinary people. Many concerns call ASOR to Cyprus, the bridge between east and west. Strategi-

---

[2]In the academic year 1979-1980 Richard L. Zettler of the University of Chicago was ASOR's Mesopotamian Fellow. His project was to prepare the final report on the Inanna temple. In the process he spent time in the National Museum in Baghdad, where he studied tablets and objects from the Inanna temple. He received considerable help from Muayyad Said Damirji, Director General of the State Antiquities Organization. In view of the fact that ASOR and the University of Chicago had between 1951 and 1963 jointly sponsored six seasons of excavation at Nippur, concentrating on the successive structures of the Inanna temple, it was appropriate that ASOR's Mesopotamian Fellow should prepare the final report.

cally situated in the East Mediterranean Basin, Cyprus is a crossroad of ancient and modern cultures and a natural meeting ground for Mideastern and classical archaeologists.

The location of Cyprus helps to explain why the island has constantly been drawn into the vortex of the Mideast; it is also responsible for Cyprus's turbulent history, involving Greeks, Phoenicians, Assyrians, Egyptians, Persians, Romans, and other peoples. The fact that Cyprus was an important source of copper in the ancient world also accounts for its international entanglements.[3]

The Archaeology of Cyprus

The archaeology of Cyprus spans more than 6,000 years, extending from the Neolithic to the end of the Roman period. The earliest settlements thus far discovered date to the Neolithic period (about 5800 B.C.), though some may go back further, to the Paleolithic period. Porphyrios Dikaios excavated Khirokitia, in the Larnaca district. It was probably the most important Neolithic settlement in Cyprus and dates to the mid-sixth millennium. Excavators affiliated with ASOR have also uncovered Neolithic remains, Yechiel M. Lehavy at Dhali-Agridhi on the Yalias River near the modern village of Dhali, and Ian A. Todd at Kalavassos-Tenta in the Vasilikos Valley of the Larnaca province. The village of Tenta, according to Todd, was composed of circular buildings with mudbrick or stone walls. They were surrounded by an outer stone wall with a ditch outside it. Todd has also discovered at Tenta the oldest wall painting to come to light in Cyprus; it represents two human figures standing side by side. The Kalavassos-Tenta project included a complete field survey of the area, incorporating environmental and socioeconomic factors.

The systematic excavation of Cypriot sites has a short history. The Swedish Cyprus Expedition, working in Cyprus from 1927 to 1931 under the direction of Einar Gjerstad, set the archaeology of the island on a scientific foundation. Prior to the Swedish survey of the island, the archaeology of Cyprus had been for the most part at the mercy of amateurs, who occupied themselves with treasure-hunting and grave-robbing.

One of the leading native Cypriot archaeologists was Porphyrios Dikaios, who excavated many sites on the island, in addition to Khirokitia. He was curator of the Cyprus Museum and later director of the Department of Antiquities, a position he held for over thirty years. Dikaios is justly regarded as the father of prehistoric archaeology in Cyprus.

[3]Copper takes its name from that of the island. In Roman times the metal was known as *aes Cyprium*, "metal of Cyprus"; it was abbreviated to *cyprium* and later corrupted to *cuprum* (Latin for "copper").

Excavation at Idalion

One of ASOR's goals in undertaking archaeological work in Cyprus was to learn more about the Phoenicians who settled on the island in the tenth century B.C., thereby making Cyprus in all likelihood the first Phoenician colony. Ernest Wright, the main force behind ASOR's foray into Cyprus, also hoped to contribute through stratigraphic excavation to the needed restudy and reclassification of Cypriot pottery.

The name of Idalion, an ancient city situated about twelve miles south of modern Nicosia near the village of Dhali, appeared among the ten Cypriot kingdoms listed on the prism of the Assyrian king Esarhaddon (680-669 B.C.). In 1931 the Swedish Cyprus Expedition made soundings at Idalion, discovering occupational levels extending from the thirteenth century B.C. to the Early Roman period. An independent kingdom from 700 B.C., Idalion was eclipsed about 450-425 B.C. by the Phoenician Kingdom of Kition on the southeast coast, near modern Larnaca.

Before Paul Lapp drowned off the northern coast of Cyprus in 1970, he had planned to excavate at Idalion. Afterwards, Ernest Wright, assisted by two former students, Lawrence E. Stager of the University of Chicago and Anita Walker of the University of Connecticut, undertook the project and strove to make it a model dig, incorporating into the project specialists in the natural and social sciences. During the excavation Frank Koucky, a geologist from the College of Wooster, conducted a survey in an effort to locate the copper mines and smelting sites for which Cyprus was renowned.

The Turkish Invasion

The Turkish invasion of Cyprus in July 1974 was occasioned by a Greek coup against Archbishop Makarios, president of the Republic of Cyprus. When the revolution erupted between the Greek Cypriots, who supported Makarios and independence, and the leaders of the Greek military junta, who advocated *enosis*, unity with mainland Greece, the ASOR archaeologists working at Idalion had to be evacuated. After several anxious days of waiting, they took a tortuous route by land, sea, and air to Beirut. The abandonment of the ambitious plan for the 1974 dig season made it one of the shortest on record.

Lawrence E. Stager, director of the Idalion excavations described the conversion of ancient Idalion as it changed hands from excavators to soldiers:

> Few of us were surprised when at 3:00 a.m. the morning of July 20 [1974] we were awakened to the news that the Turks had landed on the north coast around the port of Kyrenia. In the pre-dawn light from our rooftop beds we watched the mountains aflame on the northern horizon. Later jets moved south, pounding Nicosia. That morning we knew the dig was over.

Friday we had used the probe trenches, dug one meter wide and five meters long, on the East Acropolis to give us a stratigraphic preview of soil layers soon to be excavated over the entire square. The next morning Greek Cypriot soldiers occupied these archaeological probes, using them as slit trenches.[4]

Tensions between the Greek and Turkish Cypriots have continued since 1974, exacerbated by Turkish control of the northern third of the island. The disturbed situation has not prevented the team from returning to Idalion, on whose west section they have been concentrating. The west acropolis, together with its lower terrace, formed a citadel area protected by a spectacular wall surviving to a height and width of about twenty-four feet. The 1980 season at Idalion was spent exploring the public buildings within the citadel, which dates to 500-450 B.C.

Other Sites for Excavation

In addition to his excavation at Kalavassos-Tenta, Ian Todd and Alison South are digging at the nearby site of Kalavassos-Ayios Dhimitrios, which is a major Late Bronze Age (thirteenth century B.C.) settlement with well-preserved architecture. This project is proceeding under the auspices of Brandeis University and ASOR. The excavators have uncovered evidence of metallurgic activity, which suggests that the economy of Ayios Dhimitrios had some connection with the copper mines located north of Kalavassos village.

The other excavation under ASOR auspices in Cyprus is being directed by Stuart Swiny at Sotira Kaminoudhia, located west of Limassol. This small prehistoric site is shedding light on the Cypriot Early Bronze Age, at least the transition between Late Chalcolithic and Early Bronze. At present there is a great deal of confusion about these periods in Cypriot archaeology. The Late Chalcolithic is a shadowy period; similarly, no Early Bronze Age settlement has ever been excavated in Cyprus, although survey has revealed the existence of Early Bronze sites. The Early Bronze pottery that has surfaced comes from the contents of family cemeteries along the north coast, not from settlements. For these reasons, the transition from Late Chalcolithic to Early Bronze in the south of Cyprus remains a moot point; whatever Swiny does to clarify it will be a contribution to the archaeology of Cyprus.

Several other excavations have taken place in Cyprus under American auspices: John E. Coleman worked at the Middle Bronze Age (about 1900 B.C.) site of Alambra; James Carpenter at the Bronze Age site of Phaneromeni,[5] near Episkopi; Paul W. Wallace at Akhera, situated in the area of ancient copper mines in central Cyprus; David Soren and

---

[4]*ASOR Newsletter* 6 (1974-1975).

[5]Saul S. Weinberg of the University of Missouri discovered the Bronze Age site of Phaneromeni in the early fifties and then conducted excavations there.

Diana Buitron at Kourion, where they excavated the sanctuary of Apollo Hylates, the god of the woodland. Kourion, located in the Limassol district, was first excavated from 1934 to 1952 by George McFadden of the University of Pennsylvania Museum.

In addition to the Swedes and Americans, the French, British, Polish, and Australian missions have been actively engaged in field archaeology in Cyprus. Also, the Department of Antiquities under the leadership of Vassos Karageorghis has been excavating at such important sites as Salamis, Kition, and Paphos. Karageorghis, a native Cypriot, is the leading archaeologist on the island, with a firsthand knowledge of its history and culture.

CAARI

From its long experience in the Mideast, ASOR has found that overseas centers facilitate the work of archaeologists by providing support services and research facilities. Ernest Wright hoped to establish such a center in Cyprus for the archeology of the East Mediterranean, but he died before it could take place. In 1978 ASOR founded the Cyprus American Archaeological Research Institute (CAARI) in Nicosia to promote dialogue between American and Cypriot scholars and to provide facilities comparable to those offered by other American overseas advanced research centers in the Mediterranean area and the Mideast. The only institution of its kind in Cyprus, CAARI serves a special need; the island has no university, and in the absence of other national research centers in Cyprus, CAARI welcomes archaeologists of all nationalities. The institute thereby serves in a unique way as a center for the exchange of information about the archaeology of Cyprus. In all areas CAARI cooperates wholly with the Cypriot Department of Antiquities.

Conveniently located in the center of Nicosia near the Cyprus Museum, CAARI occupies a two-story building with its hostel, library, and other research facilities. As artifacts excavated by foreign teams may not be removed from Cyprus, CAARI provides space for archaeologists to analyze their materials in preparation for publication.

Thus far CAARI has had three directors, who have worked to transform an untried facility into a permanent research institute. Anita Walker established the center in its present quarters; she also forged good relations with local authorities, making CAARI acceptable to them and the community at large. Ian Todd of Brandeis University succeeded to the directorship in 1979. Building on the solid foundation laid by Walker, Todd improved the modest research facilities of the center. Thanks to Todd, the "collections room" now contains over a hundred trays of sherds, lithics, geological samples, and metallurgical and other specimens not easily available outside CAARI.

Stuart Swiny, a British archaeologist who has long resided in Cyprus, became director of CAARI in 1980. His success in attracting some financial support for CAARI from the Cypriot community indicates the favor that the organization enjoys locally. Swiny is also striving to develop the resources of CAARI to make it more than a hostel; he is placing special emphasis on new library acquisitions.

The United States government, through the Fulbright Commission and the International Communication Agency, has assisted CAARI in a time of great need. This federal support is an indication that CAARI is valued not only by the scholarly community but also by the United States foreign service personnel, who see it as an important cultural arm of America.

Excavations at Carthage

Most historians believe that the Phoenicians of Tyre founded Carthage in 825 or 814 B.C. Today Carthage is a residential suburb of modern Tunis, as well as a key site for the history of North Africa. In 1972 the UNESCO director general launched an international campaign to save ancient Carthage from depredation by ubiquitous modern developers; nine countries responded to the appeal.

The ASOR Projects

ASOR represented the United States in the international effort, sponsoring two projects simultaneously, Punic Carthage and Roman Carthage. Lawrence E. Stager conducted the excavations of the Punic phase, with Frank M. Cross as adviser. The Roman phase was entrusted to John H. Humphrey, with John G. Pedley as adviser; both Humphrey and Pedley are associated with the Kelsey Museum of the University of Michigan. These projects were executed in cooperation with Azzeddine Beschaouch, director of the Tunisian National Institute of Archaeology and Art, and Abdelmajid Ennabli, conservator of Carthage. The five seasons of excavation (1975-1979) were financed by the fund of excess United States foreign currency (counterpart funds), administered by Public Law 480 through the Smithsonian Institution.

The Tophet

Stager concentrated on the Precinct of Tanit, also called the Tophet,[6] as well as on the rectangular commercial harbor. The Carthaginian Tophet was dedicated to the fertility goddess Tanit and her consort, Baal Hammon, the chief god of Carthage. As the name suggests, this was the

---

[6]The word *tophet*, which may mean "roaster," is used in the Hebrew Bible to designate the notorious high place in the valley of Hinnom, near Jerusalem, where human sacrifices were offered. At this idolatrous cult shrine, children were cremated in honor of the gods Baal and Molech. Human sacrifice is first attested in Judah during the reign of King Ahaz (735-715 B.C.).

Carthage "Precinct of Tanit," or "Tophet." Looking west across field of monuments erected over urns filled with the charred remains of children sacrificed to Tanit and Baal Hammon, the patron deities of Carthage during the Punic period (about 725-146 B.C.). From the Oriental Institute, University of Chicago, comes the field staff for this ASOR project. In the foreground are Lawrence Stager (director, left) and Douglas Esse (supervisor, right). In the center is Joseph Greene (supervisor) and behind him Samuel Wolff (supervisor). (Photo by James Whitred.)

sacred area for the sacrifice of children. First excavated in 1922, it contained carved limestone stelae (upright slabs with inscriptions) and pottery urns filled with charred human and animal remains. This precinct had been used as the burial place of sacrificed children from the eighth-seventh centuries B.C. to the year 146 B.C., when Carthage fell to the Romans at the end of the Third Punic War. The highest concentration of burial urns in the Tophet dated to the fourth century B.C.

Stager's statistics are unsettling—the number of child sacrifices increased, rather than decreased, with the passage of time, contrary to the common understanding of cultural evolution. In the earlier period, animals had occasionally been substituted for children as sacrificial victims, but not in the fourth-third centuries B.C. Stager conjectures that between 400 and 200 B.C. about 20,000 urns were deposited in the Tophet at Carthage. This statistic suggests that child sacrifice was a systematic practice among the Carthaginians, motivated by economic and religious reasons. The usual interpretation is that sacrifice of the first-born would ensure fertility and protection against disease and other blights; there are other possibilities, including population control. While the final word has not been said, Stager's inferences are based on the combined research of archaeologists, osteologists, and epigraphists.

It was also Stager's task to determine the physical dimensions of the Tophet at Carthage and its relationship to the harbor, which had been built in the fourth century B.C., before the First Punic War (264-241 B.C.). The standard description of this harbor comes from Appian of Alexandria, Greek historian of the second century A.D., whose writings about the Roman conquests are a valuable historical source. According to Stager, the Tophet and the commercial harbor may have been located in close proximity to facilitate the transport of the sandstone stelae, which were erected in the sanctuary of Tanit.

Kelsey's Expedition

It was fitting that American archaeologists conducted excavations at Carthage in the 1970s in view of the fact that other Americans had carried out an earlier campaign at this site. In 1925 Francis W. Kelsey, a classicist associated with the University of Michigan, led a Franco-American expedition to Carthage, becoming the first American archaeologist to work at this site. Kelsey was assisted by Donald B. Harden of the Ashmolean Museum, Oxford. In the course of excavating, Kelsey identified only three strata of urn burials in the Tophet precinct, although Stager later recovered stratigraphic evidence for at least eight phases. During one of Stager's seasons in the field, a happy coincidence took place: as he was in the process of linking his trenches with those of Kelsey and Harden, Harden paid a visit to the site and shared with Stager some conclusions reached from his own excavations in the Tophet a half century earlier.

John Humphrey

At the same time that Stager was excavating at Punic Carthage, John Humphrey, ASOR's project director of Roman Carthage, was also working there, under the auspices of the University of Michigan's Kelsey Museum, which was so named to honor the memory of the first American excavator of Carthage. It was Humphrey's task to concentrate principally on the later history of Carthage—the Late Roman, Vandal, and Byzantine periods—extending approximately from A.D. 400 to 698, when the Arabs conquered and then completely destroyed the city. He excavated a Late Roman house and an adjacent major parish church roughly contemporary with Augustine of Hippo (A.D. 354-430).

As part of the overall plan to save Carthage, the area dug by Humphrey's team will be conserved and the house and church complex reconstructed. When the whole site of ancient Carthage has been converted into an archaeological park with a museum, as planned, it will be one of the major tourist attractions in North Africa. At the same time, UNESCO's goal of saving Carthage will have been achieved. No longer *delenda est Carthago* (Carthage must be destroyed), but now *salvanda est Carthago* (Carthage must be saved).

The Carthage Research Institute

While the American teams were engaged in excavating Punic and Roman Carthage, ASOR supported a center in the vicinity, the Carthage Research Institute. The institute served as a base camp during the dig seasons and as an advanced study center for the remainder of each year. Scholars intent on studying the Phoenicians of the West Mediterranean were welcome there. In keeping with the original plan, the institute operated only during the five-year period when the digs were actually in the field. While a permanent American archaeological presence in Tunisia would have been highly desirable, the maintenance of the institute would have put an undue strain on ASOR's financial and scholarly resources, which were already designated for more immediate concerns of ASOR than the region of the West Mediterranean.

Explorations in the Buqeah Valley

In 1954, while excavating the ruins of Qumran on the west coast of the Dead Sea, F. M. Cross and J. T. Milik became curious about an Iron II site in the nearby desert region of the Buqeah, which they later visited. The Buqeah, meaning "little valley," is located in the Judean hills southwest of Jericho, about three miles west of the Dead Sea. In biblical times this desolate area was called the Valley of Achor (literally, the "valley of trouble"). References in the Books of Joshua, Hosea, and Isaiah indicate that the designation is accurate; today it remains an extremely inhospitable place.

In 1955, with assistance from ASOR, Cross and Milik conducted surface surveys and soundings in this area. In the course of their work they investigated three fortresses and related structures dating to Iron II (918-587 B.C.): Khirbet Abu Tabaq, Khirbet es Samrah, and Khirbet el Maqari. In antiquity all three fortresses played a role in the agriculture of the desert region.

In 1972, while a Fellow at the Albright Institute in Jerusalem, Lawrence Stager continued the earlier soundings of Cross and Milik in the Buqeah, to salvage as much information as possible before these remains were obliterated by modern highway construction and military maneuvers. In his investigation, Stager was able to utilize new methods for the retrieval of archaeological data. At the same time, he was guided by an understanding of the desert agriculture developed since the Cross-Milik investigation of these sites. Concurring in general with the interpretation of Cross and Milik, Stager concluded that in the Iron Age the Buqeah had functioned as a hazardous passageway between Moab and Jerusalem, with the forts in question serving as paramilitary outposts providing protection for travelers en route.

These forts may well have served in this wilderness area to protect people engaged in farming and retrieving mineral deposits from the Dead Sea. Stager's systematic examination of the Buqeah addressed the question of how the farmers of the Iron Age had survived in the Judean desert. His work resulted in a valuable study, *Outposts in the Judean Wilderness*, which has increased understanding of the settlement patterns in the seventh century B.C., though the topic continues to be elusive. According to Stager, despite the aridity of this forbidding region, the Buqeah would have been able to support settlements by irrigation. Irrigation, in turn, would have been made possible by terrace dams and floodgates to contain the waters rushing headlong down the Judean mountains.

William F. Albright

When Albright left the directorship of the Jerusalem School in 1929 to become the W. W. Spence Professor of Semitic Languages at Johns Hopkins University, he did not sever his ties with ASOR. He continued to exercise a leading role for the next forty years, despite heavy teaching responsibilities. It was the year of his death, 1971, that marked the end of an era in ASOR's history and in Near Eastern scholarship.

His Expertise

Albright was exceedingly diversified in his interests. Although trained in Akkadian, he was both a humanist and an orientalist; his research interests extended to every aspect of Near Eastern studies, including history, religion, languages, literature, archaeology, and geography. His professional breadth made him a welcome member of other learned societies besides ASOR. In 1935 he was elected president of the American Oriental Society, and in 1939 he was president of the Society of Biblical Literature. Some have been surprised to learn that Albright never served as president of ASOR, though he did hold the office of first vice-president, beginning in 1938 when he replaced Torrey. Albright explained that he always shied away from the ASOR presidency because of its heavy administrative responsibilities, for which he did not feel temperamentally qualified.

Albright had many teachers, but few masters. He soon surpassed his mentors through extraordinary ability combined with great diligence.

William Foxwell Albright. (Portrait by Fabian Bachrach.)

He learned pottery chronology from Petrie, Vincent, Phythian-Adams, and Fisher in Jerusalem, then he so rapidly developed his own ceramic typology of Palestine that they could not keep pace with him. Similarly, with regard to the historical geography of Palestine, Albright profited greatly from the pioneer work of Robinson and later of Alt and others, but he went beyond them. They had been able to identify many ancient sites but could not date their remains; Albright, by means of his pottery typology, was able to determine the chronology of these sites.

Albright also distinguished himself as both a theoretical and a practical linguist. In addition to having a speaking knowledge of several European languages, he was fluent in modern Hebrew and Arabic. Knowledge of the latter two languages was a distinct asset for the director of the Jerusalem School, especially in the 1920s, when a sympathetic ear (and tongue) were appreciated by both political sides.

His Bibliography

A prolific writer, Albright produced almost 1,100 works, touching on almost every area of ancient Near Eastern studies. Scholars are indebted to David N. Freedman of the University of Michigan for editing the comprehensive bibliography, which ASOR published in 1975. A cursory reading of titles of Albright's articles makes it evident that he was in the vanguard of scholarship, especially in relation to newly discovered literary remains; the following selected instances are illustrative.

In 1928 a peasant with a plow made a chance discovery of a tomb at Ras Shamra, the site of the ancient city of Ugarit on the coast of northern Syria. The following year the first tablets in Canaanite alphabetic cuneiform were found under controlled conditions in a dig conducted by Claude F. A. Schaeffer. Albright recognized early the great value, especially for biblical studies, of the Ras Shamra tablets. These texts have pointed to striking parallels between Canaanite and Hebrew literature and have provided valuable insights into the religious practices of the Middle and Late Bronze Ages.

Albright was also quick to appreciate the importance of the 20,000 tablets unearthed at the royal city of Mari (Tell el Hariri) on the middle Euphrates during Parrot's excavations there in the 1930s, especially for the light they have shed on the chronology of the early second millennium B.C. Parrot's identification of Mari with modern Tell el Hariri was gratifying for Albright, who had proposed that identification nine years earlier.

The classic example of Albright's genius relates to the dating of the Dead Sea Scrolls; he was one of the first scholars to declare them authentic, despite strident voices to the contrary. His dating was based

on his prolonged study of documents and inscriptions of the last pre-
Christian centuries and the first post-Christian centuries, and especially
his detailed paleographic analysis of the Nash Papyrus a decade before
the Dead Sea Scrolls appeared.

Like all creative scholars, Albright made his share of mistakes
concerning both texts and sites. He sometimes changed his mind,
retracting the proposal or interpretation, but he almost always suggested
another one based on new evidence and fresh arguments. As Freedman
has pointed out, with Albright it was part of the continuing process of
trial and error in the pursuit of truth on a scientific and inductive level.
Without venturesome minds, scholarship would be static; simply to
concur with consensus contributes little and requires even less courage.

His Teaching

Despite complete absorption in personal research, Albright still
found time to encourage his students at Johns Hopkins and other
serious inquirers. His abiding concern for younger scholars and his own
scholarly research were responsible for the creation of the "Albright
School." His bright and well-prepared students saw no dichotomy
between Albright the scholar and Albright the teacher. He invited his
students to join him in his research, thereby conducting his research as
part of his teaching. This method was ideal for the best students but not
the most effective pedagogical technique for the ordinary students.

Through his students Albright continues to exert an extraordinary
influence on Near Eastern studies and associated disciplines, especially
the Old Testament. His students and his students' students occupy many
of the prestigious positions in this country and abroad. While Albright's
disciples bear his mark, at the same time they are independent scholars,
holding positions at variance with the master's. Positions put forth by
Albright are being challenged today. Naturally there have been changes
and there will be more changes; Albright knew this, and he encouraged
it. What better sign of a great scholar.

The Biblical Tradition

Some have caricatured Albright as a "galloping fundamentalist" or
have charged him with "tradition fundamentalism" (the insistence that
the traditions lying behind the Bible's presentation of Israel's history are
almost entirely based in history). In the course of his scholarly career
Albright made a shift in his philosophical presuppositions, leading to a
more positive attitude toward the early traditions of the Old Testament.
As a student he was under the influence of Paul Haupt but did not
espouse his radical biblical scholarship. In keeping with his own conservative religious point of view, which he inherited from his family,
Albright's scholarly life did move in a more conservative direction. By

bringing archaeological evidence to bear on biblical criticism, Albright became more confident about the value of the biblical tradition for historical reconstruction. In no sense was he a fundamentalist, however; for example, Albright followed Wellhausen on the documentary hypothesis far beyond many of his students.

It was Albright's respect for the biblical tradition that inspired confidence in the more conservative religious groups in the United States, including Jews and Roman Catholics, whom he influenced considerably. The resurgence of interest in biblical studies among Roman Catholics in the United States during the 1950s owes much to Albright, if only indirectly. At Johns Hopkins University several priests studied under Albright; later they became seminary teachers and imparted to their students the Albrightian position. To be sure, Pius XII's liberating encyclical on the Bible, *Divino afflante spiritu*, had been promulgated in 1943, but this Magna Carta might well have been ignored had there not been trained scholars to implement it in the United States.

Augustin Bea, a Roman Catholic biblical scholar who served as rector of the Pontifical Biblical Institute in Rome, also came under the influence of Albright as friend and colleague. Bea was a good but not a great scholar whose earlier writings were cautious so far as modern critical methods were concerned. More important he was involved in church life at the highest level and, without doubt, exerted a strong influence on the formulation of *Divino afflante spiritu*. The papal encyclical appears to have adopted positions espoused by Albright.

Moreover, at the invitation of Albright and Freedman, as general editors of the Anchor Bible series, Roman Catholic and Jewish scholars became participants in this ecumenical endeavor. When completed, this series will comprise well over sixty individual book translations of the Old and New Testaments and the Apocrypha, with accompanying commentaries based on the most up-to-date and reliable research.

His Honors

In the course of his long career Albright received many honors, including three Festschrifts on the occasion of his sixtieth, seventieth, and eightieth birthdays. In 1951 when he reached sixty, his colleagues dedicated *BASOR* 122 (1951) to him. So enthusiastic were prospective contributors that Ephraim A. Speiser, editor of the issue, had to limit acceptance to those scholars who were actively engaged in field projects at the time. Its table of contents summarizes the central scholarly concerns of the mid-twentieth century, including the dating of the Dead Sea Scrolls (Millar Burrows), the survey of Transjordan (Nelson Glueck), early Hittite chronology (Albrecht Goetze), Sumerian wisdom literature (Noah Kramer), and the Chalcolithic cultures of Palestine and Syria (Ernest Wright).

William Albright speaking at the home of Israel's president on the occasion of the presentation of a Festschrift in honor of Albright's approaching eightieth birthday. From left to right: Abraham Malamat, Ernest Wright, Nelson Glueck, William Albright, Mrs. Zalman Shazar, President Zalman Shazar, Yigael Yadin, Mrs. Ruth Albright, Benjamin Mazar, Joseph Aviram, Israel Goldstein, and others. (Ross Photo, Jerusalem.)

Ten years later, Wright edited a substantial volume in Albright's honor, *The Bible and the Ancient Near East*. Its fourteen commissioned articles touched on all the scholarly issues close to Albright. This collection of essays was presented during a special ceremony held at the Hebrew Union College in Cincinnati, where Albright was serving as a visiting professor in 1961.

In 1969 Albright's Israeli friends prepared an impressive Festschrift in acknowledgment of his abiding interest in Israel and its people. Edited by Abraham Malamat of Hebrew University, the collection is included in the well-known *Eretz Israel* archaeological series. In a prefatory article, Yigael Yadin assessed Albright's place in the development of Near Eastern studies; linking him with Petrie and Vincent, Yadin called them "a trio of giants." This Festschrift was formally presented at the Jerusalem residence of Israel's president during Albright's final visit to Israel, when he was an official guest of the government. On that auspicious occasion he was declared *yaqqir Yerushalayim*, "notable of Jerusalem," in public recognition of his friendship with Israel.

Prior to the sovereignty of Israel in 1948, Albright had favored the formation of a binational Arab-Jewish state; after 1948 he supported the new Jewish state and continued his close friendship with its citizens, especially Israeli scholars. As inevitably happens in the Mideast when a scholar is perceived to favor one political side, his or her relationship with the opposing side is diminished; indeed, Albright's position with the Arabs in the Mideast suffered from his friendship with Israel.

In 1970 Albright's colleagues dedicated *BASOR* 200 (1970) to him; this issue marked the golden jubilee of the journal, which Albright had edited for thirty-eight of those fifty years. (In all, he had edited 152 of BASOR's 200 issues). Contributors to this special issue honoring Albright were selected from the board of editors of BASOR: Delbert R. Hillers, Frank M. Cross, William G. Dever, Jonas C. Greenfield, and William L. Moran.

On his eightieth birthday in 1971, also the year of his death, Albright was presented another Festschrift, edited this time by Hans Goedicke of Johns Hopkins University. This volume included thirty-five contributions by leading scholars in Old Testament and Near Eastern studies. It was appropriate that the final tribute to Albright should have emanated from Johns Hopkins; this university and ASOR were the major foci of his scholarly career.

H. Dunscomb Colt

In 1973 ASOR lost another good friend and trustee in the person of H. Dunscomb Colt of New York, who had served on the ASOR board of trustees as the official representative of the Archaeological Institute of America; he had also been a trustee of the American Center of Oriental Research (Amman). His name is identified with several expeditions in the 1930s, especially Tell ed Duweir (Lachish), where he assisted James Starkey. He also actively engaged in the excavation of three Negev sites that formed a network of Nabatean settlements: Nessana, Subeita (Shivta), and Eboda (Avdat).

Colt generously supported the publication of archaeological reports, notably Callaway's volumes on Ai. In 1966 Colt donated steel shelving to the library of the Jerusalem School, doubling the library's capacity. In recognition of his gift, the library of the School is now called the Colt Library.

G. Ernest Wright

The death of G. Ernest Wright in 1974, the eighth year of his ASOR presidency, prematurely deprived Near Eastern archaeology of the valued services of another leader in the field. His passing would have caused an even greater void had he not recruited so many younger archaeologists, who were able to fill the vacuum. They were the new generation trained in field archaeology principally at Shechem and Gezer, also at other sites in Jordan, Cyprus, and Tunisia.

The Memorial Volumes

The contents of the two memorial volumes that appeared shortly after Wright's unexpected death are a measure of his considerable influence on biblical studies and Syro-Palestinian archaeology. So many wanted to pay tribute to their friend and mentor by contributing articles that the editors had a difficult task keeping the contents within reasonable bounds.

Frank M. Cross—Wright's student, colleague, and friend—edited one of these collections of essays. The title, *Magnalia Dei, the Mighty Acts of God*, was appropriate, for the divine activity in history was central to Wright's theology. Not only did he write about this dominant biblical theme, but he was deeply conscious of it in his daily life. Those who knew him were aware that Wright' personal piety was an important factor in his life and career. The second memorial volume took the form of a special double-issue of *BASOR* 220 (1975) and 221 (1976), edited by Edward F. Campbell and Robert G. Boling, two of Wright's protégés. To simplify the selection process, the editors limited potential contributors to Wright's Harvard students, with whom he had enjoyed a remarkable rapport. As well as being a charismatic teacher, Wright belonged to that unusual breed of professors who encourage their students to surpass them. In turn, he was always ready to learn from them and willingly acknowledged his indebtedness to them.

His Development

A comparison between his first dig at Shechem and his last at Idalion illustrates Wright's own development, especially in field techniques over two decades. He had employed the best methods then available at his Shechem excavations but was aware of the need for improvement; the amount of information retrieved had been small, and some of the larger questions had not been addressed. Influenced by the prehistorian Robert J. Braidwood, who had achieved excellent results for the Neolithic period (about 7000 B.C.) at Qalat Jarmo, in the Kirkuk province of Iraq, by utilizing an interdisciplinary team of natural and social scientists, Wright introduced the same technique at Idalion. In addition to archaeologists, his core staff consisted of the following specialists: geologist, agronomist, metallurgist, ceramicist, anthropologist, and zoologist. Wright's openness to new scientific and interdisciplinary possibilities in his later life is one measure of the man.

Although Wright always repudiated the "archaeology proves the Bible" mentality, with the passing years he became even more aware of the limitations of archaeology. In 1971 he published an article entitled "What Archaeology Can and Cannot Do," in which he stated:

With regard to Biblical events, however, it cannot be overstressed that archaeological data are mute. . . . Yet the mute nature of the remains does not mean that archaeology is useless. . . . What archaeology can do for Biblical study is to provide a physical context in time and place which was the environment of the people who produced the Bible or are mentioned in it.[7]

It is interesting that Roland de Vaux, whose career paralleled Wright's in many ways, also spoke in his later life of the finitude of archaeology in an essay, "On Right and Wrong Uses of Archaeology."[8]

Development in Wright the archaeologist was matched by growth in Wright the theologian, if one compares his statement on the historically oriented faith of ancient Israel in *God Who Acts: Biblical Theology as Recital* (1952) with his later *Old Testament and Theology* (1969). The earlier book proclaims straightforwardly the thesis that God has acted in history, while the second reduces the emphasis on the concept of revelation in history. The fact that Wright espoused the revelation-in-history formula was consistent with his interest in both archaeology and theology, which belonged together in his estimation.

There were so many facets to Ernest Wright's personal and professional life that it is difficult to do justice to any of them in a few words. His historical theology, his archaeology, his interest in popularization, his enthusiasm for biblical and archaeological studies, his teaching, and his service to the Church all worked together to make him the person he was and are responsible for the influence he had. No summary statement can characterize a person of G. Ernest Wright's stature, but Edward Campbell's epitome is memorable, "Great scholar and teacher, he was, plain and simple, a good man."

Frank Moore Cross

The officers and trustees of ASOR were devastated by the unexpected death of Ernest Wright; nonetheless, they immediately had to confront the problem of finding a scholar of Wright's versatility to succeed to the presidency of ASOR. Frank Moore Cross, a colleague of Wright's at Harvard, was the obvious candidate, but he was already overburdened with teaching and publication responsibilities. In addition, like his mentor Albright, Cross had misgivings about his administrative abilities. But his commitment to ASOR and to the memory of Ernest Wright prevailed over his lingering doubts. Agreeing to become an interim or transitional president (that was the condition of acceptance), Cross was elected as ASOR's sixth president in 1974.

ASOR had secured in Cross a scholar of first rank, with an international reputation as epigraphist of Northwest Semitic languages. His

---

[7]*Biblical Archaeologist* 34 (1971) 73.

[8]J. A. Sanders, ed., *Near Eastern Archaeology in the Twentieth Century: Essays in Honor of Nelson Glueck*, Garden City, 1970, pp. 64-80.

demonstrated competence in ancient orthography, epigraphy, and text-critical study was recognized by his being chosen a member of the international team of experts responsible for editing the Dead Sea Scrolls. His splendid volume, *The Ancient Library of Qumran and Modern Biblical Studies* (1958) shows that his interest is not limited to the texts alone. That work dealt with the life and times of the people who preserved the Qumran manuscripts.

Cross served as ASOR's president for two years, giving prudent and balanced direction to the organization as it continued to expand its scholarly work in both Israel and the Arab world, while maintaining field projects in Cyprus and Tunisia. It was not an easy time to be at the helm, especially as ASOR was laboring under fiscal constraints in that period. In 1975 Cross played a key role in planning the seventy-fifth anniversary celebrations of ASOR both in Jerusalem and at home and made them scholarly and social events worthy of the occasion.

In 1976, realizing that they had imposed long enough on Frank Cross, the trustees allowed him to resign in order to complete his important work on the Cave Four texts of Qumran. In that year Philip J. King of Boston College succeeded to the presidency of ASOR and served for two three-year terms.

The Seventy-Fifth Anniversary of ASOR

In 1975 ASOR celebrated the seventy-fifth anniversary of its establishment. The official observance appropriately took place in Jerusalem in June of that year, featuring an international symposium entitled "The Archaeology and Chronology of the First Period of the Iron Age: Problems of Early Israelite History," made possible by grants from the Zion Research Foundation of Boston and the American Council of Learned Societies. In the course of the two-day symposium scholars from America, Europe, and Israel made formal presentations, which were followed by lively discussions.

On June 11, 1975 the ASOR board of trustees held a public meeting in Jerusalem to honor both the anniversary and the city in which ASOR was founded. President Cross chaired the session, and Philip J. King, president of the Albright Institute (AIAR), delivered the main address. Under the heading "The American Schools of Oriental Research: Retrospect and Prospect" King reviewed the history of the organization during the first seventy-five years of its existence, emphasizing the role of leading figures who gave ASOR its direction.

Other festive events included a reception and formal dinner in the garden of the Albright Institute, with the symposium speakers and ASOR trustees as honored guests. Another highlight was a guided tour of the major excavations under ASOR auspices in Israel and Jordan; at several of these sites archaeologists who had dug there spoke to explain their work and finds. When the trustees crossed into Jordan to visit the

A dinner party in the garden of the Albright Institute, Jerusalem, in June 1975 on the occasion of the seventy-fifth anniversary of the founding of ASOR. From left to right: Philip King, president of the Albright Institute, Frank Cross, president of ASOR, and William Dever, director of the Albright Institute.

American Center of Oriental Research in Amman, George E. Mendenhall, director of ACOR, welcomed them. On the site visits in Jordan James A. Sauer and Larry G. Herr served as principal guides for the ASOR trustees.

ASOR's seventy-fifth anniversary observance in the United States took place in Chicago in the autumn of 1975 on the occasion of the joint annual meeting of the Society of Biblical Literature, the American Academy of Religion, and ASOR. Ruth Amiran of the Israel Museum in Jerusalem delivered the major address, "Arad: An Example of Urban Life in Early Bronze II Canaan in the Setting of the Ancient Near East." Amiran, an authority on the Early Bronze Age, in 1962 began excavating at the important eastern Negev city of Arad. In addition to Amiran's presentation, ASOR's seventy-five years of scholarly work were honored by a symposium entitled "Temples and Sanctuaries in the Ancient Near East," with papers by Richard J. Clifford, Yigal Shiloh, and Edward F. Campbell. ASOR has published the proceedings of the Jerusalem and Chicago symposia, edited by Frank Cross, as the first volume of a new series, The Zion Research Foundation Occasional Publications.

Excavations in Syria

Syria's favorable location at the crossroads of trade routes contributed to its prosperity in ancient times and continues to bring advantages today. Syria is one of the most promising countries from the point of view of Near Eastern archaeology, but political instability, resulting from the Arab-Israeli war and internecine conflict, has hindered the systematic exploration of that country. Even so, some of the most exciting discoveries in the Mideast have been made in Syria. It would be difficult, for example, to find sites richer in literary remains than Mari, Ugarit, and Ebla.

Palmyra ("the place of the palms"), one of the most spectacular sites in the Mideast, abounds in history and architecture. This caravan city is located in a fertile oasis of the Syrian desert, about 120 miles northeast of Damascus. Its ancient Aramaic name, Tadmor, is preserved in the name of the modern village, Tudmur. Palmyra, as it was known in Hellenistic and Roman times, reached the height of its power in the third century A.D., then suffered destruction under the Roman Emperor Aurelian in 273. The language of Palmyra was Aramaic, and the Palmyrene inscriptions discovered there have provided valuable insights into the life and economy of the desert city. The archaeological missions that have worked at this site since 1900 are too numerous to list, but much still remains to be done.

The Period before World War II

While early explorations in Syria took place in the seventeenth century, actual excavations did not get underway until the beginning of the present century. Some projects were in the field before World War I, but the Ottoman Turks offered little formal encouragement for such undertakings in any part of their empire. Among foreign archaeologists, the French dominated the scene, at least until Syrian independence, in view of the French mandate in Syria between 1920 and 1941. When the Syrians achieved independence at the end of world War II, they began to take an active interest in the archaeology of their country.

Although the land of Syria and its rich cultural heritage are central to ASOR's concerns, there has been limited involvement there on the part of ASOR until recently. In 1925 under ASOR auspices William F. Albright and Raymond P. Dougherty made a survey of some of the oldest tells in northern Syria and the Euphrates Valley. Others have undertaken additional surface explorations, but there is still a great need for this kind of investigation in Syria.

In addition to excavations at such well-known sites as Dura-Europos, Ugarit, and Mari, several other significant field projects have taken place in Syria. Harald Ingholt, a Dane who was a Fellow of the Jerusalem School from 1924 to 1925, directed the Danish excavations at the citadel of Hamath (modern Hama) from 1932 to 1938. The twelve strata uncovered by the excavators indicate that this city in central Syria on the banks of the Orontes River was occupied from the fifth millennium to about A.D. 1400. This site is famous for the discovery of Hittite hieroglyphic inscriptions, identified as written in the Indo-European language used in the Syrian Hittite states principally from the tenth to the eighth century B.C., after the fall of the Hittite Empire. The fourth largest city in modern Syria, Hama has been the scene of bitter internecine feuds in recent times, unfortunately reminiscent of some of its earlier history.

Qasr el Hayr

In the 1960s another American archaeologist affiliated with ASOR, Oleg Grabar, excavated in Syria. A specialist in Islamic art and architecture, he was formerly associated with the University of Michigan and is now at Harvard's Fogg Art Museum, where he is the Aga Khan Professor of Islamic Art. He dug at Qasr el Hayr Sharqi, a medieval Islamic town located about eighty miles northeast of Palmyra; there he concentrated on the ruins of a caravanserai. Its construction dates to the eighth century A.D. (the Umayyad period); it continued to exist until the early part of the fourteenth century. This excavation illustrates the material culture of the Muslim Middle Ages in the Levant. It is hoped that American students trained by Grabar and others in Islamic art and architecture will assist in Syria and other countries of the Mideast with the excavation of Islamic sites.

Tell Mardikh (Ancient Ebla)

Since 1964 Italian archaeologist Paolo Matthiae of the University of Rome has been digging at Tell Mardikh, a 140-acre site about thirty miles south of Aleppo. In 1968 the identification of this site with the ancient city-state of Ebla was confirmed by an inscription on the bust of a man identified as the king of Ebla; the inscription refers to "the lord of the city of Ebla." The kingdom of Ebla, a great commercial center, played a key role in the ancient world from the middle of the third to the middle of the second millennium B.C.

The most electrifying discovery at Ebla, to date, is the royal archive, which contained thousands of cuneiform tablets from the third millennium, dealing with the economy, administration, trade, religion, and a variety of other subjects. Giovanni Pettinato, professor of Sumerology at the University of Rome, was the first to identify the language of the texts as Northwest Semitic. More specific evaluation of the tablets, including their language and the light they may cast on neighboring peoples and ambient cultures, must await publication of the texts. Other discoveries of this magnitude, notably the Ugaritic texts and the Dead Sea Scrolls, have occasioned wide-ranging interpretations, often accompanied by vituperative exchanges unbecoming to scholars. Rapid publication of texts and other finds may enable scholars to avoid digressions into irrelevant issues.

So far as Ebla is concerned, today there are two teams at work on the decipherment of the tablets, one reporting to Matthiae, and the other working with Pettinato. Because of an unfortunate rupture in the friendship of Matthiae and Pettinato, a spirit of rivalry has developed between them. There are occasions when competition can be healthy, but that remains to be seen in this case. At this time, Pettinato and his assistants have several publications to their credit, including a few large volumes. The other side will catch up and ultimately surpass them because they have access to the whole collection of tablets, while Pettinato has pictures of only about half or fewer of them. When all the materials have appeared, competent scholars will have to make their own judgments about the content of the tablets and the implications for the history of the ancient Near East.

Syrian Archaeologists

Syrian archaeologists have been engaged in excavating sites throughout the country under the aegis of the Directorate General of Antiquities and Museums, currently headed by Afif Bahnassi. Adnan Bounni, director of the archaeological excavation division of the Directorate General, has dug at several important sites and is associated especially with Palmyra, the subject of several of his publications. He has also worked at Tell Kazel to the north of the Eleuthera River. This Late Bronze settlement may be the site of Sumuru, the administrative center of the province of Amurru in the reign of Amenhotep III of the eighteenth Egyptian dynasty (about 1403-1364 B.C.). Sumuru was known as Simyra in the Hellenistic period. Kassem Toueir of the Directorate is also an active excavator in Syria. Recently he dug at the Abbasid site of Raqqa, east of Aleppo in northern Syria, with New York University Professor Frank Peters. Alexander the Great founded the city of Raqqa, called Nikephorium in the literary sources.

American and British Missions

Several important sites in Syria have been entrusted to American archaeological missions. Giorgio Buccellati of the University of California (Los Angeles) has been working at Tell Ashara on the middle

Euphrates, the site of ancient Terqa, about forty-five miles north of Mari. It was the chief town of a district during the time of Zimrilim of Mari (about 1779-1761 B.C.). In the town of Terqa there had been a temple to Dagan, the West Semitic god of crop fertility (*dagan*, the common Hebrew noun for "grain"). Ancient Terqa may have been on a level of importance with Ebla and Mari.

Harvey Weiss of Yale University is excavating at Tell Leilan, an impressive Early Bronze Age site in northeastern Syria; it is thought to be ancient Shubat-Enlil, the capital city of the North Mesopotamian Empire of Shamshi-Adad of Assyria (1813-1781 B.C.), the contemporary and rival of Hammurabi of Babylon. Tell Leilan was a continuously occupied town from as early as the Ubaid period (about 5500-4000 B.C.). The city wall, which dated to 2400 B.C., measured sixty feet wide and forty-five feet high; it surrounded a settlement twice the size of ancient Ebla.

Rudolph H. Dornemann of the Milwaukee Public Museum dug at Tell Hadidi, identified as Azu, a Bronze Age city on the Euphrates which served as an administrative center in antiquity. This was one of the sites endangered by the construction of the dam at Tabqa. In the course of excavating between 1974 and 1977 Dornemann uncovered a private archive of a wealthy citizen; it consisted of a small collection of clay tablets inscribed with cuneiform writing. These tablets identified the ancient name of the city as Azu, which is also mentioned in the tablets found at Alalakh in the Orontes Valley. The results of the excavations at Tell Hadidi have led Dornemann to conclude that settled urban sites were the norm in northern Syria in the latter part of the Early Bronze Age.

The British archaeologist, Peter J. Parr, is excavating at Tell Nebi Mend, the site of ancient Kadesh on the Orontes, southwest of Homs. There the famous battle between Rameses II of Egypt and the Hittites took place in 1288 B.C. Neither side emerged as outright victor, but it was a strategic defeat for Egypt, inasmuch as the Hittites continued to control Syria.

These archaeologists are doing excellent work in Syria. When the results of their projects have been coordinated with several other Syrian and foreign expeditions excavating in the country, a clearer picture of Syria's role in the ancient Near East will come into focus. Thirty years ago W. F. Albright predicted that Syria would be "one of the most important foci of archaeological activity in the world," if unimpeded by political unrest.

The Euphrates Valley

In 1967 the Syrian government appealed for help in rescuing many significant sites in the Euphrates Valley, sites threatened by the construction of the Thawra Dam, near Tabqa (the present-day Al Thaoura).

Completed in 1973, the dam was responsible for the creation of an enormous artifical lake, Al Assad. The results of this international salvage operation have been published, in part, by ASOR in its *Annual* 44 (1977). This collection of reports represents the archaeological periods from Epipaleolithic to Islamic, especially the Bronze Age. ASOR was pleased to have this opportunity to demonstrate to the Syrians its unbiased interest in the archaeology of the whole Mideast.

Sauer's Survey

In 1977 when ASOR officers approached the Directorate General of Antiquities in Damascus to seek permission for a preliminary survey, a sounding, and eventually a dig, Afif Bahnassi issued a license for a survey to be conducted by James A. Sauer, director of ACOR in Amman. In the course of visiting nine major geographical regions in Syria, Sauer and his team inspected eighty-three sites; from seventy of them they collected artifacts representing all archaeological periods from Lower Paleolithic to Ottoman. As a result of the survey, Sauer pinpointed the northern Ghab and the Rouj in the Orontes Valley as appropriate areas for more intensive survey and subsequent excavation.

Tell Qarqur

The ancient site of Tell Qarqur captured the attention of the survey team as a promising spot for a dig. Undoubtedly they were influenced by the similarity of the modern name with ancient Qarqar, the fortress on the Orontes that was the site of two major battles: in 853 B.C. when a coalition of western states, including Syria and Israel, fought Shalmaneser III of Assyria, and again in 720 B.C. when another coalition opposed Sargon II of Assyria, who in turn defeated them and burned Qarqar.

Tell Qarqur is a twin mound covering sixty acres on the east of the Orontes. Sherds lying on the surface of the tell indicated that it had several major periods of occupation, principally Early Bronze IV (about 2400-2000 B.C.) and Middle Bronze I and II (about 2000-1600 B.C.); the Late Bronze and Iron Ages are also represented. However, the mound shows little evidence of occupation in Iron II, the period of Assyrian domination in the region. ASOR has planned a long-term excavation at Tell Qarqur during the eighties; political unrest in neighboring Hama has temporarily delayed the project.

The Ghab and the Rouj

During the second phase of the survey project in 1979 Sauer's team concentrated on the Ghab and the Rouj in the northern Orontes Valley. There they studied remains from eighty-nine sites preparatory to reconstructing the occupational history of the region from earliest times to the modern period. This systematic survey will help in providing archaeologists with a comprehensive view of the whole region, including its patterns of settlement.

The Need for a "Cultural Bridge"

In 1977 the Syrian Arab Republic and the United States signed a cultural agreement covering the years 1978 to 1980; the agreement spoke of "cooperation in scholarly research." While there was no provision for an American research center in Syria, it would have been the most effective way to cooperate. For almost two decades ASOR has been expressing an interest in establishing an institute in Damascus; the final decision may have to be made by the governments of the two countries involved.

Like other ASOR institutes abroad, a Damascus center would serve as the base for American archaeological research projects in Syria. It would disseminate information regarding Syrian archaeological undertakings and would provide educational resources for both Syrian and American students. In short, such an institute would be an ideal cultural bridge between Syria and the United States.

History has demonstrated that when diplomatic relations between the United States and other countries have been severed, American overseas cultural centers have functioned as goodwill embassies. In the years immediately after the War of 1967, for example, when relations between Egypt and the United States were broken, the American Research Center in Egypt (ARCE) filled the void effectively. In the words of S. Dillon Ripley, secretary of the Smithsonian Institution, "In times of world tensions, our American scholarly centers abroad keep vital human channels open."

An Excavation in Egypt

Although the exploration of Egypt has a long history, archaeology in the modern sense began at the start of the nineteenth century, specifically when the French occupied Egypt in 1798 under Napoleon Bonaparte, who arrived in the country accompanied by scientists and scholars. Egypt is so rich in monuments, reflecting its long and complex history, that Egyptian archaeology cannot be treated adequately in short scope. As ASOR's direct involvement in Egypt has been minimal, it will suffice to recall three leading scholars in the history and archaeology of Egypt, Petrie, Reisner, and Breasted, who also influenced the work of ASOR in Syria-Palestine.

Despite the close geographical and historical relationship between Palestine and Egypt, ASOR only recently for the first time sponsored a field project in Egypt. Syro-Palestinian archaeologists have valuable insights to share with Egyptologists about the archaeology of Egypt,

especially in the region of the Nile Delta. Egyptologists also have much
to offer Syro-Palestinian experts as Petrie's experience, first in Egypt,
then in Palestine, demonstrates.

Holladay's Excavations

In 1977 John S. Holladay of the University of Toronto initiated
ASOR's first field project in Egypt.[9] On the basis of his experience in
Palestinian archaeology, he chose to work in adjacent Lower Egypt,
concentrating on the eastern Delta's Wadi Tumilat, which serves as a
land corridor between Egypt and Arabia and between Egypt and the
Levant. As part of an interdisciplinary investigation of Wadi Tumilat's
role in international commerce, Holladay planned a site by site survey of
the wadi with the hope that it would shed light on the historical,
cultural, and economic problems of the region.

In addition, Holladay undertook the excavation of Tell el Maskhuta,
located about eight miles west of modern Ismailia. Edouard Naville, a
Swiss archaeologist, had dug this site in 1883 under the auspices of the
Egypt Exploration Fund, subsequently identifying it as ancient Pithom.
The Book of Exodus (1:11) describes Pithom and Raamses as store-cities
that the Hebrews were forced to build for the Pharaoh. In 1918 British
Egyptologist Alan Gardiner proposed Tell el Ratabah, about nine miles
west of Maskhuta, as the likely site for biblical Pithom; Maskhuta was
then thought to cover the ruins of Succoth, a station on the route of the
biblical exodus. Petrie was inclined after his investigation of Ratabah to
identify it as biblical Raamses, complicating matters further. Obviously
the archaeological evidence is inconclusive, requiring additional excavation.[10]

---

[9]ASOR has been only indirectly involved in the exciting Nag Hammadi Gnostic
Papyri project, which is under the direction of James M. Robinson of the Claremont
Graduate School. While the precise details of the find remain unclear, it would appear that
the discovery of these codices was made by a local peasant in one of a number of tombs at a
cliff called Jabal al Tarif, about six miles northeast of Nag Hammadi in Upper Egypt.
This cache represents the earliest collection of Christian manuscripts discovered to date.
These fourth-century (Christian and non-Christian) papyri, written in Coptic, are invaluable for the history of early Christianity and the study of the Coptic language.

While serving as annual professor in 1966 at the American School in Jerusalem,
Robinson visited Nag Hammadi in an attempt to view the find-spots of the Nag Hammadi
library. Robinson has set an example to his colleagues by making the Nag Hammadi texts
available in photographic reproduction for all scholars to examine. ASOR archaeologist
Bastiaan Van Elderen has been engaged in the excavation of Nag Hammadi and its
environs since 1975. Before his accidental death, Paul Lapp had been scheduled to direct
this excavation in association with Robinson.

[10]From 1966 to 1969 Manfred Bietak carried out important campaigns at Tell ed Daba
near the village of Qantir in the Delta. As a result of these excavations it seems likely that
Tell ed Daba is the site of the Hyksos capital of Avaris.

Holladay's excavations at Maskhuta make Naville's proposed identification of the site as Pithom implausible because stratified deposits at Maskhuta begin only in the mid-seventh century B.C., the period of the Saite twenty-sixth dynasty of Egypt (664-525 B.C.). Additionally, the site's storage-space areas, which suggested the "store-cities" of the Book of Exodus, are interpreted as Late Ptolemaic and Roman warehouses. Holladay's stratigraphic analysis of Maskhuta has now made it possible to construct a corpus of Egyptian pottery extending from about 609 B.C. to A.D. 135; he has also succeeded in documenting how the Wadi Tumilat transit canal functioned during the same period.

American Research Center in Egypt

In its sponsorship of the Tell el Maskhuta excavations ASOR has worked cooperatively with its counterpart, the American Research Center in Egypt (ARCE), which was founded in 1948 to promote cultural relations between Egypt and the United States. This center encourages a variety of research projects, which may explore any aspect of Egyptian civilization from ancient to modern. With headquarters in Cairo the ARCE is able to render substantial assistance to excavations and other field projects.

Joint Egyptian-Israeli Projects?

Before the assassination of President Anwar Sadat in 1981, Egypt was the closest ally of the United States among the Arab nations of the Mideast. The Camp David accords, as the Mideast peace agreement between Egypt and Israel is known, have nudged these two traditionally hostile nations a little closer and as a by-product provided a platform for dialogue between the archaeologists of the two countries. One can envision several joint Egyptian-Israeli archaeological projects in the future; the reexcavation of Tell el Areini (Erani) in the southern Shephelah with the participation of Egyptian and Israeli archaeologists is almost essential. Such a cooperative international effort would be enormously profitable for both sides.

CHAPTER IX
THE MODERN PERIOD: 1967-1980 (Part 3)

Excavations and Surveys in Jordan

In the 1970s ASOR/ACOR sponsored several detailed surveys of the land east of the Jordan River, though Edward Robinson, Selah Merrill, Claude Conder, Gottlieb Schumacher, Howard Crosby Butler, Nelson Glueck, James Mellaart, and others, had already reconnoitered the region. Even this distinguished group had not been the pioneers. Three intrepid explorers, dressed for security in native garb, had been there before them—the German Ulrich J. Seetzen, who discovered the impressive remains of Gerasa (Jerash) and Philadelphia (Amman); the Swiss Johann L. Burckhardt, renowned for the rediscovery of the lost city of Petra; the British James S. Buckingham, who claimed to be the first to travel to Bashan and Gilead.

Surveys in Jordan are urgently needed today. Ancient remains are disappearing as they are robbed for building stones in the construction of new villages; they are also the victims of industrial development. ASOR's recent surveys were undertaken to fill in earlier gaps and to provide a comprehensive view of Jordan. In fact, they are altering the traditional understanding of the settlement patterns in Transjordan during the second millennium B.C. Glueck, for example, had posited a hiatus in the population of southern Transjordan between 1900 and 1200 B.C., but pottery has been collected on the recent ASOR surveys from every period, including the Middle and Late Bronze Ages.

Bab edh Dhra

Preparatory to extensive excavation of Bab edh Dhra, Walter Rast of Valparaiso University and Thomas Schaub of Indiana University of Pennsylvania conducted a survey of the isolated southeast plain of the Dead Sea in 1973, including four sites which bear a striking resemblance to Bab edh Dhra: Numeira, Safi, Feifa, and Khanazir. These newly rediscovered settlements, two of which Glueck had also visited, apparently formed a network of occupational areas in the Early Bronze Age.

Beginning in 1975 Rast and Schaub, who had had the benefit of digging at Bab edh Dhra with Paul Lapp before the War of 1967, resumed field operations at this Early Bronze Age site in the southeastern Dead Sea plain. Their principal goal was to understand the settlement patterns of the region from about 3200 to 2200 B.C. Long-term plans also

Walter Rast and Thomas Schaub, the excavators of Bab edh Dhra, confer during a pottery-reading session taking place within the Citadel of Kerak, which serves as the dig headquarters.

A typical Bab edh Dhra tomb dating to the Early Bronze Age (about 3200 B.C.); it contained five skulls, reed matting, and a wood staff.

ASOR officers and trustees visiting Bab edh Dhra in 1979 during their annual, summer inspection tour of ASOR field projects. From left to right: William Dever (with camera), Walter Rast, James Sauer, Edward Campbell, Richard Scheuer, Melvin Lyons, Philip King, Thomas Schaub, and Joan Scheuer.

envisioned exploration of the other four sites to determine the interaction of their populations with Bab edh Dhra.

As the investigation proceeds, the archaeologists continue to pursue questions about the social and economic environment, specifically the kinds of human activity this inhospitable region could have supported. Answers to these questions would be helpful in the modern planning of settlements in this flat land of limited resources and harsh climate. Perhaps the people of antiquity had some insights that are worth sharing.

In the course of excavating Rast and Schaub must keep an eye on the progress of at least two modern construction projects, the enlargement of the multimillion dollar Jordan potash works and the new Arabah tarmac highway that connects Aqaba with the southern Ghor. The archaeologists and the developers are competing for the same land; unless the surveys are finished before the new structures are in place, the scientific data sought will be irretrievable. Modern progress, of course, must continue so daily life can go on, even if it means the destruction of ancient sites.

After four seasons of digging at Bab edh Dhra, the excavators arrived at the following chronological breakdown: in Early Bronze I A (about 3200 B.C.) nomadic pastoralists used the site to bury their dead; in Early Bronze I B (about 3100 B.C.) people began to settle here permanently; in Early Bronze II-III (about 3000-2400 B.C.) an enormous wall was built around the city; in Early Bronze IV (about 2200 B.C.) the settlers departed from this region.

Rast and Schaub have continued the exploration of the enormous Bab edh Dhra cemetery that Lapp began before the Six-Day War. Located southwest of the town, it was in use between 3200 and 2200 B.C. and consisted of shaft tombs and charnel houses. Some would argue that the cemetery was a regional one, in that it contained well over 50,000 burials; others would consider it local. Rast and Schaub hope in their work here to determine the extent of the burial area in the Early Bronze Age and the distribution of tombs.

Numeira

In association with the investigation of Bab edh Dhra work has been proceeding at the neighboring site of Numeira, located about eight miles south of Bab edh Dhra. This settlement, comprising only two acres, was occupied only during Early Bronze Age III (about 2450 to 2350 B.C.); after at most a century it was destroyed either by external assault or by an earthquake. Michael D. Coogan of Harvard University is directing the current campaign at Numeira and will be responsible for its final publication.

The fortifications and domestic installations at Numeira bear resemblance in plan to those at Bab edh Dhra in Early Bronze III. Since there is no indication of a cemetery in the environs of Numeira, the assumption may follow that the dead were buried in the charnel houses of Bab edh Dhra, especially as these charnel houses contain pottery characteristic of Numeiran ware. The excavators at Numeira have uncovered a pottery storeroom containing 300 vessels. This cache constitutes a significant corpus of Early Bronze III ceramics; its study will contribute much to modern understanding of that period.

Other Sites in the Southern Ghor

As yet, excavation has not been undertaken at the remaining three settlements in the region of the southern Ghor. However, there are plans to do so in the late eighties, after Bab edh Dhra and Numeira have been adequately published. These five Early Bronze centers prompt speculation about their relationship to the five biblical "cities of the plain" mentioned in the Book of Genesis (14:2), Sodom, Gomorrah, Admah, Zeboiim, and Bela (Zoar). Once the remaining sites have been explored, the evidence will have to be examined in conjunction with the biblical tradition. Rast and Schaub have made plans to conserve as much of these sites as possible. Meanwhile, they have been instrumental in establishing a modest museum in the Crusader castle at Kerak for the display of artifacts from the southeast plain of the Dead Sea.

Roman Fortifications

In 1976 S. Thomas Parker of North Carolina State University launched, under ASOR auspices, a topographic and ceramic survey of the *limes arabicus*, the elaborate system of fortifications that the Romans developed along the edge of the Syrian desert. Composed of camps, forts, and watchtowers linked by the Roman road system, it served as a buffer between the nomads of the desert and the sedentary population of Palestine. No comprehensive survey of this Roman frontier system has been conducted in Jordan since the turn of the century.

The *limes* extended for some 225 miles from Aqaba in the south to Bozrah (modern Busra ash Sham) on the southern Syrian border, the city which served as the capital of the Roman province of Arabia. Parker's project has concentrated on that part of the frontier which is located in central Jordan and primarily dates to the Byzantine period (about A.D. 300-500). In his effort to reconstruct the history of the *limes* system, Parker has also been excavating one of two major military sites, the Roman legionary camp at Lejjun (Latin *legio*), east of the Dead Sea in the region of Moab. The other legionary fortress is located at Udruh near Petra, in the region of Edom; it is scheduled to be excavated by a British team. (The 1982 Edom survey revealed another, even larger, Roman military camp.)

This project will illuminate the history of the Roman army in Arabia and of the Arabs before the birth of Islam. Preliminary excavations at Lejjun in 1980 have provided a view of a military camp by means of probes into the barracks, the officers' mess, the lounge area, and even the local treasury, which yielded coins.

The Ras en Naqb Basin

In 1977 Donald O. Henry of the University of Tulsa launched a long-term study of prehistoric sites in southern Jordan, concentrating on the Ras en Naqb Basin. In 1979 he discovered sixty sites near the modern village of Ras en Naqb. To understand how populations adapt to their environments, he plans to undertake test excavations at eight small Paleolithic campsites occupied from 500,000 to 8000 B.C. Henry's research is revealing Jordan's wealth of prehistoric remains.

McGovern's Cave Excavations

Patrick E. McGovern and Robin M. Brown went in 1977 to the Umm ad Dananir region of the Baqah Valley, about fifteen miles northwest of Amman, to excavate a partially robbed Late Bronze burial

cave. On earlier surveys Glueck and de Vaux had found no evidence of
Late Bronze occupation; they concluded that the area was unoccupied in
the Late Bronze Age. The discovery of a Late Bronze tomb shows that
there were people in the Baqah Valley during that period, although a
tomb is not a stratified settlement or even an occupation level. To the
extent that the discovery of a Late Bronze tomb shows there is material
from the Late Bronze Age, the conclusion of Glueck and de Vaux must
be revised.

In an attempt to locate additional caves that might shed light on the
Late Bronze period, as so few sites of this era have thus far been
excavated in Jordan, McGovern made use of geophysical prospecting
instruments. Affiliated with the University of Pennsylvania Museum's
Applied Science Center for Archaeology (MASCA), McGovern carried
out a cesium magnetometer and resistometer survey in the Umm ad
Dananir region under ASOR's auspices. In the process he discovered a
completely undisturbed Iron I A (about 1200 to 1050 B.C.) burial cave,
which contained more than 225 burials secondarily deposited and a
unique assemblage of Iron I A whole vessels, iron and bronze anklets,
pendants, and a variety of other artifacts.

These finds will be invaluable in illuminating the transitional
period, when the Late Bronze Age culture was coming to an end and
such new arrivals as the Ammonites and Israelites were making their
appearance. McGovern has continued to make soundings at Khirbet
Umm ad Dananir in an effort to find the settlement site associated with
the Late Bronze and Iron I A cemetery.

The Hisma Desert

In 1978 David F. Graf of the University of Michigan undertook a
survey of Nabatean-Roman military sites in the Hisma Desert of southern
Jordan. Graf intended to learn more about the defensive system in that
era by focusing on forts, watchposts, and caravanserai. In 1980, he
continued his survey of the region and collected a corpus of Nabatean
and Thamudic inscriptions, generally thought to be the handiwork of
the Thamud, the famous North Arabian tribe that is known to have
occupied the region from the eighth century B.C. until the dawn of
Islam. Graf's concentration on the southern section of the defensive
system complemented Parker's *limes arabicus* survey. In conjunction
with John W. Eadie, also of the University of Michigan, plans are being
made for excavations at Humayma, an important frontier settlement in
the Hisma.

The Central Moab Region

J. Maxwell Miller of Emory University launched his survey of the
Central Moab region in 1979, concentrating on the plateau between the

Wadi Mujib and the Kerak-Qatrana road. Albright and Glueck had surveyed this area earlier under ASOR's auspices. During the first season Miller's team registered more than 270 sites and confirmed that there had been occupation in Iron Age I (1200-1000 B.C.) in Moab. Perhaps more important, they found evidence for the first time of occupation in the Late Bronze Age (1550-1200 B.C.). In the long view occupation of the Moabite plateau reached back to the Paleolithic period. Miller plans to continue the survey southward, focusing on the area between the Kerak-Qatrana road and the Wadi el Hesa.

The Rift Valley and the Arabah

In 1979 David W. McCreery, a paleoethnobotanist, directed an archaeological survey of the southern Ghor or Rift Valley and the Arabah, moving south from the Dead Sea to the Gulf of Aqaba. This project was conducted at the request of the Jordan Valley Authority, which was about to develop townships and construct schools in the region. Sites considered suitable for modern development, mainly on the basis of the availability of water and good farm land, had been the same highly prized sites in antiquity.

The Wadi el Hesa

Burton MacDonald of St. Francis Xavier University in Antigonish, Nova Scotia, directed the first season of the Wadi el Hesa survey while serving as annual professor at ACOR during the academic year 1979-1980. The area under intensive survey included the south bank of the Wadi el Hesa and the area to the north of Tafila (in south central Jordan). Wadi el Hesa, identified with the Valley of Zered, had been the southern boundary of the Kingdom of Moab and the northern boundary of the Kingdom of Edom. In all, MacDonald explored over 1,000 sites that contained evidence of occupation from 500,000 B.C. to the end of the Ottoman Empire (A.D. 1918). Previously only twenty of these Edomite sites had been reported. Although earlier surveys had located no pre-historic settlements, MacDonald found lithic materials from the Paleo-lithic, Epipaleolithic, and Early Prepottery Neolithic periods, extending from about 500,000 to 6000 B.C. He also found evidence of Iron Age I occupation (1200-930 B.C.), unlike earlier surveys in Edom. The report of the 1981 season indicated no evidence (with the exception of one possible Middle Bronze sherd) that dates to the Middle Bronze or Late Bronze Ages.

The Area of Quwelba

W. Harold Mare of Covenant Theological Seminary in St. Louis launched a survey in 1980 of Quwelba and its environs. Located ten miles northeast of the modern city of Beit Ras in northern Jordan, Quwelba is the site proposed as the ancient Decapolis city of Abila. It has never been excavated, but Mare's surface sherding in this vicinity yielded pottery from the Early Bronze Age to the Umayyad period (A.D. 661-750), with a concentration in Byzantine and Umayyad. As part of a survey of Transjordan in the previous century, Gottlieb Schumacher published in 1899 a general plan of Abila, which Mare's team will be in a position to evaluate and complete.

The Decapolis

The Decapolis, the league of ten Greek cities in Palestine, was probably established by the Roman general Pompey in 63 B.C. Strategically situated along the trade routes and military highways, this loose federation survived until the second century A.D. The location of some of these cities is uncertain, but with development in field archaeology and historical geography, all may someday be identified. Scythopolis (Beisan), Philadelphia (Amman), Gerasa (Jerash), Pella (Khirbet Fahl), Gadara (Umm Qais), and Damascus are well known as a result of intensive excavation and survey. The remaining Decapolis cities have not been identified with certainty, although there are many conjectures. Dion, for example, may be located at Tell el Husn in northern Jordan; the validity of this identification can be determined only by future excavation at the site.

Qasr al Kharanah

The East Jordan desert holds several castles built in the Umayyad period by the Damascus caliphs for their use as hunting lodges and retreats. As the Umayyads had come from the desert, it is not surprising they liked to return there occasionally. In 1979 Stephen Urice of Harvard's Fogg Art Museum made an architectural study of the Qasr ("castle") al Kharanah, the only desert castle that appears to have been built for defensive purposes. The architecture of the building is indicative of a fortress; it is cornered by round towers and has slits in place of windows. In the course of his work Urice made a new set of floor plans for the building. Studies of this kind must continue, to gain a better knowledge of Islamic architecture and of early Islamic history.

Umm el Jimal

During the seventies Bert De Vries of Calvin College conducted under ASOR's auspices a topographical and archaeological survey at Umm el Jimal, a prosperous desert city situated in a barren northeast corner of Jordan, twelve miles east of Mafraq. The site is covered with the remains of over 150 buildings constructed of basalt, a volcanic lava stone; hence its name, "the black city of the desert." Umm el Jimal was settled by Arabs, who built this city under the protection of the Roman Empire. Ultimately destroyed by earthquake, it had an excellent irrigation system able to support as many as 5,000 to 10,000 people, despite the barrenness of the region.

Selah Merrill visited Umm el Jimal in September 1875 under the auspices of the American Palestine Exploration Society. According to Merrill's detailed account, only two Europeans (Graham and Waddington) had managed to reach the site previously because of the remoteness of its location and desolateness of the region. Merrill seemed to take pride in the fact that he succeeded in visiting Umm el Jimal, while Burckhardt and Buckingham, both intrepid and adventurous explorers, had failed despite their attempts. Merrill's description of his visit to Umm el Jimal includes these lines:

> We reached Um el Jemal (from Bozrah) after a ride of about five hours. The ruins do not abound in columns and temples, like those of Kunawat or Gerash; still they are imposing, and make a peculiar impression upon one, because they stand alone in the desert. They are remarkable, in the first place, from the fact that they present only two prominent styles of architecture, namely, Roman and Christian, or Byzantine, and not half a dozen, as is so often the case in other places. They are remarkable, again, because they afford a good example of an *unwalled* town. Indeed, in this respect they are very instructive. But the walls of the houses, in many cases, joined each other, and this would give the appearance of a city wall separate from the houses. Such an arrangement would no doubt add to the facilities for defence. If there was no wall, there was at least a gate to the city.[1]

Howard Crosby Butler of Princeton University also led an expedition to Umm el Jimal in the first decade of the present century; he made a detailed plan of this complex city.

De Vries has excavated some of the principal structures, such as the barracks, praetorium, and segments of the city walls, while completing and updating Butler's plans. The impressive ruins of this caravan staging post from Nabatean, Roman, Byzantine, and Umayyad times, spread over 150 acres, will be one of the major tourist attractions of Jordan when the Department of Antiquities completes its consolidation of the city's walls and buildings.

Other ASOR Field Projects in Jordan

Several other field projects affiliated with ASOR are in progress east of the Jordan, covering most of the cultural periods.

---

[1]Selah Merrill, *East of the Jordan*, New York, 1883, pp. 81-82.

Ain el Assad

Gary O. Rollefson has been investigating the Lower Paleolithic deposits at Ain el Assad, an oasis in the desert east of Amman, near Azraq. Despite the presence of much material evidence, the Pleistocene prehistory of Jordan has been neglected in the past. Rollefson and others want to make up for that deficiency by examining sites like Ain el Assad and relating them to other Paleolithic remains in the Mideast. This site, which has been known through survey since the twenties, should be helpful in the reconstruction of Late Pleistocene environments and climates.

Tulul edh Dhahab

Robert L. Gordon has been concentrating on Tulul edh Dhahab, a site with twin peaks situated halfway between the Yarmuk River and the Dead Sea. He is excavating the western peak, which is a one-period site with the Hellenistic level almost completely exposed at the surface. A Greek fortified settlement or military outpost, it is comparable to Tell Sandahannah, identified with Marisa, in the Shephelah; Bliss and Macalister dug at Tell Sandahannah at the turn of the century. Gordon expects Tulul edh Dhahab to play a key role in the study of settlement patterns in the Hellenistic Levant.

Khirbet Iskander

Suzanne Richard is at Khirbet Iskander, about thirty miles south of Amman, conducting a preliminary survey and soundings. This Early Bronze Age site is strategically located on the King's Highway where it crosses the Wadi Wala; it may have been an important political, military, and economic center. Although Khirbet Iskander was known in the nineteenth century, Glueck was the first to study the site systematically in 1939; in 1955 Parr did a preliminary excavation here. From early reports, Iskander has much in common with settlements such as Bab edh Dhra and Ader, near Kerak. (Albright made soundings at Ader in 1933 on behalf of ASOR and in cooperation with the British School.) Excavation of Khirbet Iskander should help to illuminate the Early Bronze IV period (about 2400-2000 B.C.), a dark age in Palestinian history. Archaeologist Roger Boraas has joined the Iskander project as its stratigrapher.

Redford's Survey

Donald B. Redford of the University of Toronto has been engaged in a survey of Jordanian sites, attempting to identify place-names mentioned in the annals of Pharaoh Thutmose III (1504-1450 B.C.) and inscribed in the halls of the temple of Amon-Re at Karnak in Upper Egypt. In pursuit of the toponyms of Thutmose III, the greatest military conqueror of ancient Egypt, Redford must visit Syria, Lebanon, Israel, and Turkey, in addition to Jordan, because the expansionist policy of the pharaoh was so successful.

The Future of Jordanian Archaeology

The past two decades have witnessed extraordinary growth in Jordan's archaeological activity, undertaken by both native and foreign archaeologists. The Jordanian government is eager not only to preserve its historical and archaeological heritage but also to develop this rich resource. As industrial, agricultural, and urban development within the country threatens this legacy, practical steps must be taken to protect endangered sites. Jordan's five-year plan (1981-1985), dealing with every aspect of antiquities, is one important response to the present critical state of the archaeology of the country. The profound concern of the Jordanians for their important history and rich archaeological heritage has been succinctly stated by His Majesty King Hussein, "We are caretakers of a legacy that belongs not only to us, but to the world."

The Amman Center

His Royal Highness Crown Prince Hassan bin Talal has proposed the establishment of a Historical and Archaeological Center in Amman. International in character, it would serve the countries of the region by functioning as an information center, a meeting place for foreign scholars, and a research facility with an international library and other resources. Such a center would ensure high standards for the archaeology of Jordan while setting the same scientific tone for neighboring countries.

Salvage Archaeology in the Negev

Discussion of the Negev region immediately raises two questions: why did ancient people settle in such a marginal area, and how did they manage to survive in such an arid climate? Recent explorations of the Negev, including archaeological, geomorphological, climatological, and geobotanical surveys, are beginning to illuminate the way of life of its ancient inhabitants and the ecological and environmental history of the region.

Yohanan Aharoni

Tel Aviv University's Institute of Archaeology and its founder Yohanan Aharoni have made a substantial contribution to present-day knowledge of the Negev. Since its establishment in 1969 the Institute of Archaeology has produced an impressive group of Israeli archaeologists and sponsored important field projects throughout Israel, especially in the southern region of the country. When Aharoni died in 1976 Israel lost one of its outstanding historical geographers, but his achievements continue to influence a new generation of archaeologists. His regional surveys of Upper Galilee and the Negev, as well as his excavations at Arad and Beer-sheba, guarantee him a prominent place in the history of Israeli archaeology.

Tell Malhata

Beginning in 1967, as part of the Beer-sheba Valley regional archaeological project, Moshe Kochavi of Tel Aviv University excavated Tell Malhata at the confluence of the Malhata and Beer-sheba Rivers. This site was first inhabited in the Middle Bronze II B and C period (about 1750-1600 B.C.). Aharoni held that Malhata was the site of Canaanite Arad; Mazar thought it was biblical Hormah, a city of the tribe of Simeon; Kochavi suggested Baalath-beer, which is probably the same as Bealoth of the Book of Joshua. At the foot of Tell Malhata there is a Hellenistic and a Roman-Byzantine site that flourished in the time of the Hasmoneans, the dynasty that ruled Judea from the Maccabean wars (about 161 B.C.) to the Roman conquest under Pompey in 63 B.C.

Tell Masos

In 1972 the first joint Israeli-German expedition, codirected by Volkmar Fritz of the University of Mainz and Aharon Kempinski of Tel Aviv University, began excavating at Tell Masos. This is the largest and one of the most important Iron I sites in the northern Negev. Like Malhata, this tell is also difficult to identify with certainty. Following Aharoni, Kempinski is of the opinion that Masos is biblical Hormah. Kochavi, on the other hand, is inclined to identify it with the "City of Amalek" (Ir Amalek), which King Saul conquered. Kempinski has challenged Kochavi to provide evidence that Masos was an Amalekite settlement. Masos is one of the Early Iron Age villages which is shedding light on the much disputed question of the manner of Israelite settlement in Canaan.

Ramifications of the 1979 Camp David Accords

Once again, politics became a determining factor in field archaeology when Israel and Egypt signed the 1979 Camp David accords in Washington, D.C. This agreement required adjustment of the borders between the two countries and involved the relocation of Israeli military bases situated at that time in the Sinai. Development of new airfields in the Negev to guarantee the security of Israel meant the demolition of ancient sites, several still unexcavated, invaluable for the reconstruction of the region's cultural history. In many cases, this activity left time only for survey and sounding, not for excavation.

The complete survey of sites in the Negev was done principally by Israeli archaeologists, but other groups, including ASOR, also helped. Rudolph Cohen, the Department of Antiquities' representative in the Negev, directed the Negev emergency survey in anticipation of the new airfields, while Moshe Kochavi coordinated the salvage work in the Beersheba Valley.

The planned construction of the Tell Malhata Air Base threatened three important sites in the northern Negev, Tell Malhata (Tell el Milh), Tell Masos (Khirbet el Meshash), and Tell Ira (Ghara). Of these three major sites, only two had been excavated; Ira had never been dug.

Tell Ira

Ira, the largest mound in the Negev of Judah, contains evidence of settlement from the Early Bronze Age to the beginning of the Arab era, with the longest period of habitation during the Judean monarchy. To make way for the new military zone, the Israelis have been digging intensively at Ira. In an attempt to identify the tell, Aharoni suggested Kabzeel, a town reoccupied by the Judeans after their return from exile; Manfred Weippert and Anson Rainey conjectured that it may be the site of Ramat-negev, a town of Simeon.

Uncertainty about the identification of sites in the Negev is so widespread that the prospects for interpreting data and correlating sites will remain dim until the region is explored and excavated in systematic fashion. The modern military occupation can only be expected further to impede the steps requisite for real understanding of the area.

The Central Negev Highlands

In 1978 William G. Dever of the University of Arizona joined Rudolph Cohen of the Department of Antiquities in launching an interdisciplinary project in the central Negev highlands to study such questions as patterns of settlement and adjustment of populations to arid climate, as well as ancient agricultural and technological systems. Although Glueck, Rothenberg, and Aharoni had conducted earlier surveys of the Negev, many questions remained to be explored.

Beer Resisim

In addition to surveying the Nahal Nissana area near the Sinai border, where there is a concentration of Middle Bronze I (about 2000 B.C.) settlements, Dever and Cohen focused on one of the settlements, Beer Resisim, a town site composed of at least eighty-five structures. A major excavation at Beer Resisim in 1980 provided an excellent insight into the material culture of this village, whose economy was based on herding, trading, and perhaps agriculture. The town plan also came to light, showing several houses clustered around a common courtyard. As a result of the surface exploration in the central and western Negev, where over 3,000 sites of Middle Bronze Age I have been unearthed, this archaeological period is no longer as obscure as it once was.

Recent Developments in ASOR

The foregoing descriptions of ASOR's field projects attest to the quickened pace of archaeological activity conducted under its auspices in the Mideast. At the same time quality of work holds a place of high importance in all projects; ASOR is committed to responsible research and publication.

The Committee on Archaeological Policy

To maintain excellence in all areas of the archaeological enterprise, ASOR President Frank Cross in 1975 developed the Committee on Archaeological Policy, charging it with the oversight of all field projects. Every aspect of a project comes under the scrutiny of this committee: planning, staffing, recording, publishing, etc. To fulfill its mandate the committee issued a statement of standards and a set of procedural guidelines, which are made available to directors of prospective projects.

The Committee on Archaeological Policy is also responsible for long-range planning as a way of coordinating various projects and guaranteeing that all geographical regions and archaeological periods will be covered adequately. This overall strategy is formulated in conjunction with the Department of Antiquities of each country where ASOR excavates.

As an ASOR vice-president and chairman of the Committee on Archaeological Policy Edward F. Campbell has played a substantial role in raising the standards of archaeological undertakings affiliated with ASOR. Through annual visits to the sites of ASOR's projects Campbell has served as an effective liaison between ASOR and its field directors. Michael D. Coogan, who has occasionally served as chairman of the Committee on Archaeological Policy, has ably assisted Campbell; other members of the committee are drawn from the pool of ASOR archaeologists. When project directors submit their proposals to this committee of their peers, the responses they receive can enhance their fieldwork considerably. Sometimes the committee denies approval because of a project's failure to conform to standards.

David Noel Freedman: Editor of ASOR Publications

During the presidency of Frank M. Cross, ASOR's publications program was rejuvenated by the editorial skill and experience of David N. Freedman, ASOR's vice-president for publications. Few scholars can match Freedman in the quality and quantity of the material he has edited during his academic career. In addition to ASOR publications, there had been the *Journal of Biblical Literature* and now the Anchor Bible series, a Doubleday publication. Any one of these projects would assure Freedman a prominent niche in the history of Near Eastern scholarship.

ASOR's professional journal, the *Bulletin of the American Schools of Oriental Research (BASOR)* has always been edited by leading scholars: James A. Montgomery (1919-1930), William F. Albright (1931-1968), Delbert R. Hillers (1969-1974), David N. Freedman (1974-1978), and William G. Dever (1978-1982). The first major change in the journal in fifty years occurred in *BASOR* 215 (1974), edited by Freedman. This issue appeared in an enlarged and attractive format to accommodate diagrams, photographs, plans, and maps, all indispensable parts of archaeological reporting today.

The Annual of the American Schools of Oriental Research, inaugurated in 1920 under the editorship of Charles C. Torrey, was instituted to guarantee regular publication of the scholarly research generated by ASOR appointees overseas; it too has had a succession of distinguished editors. Of the ASOR *Annuals* published during Freedman's vice-presidency, he edited two of them: *Annual* 43 (1976), preliminary excavation reports on Bab edh Dhra, Sardis, Meiron, Tell el Hesi, and Carthage, and *Annual* 44 (1977), archaeological reports from the Tabqa Dam project in the Euphrates Valley.

Under Freedman's editorship the March 1976 issue of the *Biblical Archeologist* appeared in new dress, an elegant and enlarged format, with feature articles of general appeal. The purpose of the quarterly is to provide the ordinary reader with an accurate and understandable account of archaeological activities; at the same time the journal attempts to explain the meaning of new discoveries for biblical studies. With the passage of time the *Biblical Archeologist* has had a tendency to become more technical than its intended audience requires, so it has periodically needed revamping.

With the able assistance of H. Thomas Frank of Oberlin College, Freedman chose articles written in a straightforward style and appealing to the general reader interested in the Holy Land. More technical articles (detailing, for example, the results of digs and other field projects) were designated for publication in *BASOR*. Even Freedman's monitoring of the *Biblical Archeologist*, however, has not kept it completely free of the arcane. This perennial problem arises when scholars attempt to communicate their science to the lay person.

In addition to Frank, there are at least two others who deserve laudatory mention for their contribution to the well-being of the *Biblical Archeologist* during Freedman's years as editor: John A. Miles, who inaugurated the new *Biblical Archeologist* in great style, and David F. Graf, who has been a faithful and effective assistant editor and more recently associate editor of the journal.

As vice-president for publications, Freedman not only oversaw the production of all ASOR's standard books and journals but also introduced several new series consisting of special volumes, doctoral dissertations, and monographs. Unfortunately, after an auspicious beginning, financial constraints made it necessary to curtail temporarily the ASOR publications program.

The New Testament and Archaeology

New Testament archaeology has never been a vibrant discipline; in the opinion of some, it may even be nonexistent. Herein lies an irony. ASOR owes its existence in large measure to the catalysis of an eminent New Testament professor, J. Henry Thayer of Harvard University. The lack of development in New Testament archaeology has been attributed to the separation between New Testament studies on the one hand and the classics and classical archaeology on the other.

Helmut Koester, also a New Testament professor at Harvard, maintains that there is no such discipline as New Testament archaeology; he explains that the New Testament pertains to a non-Christian culture of the Mediterranean world in the Hellenistic and Imperial Roman periods. Untrained in epigraphy, art history, and architecture, many New Testament scholars, he asserts, must depend upon other specialists to assist them in their investigation of the religion and culture of the Graeco-Roman world.

Recent developments have been encouraging, however; Koester has been directing under ASOR's auspices a venture of relevance to students of the New Testament and of archaeology. Koester and his students have been making significant progress in their quest for relevant archaeological data. With concentration on the countries surrounding the Aegean Sea, starting at Greece and ending at western Turkey, they have been studying remains from the periods of Hellenism and Imperial Rome and from the Byzantine era. In their efforts to assemble a meaningful corpus of material, they have been collecting published reports from selected sites. They have also been visiting the sites and local museums for firsthand study and the opportunity to photograph; they have formed an impressive slide collection which they will publish with appropriate commentary. The project is long and tedious, but it is also an excellent way to pursue the subject of the New Testament and archaeology.

The Medical Handbook

In addition to the perceived need for improving the scientific standards of its field projects, ASOR felt the necessity for greater attention to the health of excavators and the hygienic standards of dig camps. Good health is the prerequisite for effective field work and the guarantee of high morale. Living conditions on excavations are never ideal, but preventive measures can be taken to eliminate serious illness, which can easily disrupt a field project. The issues of health care and hygiene have been addressed by ASOR's medical director, Melvin K. Lyons, who has personally participated in several excavations. On the basis of his extensive dig experience, he prepared a handbook, *The Care and Feeding of Dirt Archaeologists*, which ASOR published in 1978. A manual of sanitation, hygiene, and medicine for archaeological expeditions in the Mideast, it has been a ready reference and constant companion for hundreds of staff members and volunteers associated with excavations. Its sound medical counsel has helped to eliminate serious illness from ASOR dig camps.

The 1980 Task Force

At the end of the first eighty years of ASOR's existence, the organization looked back to assess its achievements and the means used to accomplish them; it endeavored to look ahead before beginning its ninth decade. At this time ASOR, desiring to respond to the scholarly demands of the times rather than moving haphazardly into the future, named a task force chaired by Edward Campbell to review the past and plan for the future. The following goals emerged from the task force's in-depth study; the trustees adopted them as guidelines for the critical half-decade from 1980 to 1985:

I.   To initiate, encourage and support research into and public understanding of the peoples and cultures of the Near East and their wider spheres of interaction from earliest times to the modern period, especially archaeologically-informed projects which are integrative and interdisciplinary.

II. To improve the existing institutes in Jerusalem and Amman, to continue developing the institute in Nicosia, and to revitalize when feasible the institute in Baghdad, so as to enhance their usefulness in the service of Goal I as centers for historical research in its broadest sense.

III. To respond to the changing as well as growing needs of Near Eastern peoples and governments for assistance in the conservation and disciplined study of their cultural heritage.

IV. To explore the possibilities of ASOR's expanding its research work to countries within ASOR's range of interest where there is no ASOR-associated institute.

V.   To develop means of responding more effectively to the diverse interests of ASOR's membership and to foster greater communication and participation throughout the organization.

VI. To improve and accelerate dissemination of the results of scholarly research, including that which serves the emphases of Goal I.

VII.   To develop and sustain programs for communicating to the general
       public the results and significance of research within ASOR's fields
       of interest, including influencing the educational system at all
       levels to expand attention to the roots of the human heritage that
       lie in the ancient Near East.

A comparison between the original statement of purpose and the
one at hand gives the impression that ASOR has changed noticeably in
its eighty-year history, especially concerning biblical studies. Differences
between the two statements are to be attributed to the organic nature of
archaeology as a discipline; had it not evolved, it would have stagnated.
To be sure, the original statement centered on the Bible; the present
statement lets the Bible take its place within the comprehensive discipline
called Near Eastern studies. Inasmuch as biblical studies have come of
age, such treatment seems perfectly proper.

ASOR Regional Societies in the United States

There was a time when the Northeast was the center of the intellectual and cultural life of the United States; for that reason several of the
learned societies, including ASOR, were founded in that geographical
area. Today, however, no section of the country has a monopoly on
learning and culture; so ASOR is extending its activities in the form of
regional societies throughout North America, following the model of its
parent organizations, the Society of Biblical Literature and the Archaeological Institute of America.

There is another good reason for forming ASOR regional societies.
ASOR has grown so large in recent years that only with difficulty can it
serve its constituency from a single administrative base in the United
States. To respond to its widely scattered membership, ASOR began in
1979 to organize itself regionally. D. Glenn Rose of Phillips University
and Bruce Cresson of Baylor were the first to form the Southwest
regional society; in the process they drew up a constitution and bylaws
that have served as models for additional sections. Local societies then
began to spring up elsewhere, in the Missouri-Kansas region, Pennsylvania, the Southeast, and the Midwest. Regional lectures and other
programs are being formulated as a means of nurturing the growth of
these new societies.

NEH Fellowships

The National Endowment for the Humanities, recognizing the high
standards of scholarship set by ASOR, began in 1979 to fund postdoctoral fellowships for research at the Albright Institute of Archaeological Research in Jerusalem and the American Center of Oriental

Research in Amman. Recipients may pursue any aspect of Near Eastern studies provided their research has a humanistic orientation; anthropology, archaeology, philology, history, and allied disciplines qualify. ASOR's institutes in Jerusalem and Amman were judged appropriate centers for such fellowships because of the scholarly resources available at these research institutes; in addition they are meeting places for scholars and their colleagues pursuing study in related fields.

The Dig at Tell Miqne

In addition to his duties as director of the Albright Institute in Jerusalem, Seymour Gitin is conducting with Trude Dothan of Hebrew University an excavation at Tell Miqne (Khirbet el Muqanna).[2] This long-term binational project is jointly sponsored by the Albright Institute and Hebrew University. Miqne, tentatively identified with Ekron of the Philistine pentapolis, is one of the key tells in Israel. The largest Iron Age city yet recorded in Israel, Miqne is located southwest of Jerusalem, along the slope of the northern Shephelah. This site should provide important data concerning the cultural and historical relationship among the Canaanites, Philistines, Israelites, and Assyrians. When Albright surveyed this region in 1924, he equated Khirbet el Muqanna with biblical Eltekeh, where in 701 B.C. the Assyrian king Sennacherib fought a great battle against the Egyptian-Ethiopian army, defeated them, and then invaded Judah.[3] In the course of his topographical survey in 1957, Joseph Naveh of Hebrew University identified Miqne with Ekron.

In the 1981 season, the first campaign at Miqne, it became clear that the city's two main occupational phases date to the Iron I (twelfth century B.C.) and Iron II (the end of the eighth century B.C.) periods. In addition to giving the excavators the opportunity to clarify the occupational phases of the mound and to decide its ancient identification, the dig provides the American and Israeli archaeologists working together at the site the opportunity to compare and discuss the various methods of digging and recording a Syro-Palestinian site.[4]

[2]"Miqne" is the Hebrew form of the Arabic "Muqanna"; after 1948 archaeological sites in Israel were given Hebrew names.

[3]Aqir and Qatra have also been suggested as the location of Ekron; Albright rejected Aqir and favored Qatra. The fact that Tell Miqne has never been excavated accounts in part for the uncertainty about its identification.

[4]The Israelis continue to utilize the architectural method, which is concerned with architectural levels and with understanding a building's architecture; they also emphasize the restoration of pottery vessels. Insofar as the Wheeler-Kenyon method has influenced almost all Syro-Palestinian archaeologists, among them today there are fewer differences in method, understood as the techniques for excavation and recording, than in the past. Regardless of their technical expertise in field archaeology, if the archaeologists produce

Council of American Overseas Research Centers

In the Mideast and elsewhere there are at least a dozen American overseas research institutes, including AIAR in Jerusalem, ACOR in Amman, and CAARI in Nicosia. The others are the following: American Academy in Rome, American Institute of Indian Studies, American Institute of Iranian Studies, American Institute for Pakistani Studies, American Institute for Yemeni Studies, American Research Center in Egypt, American Research Institute in Turkey, American School of Classical Studies at Athens, and the Universities Service Center, Hong Kong. The programs, services, and facilities that these centers make available to American scholars abroad constitute a valuable national resource. These advanced research centers have gone unrecognized and mostly unfunded because they have lacked broad public visibility. To correct the deficiency the overseas organizations named above have formed, with the encouragement and assistance of the Smithsonian Institution, a council named the Council of American Overseas Research Centers. It has been created to provide a forum for increased communication and cooperation among the research centers. While retaining their individual identities, the institutes will act collectively in matters of common concern. There are several areas where joint action would be more effective than individual initiative; publicity about the importance of the centers, fund raising, and research projects are obvious matters calling for cooperation.

ASOR's Photogrammetry and Computer Graphics System

Because excavation is by nature destruction, field archaeology is a discipline that relies heavily on the proper retrieval, recording, and analysis of raw data. Recently the scientific technical tools of archaeology have undergone dramatic development. Recording systems in common use were formerly both time-consuming and inadequate, while more sophisticated methods were complex and expensive. Thanks to the initiative of Maco Stewart, a trustee of the Albright Institute, ASOR is presently engaged in advancing a new photogrammetry and computer graphics system, designed to be both economical and easy to use, a system that will be applicable to any architectural or archaeological recording program in the field. In addition to generating plans, elevations, and three-dimensional images of standing architecture, it will also revolutionize the recording, analysis, and storage of inscriptional evidence and ancient texts. The new techniques being developed through ASOR represent a genuine advance in historical and cultural research and have already been greeted enthusiastically by colleagues in related fields.

---

only a ceramic sequence and an outline of a site's political history without undertaking to reconstruct the cultural process, they have done only half their work.

The Continuing Search for Funds

As ASOR moves into the last part of the twentieth century, resolved to continue as a leader in ancient Near Eastern research, the organization finds that it is exceedingly expensive even to maintain traditional programs, not to mention initiating new ones. Undaunted, ASOR has taken several firm steps to meet the demands of the eighties. Upon application in 1980, ASOR was awarded a major challenge grant by the National Endowment for the Humanities, an independent federal agency whose purpose is to encourage the pursuit of humanistic knowledge. The ASOR trustees have undertaken a capital fund drive to enable the construction of a permanent research center in Amman and the refurbishment and endowment of the existing institute in Jerusalem; Joy G. Ungerleider-Mayerson and Richard J. Scheuer have already made large gifts toward the endowment of the Albright Institute. In addition to their own gifts, other trustees of ASOR are soliciting the financial support of corporations and foundations for Jerusalem, Amman, and Nicosia.

The Friends of ASOR

At the same time a campaign is underway to reach more people among the interested public, as a source of financial assistance and as a wider audience for the results of archaeological research in the ancient Near East. These people, known as the Friends of ASOR, are encouraged to become involved in the programs of ASOR as the organization seeks new ways of serving them.

ASOR's New Officers (1982-1985)[5]

A changing of the guard took place at ASOR on July 1, 1982, when new officers were inaugurated: James A. Sauer of the University of Pennsylvania as president, Eric M. Meyers of Duke University as vice-president for publications, and William G. Dever of the University of Arizona as vice-president for archaeological projects. They succeeded Philip J. King of Boston College, David N. Freedman of the University of Michigan, and Edward F. Campbell of McCormick Theological Seminary, each of whom served two three-year terms, the maximum allowed by the ASOR bylaws.

"Biblical Archaeology": an Anachronism?

For the past fifty years the term "biblical archaeology" has been accepted as an adequately descriptive term for the discipline that many

---

[5]The present study of ASOR purports to cover the history of the organization through 1980; a few later events have been noted here to keep the history up-to-date.

Syro-Palestinian archaeologists, especially those of American back-ground, practice. As this enterprise has evolved, however, some feel that "biblical archaeology" is no longer the best name for the discipline; others are convinced that the term "biblical archaeology" is as accurate today as a half century ago. An archaeological revolution has taken place in this generation, but it has not brought with it any clear name.

Albright, the most distinguished biblical archaeologist, understood the discipline in a comprehensive way:

> Biblical archaeology is a much wider term than Palestinian archaeology, though Palestine itself is of course central, and is rightly regarded as peculiarly the land of the Bible. But Biblical archaeology covers all the lands mentioned in the Bible, and is thus coextensive with the cradle of civilization. This region extends from the western Mediterranean to India, and from southern Russia to Ethiopia and the Indian Ocean. Excavations in every part of this extensive area throw some light, directly or indirectly, on the Bible.[6]

Ernest Wright, who also exerted a strong influence on the development of archaeology in Syria-Palestine, expressed his understanding of biblical archaeology in these words:

> To me, at least, Biblical archaeology is a special "arm-chair" variety of general archaeology which studies the discoveries of the excavators and gleans from them every fact which throws a direct, indirect, or even diffused light upon the Bible. Its central and absorbing interest is the understanding and exposition of the Scriptures. It is interested in floors, foundations, and city walls; but it is also interested in epigraphic dis-coveries and in every indication of what people did with their minds as well as with what they did with their hands.[7]

William Dever is uncomfortable with the definitions of Albright and Wright; he also advocates the abolition of the term "biblical archaeology" as misleading, easily mistaken for a fundamentalist attempt to prove the Bible true through archaeology. Syro-Palestinian archae-ology has become, according to Dever, a separate discipline, independent of biblical studies, and its autonomy ought to be acknowledged. He suggests that a regional description such as "Syro-Palestinain archae-ology" would communicate more accurately the nature and scope of the discipline. Dever is convinced that "biblical archaeology" does not adequately describe what he and his colleagues do, even from the perspec-tive of chronology, as they excavate sites with occupation levels extend-ing from the prehistoric era to the Ottoman Empire, far beyond the borders of the biblical period.

---

[6]*New Horizons in Biblical Research*, London, 1966, p. 1.
[7]*Biblical Archaeologist* 10 (1947) 7.

H. Darrell Lance of Colgate Rochester Divinity School, with an impressive record of field experience, staunchly defends the term "biblical archaeology" and is opposed to substituting "Syro-Palestinian archaeology" on the same grounds of inadequacy. Lance points out that the biblical archaeologist must often look beyond Palestine for material evidence to elucidate the biblical text. In explaining that biblical archaeology is a technique for the study of the Bible, Lance states:

> Biblical archaeology, like biblical form criticism or biblical anthropology, is a *biblical* discipline which exists for the benefit and interest of biblical studies. So long as people read the Bible and ask questions about the history and culture of the ancient world which produced it, those questions will have to be answered; and the sum total of those answers will comprise biblical archaeology.[8]

Insisting that "biblical archaeology" and "Syro-Palestinian archaeology" are not interchangeable terms, Dever rejects the argument of those who maintain that the distinctions are purely semantic; for him the issue is substantive. At the same time, he is convinced that archaeology has invaluable data to contribute to the proper understanding of the Bible, as it reconstructs the setting of biblical events, their temporal context, and cultural milieu. In short, archaeology can fill the nagging gaps found on every page of the Bible, the kinds of questions often raised but seldom answered by the text. Dever concedes that the field archaeologist and the biblical scholar can cooperate on an interdisciplinary basis, each bringing his or her own competence and expertise to bear on a study best described as "archaeology and the Bible."

In many fields of inquiry there was a time before the knowledge explosion when a scholar could control multiple aspects of a discipline. A biblical scholar, for example, could also be a part-time field archaeologist, as ASOR's history attests. Today it is almost impossible for one person to possess the skills required to function as both a biblical scholar and an archaeologist. The increasingly sophisticated methods required to retrieve and interpret the data are quickly rendering the joint biblical scholar-field archaeologist anachronistic. Even the professional archaeologist cannot operate independently in the field but must be supported by a variety of specialists in the natural sciences, the social sciences, and the humanities. Only through cooperation of many disciplines can the cultural history of the ancient Near East be reconstructed.

Other considerations are making field archaeology in the Mideast more complex. For example, New World archaeology with its concentration on prehistoric sites has influenced Near Eastern archaeology for

[8]*The Old Testament and the Archaeologist*, Philadelphia, 1981, p. 95. In a forthcoming article, "Biblical Archaeology, an Emerging Discipline," to appear in L. T. Geraty, ed., *The Archaeology of Jordan and Other Studies*, Albert E. Glock of Bir Zeit University advocates the identification of biblical archaeology as a subdiscipline of biblical studies.

over a decade. By nature, New World archaeology is oriented toward anthropology. In the past, Syro-Palestinian archaeology had concentrated almost exclusively on chronological and historical matters, with little attention to the cultural aspects of the discipline. Today, as part of the anthropological approach, archaeology in the Mideast is taking into account the social and economic environment in order to complete the picture. As archaeology moves away from a narrow historical perspective, it is increasingly interested in the social and cultural reconstruction of early Israel.

The foregoing discussion is a sign that Syro-Palestinian archaeology and biblical studies contain much vibrancy. In fact, the debate has been stimulated by the extraordinary activity in the archaeology of the Mideast today. Most scholars would agree that such a condition is hardly a cause for complaint.

Special Mentions

This history of ASOR has centered, for the most part, on generations of scholars actively engaged in the archaeological research of the ancient Near East. Many have been singled out for special mention. Several others who are not professional scholars have contributed in a substantial way to the well-being of ASOR. Were it not for their dedication, the archaeological enterprise would not have flourished. Of this group, at least the following deserve special mention.

ASOR Staff

Gladys R. Walton served ASOR for a quarter-century until her retirement in 1963, managing the administrative office in New Haven during the tenure of three ASOR presidents and taking an active role in the production of the *Biblical Archaeologist* during that period. Helen Estey rendered comparable service for a decade at the Cambridge office during the terms of three later ASOR presidents, contributing her time, her understanding, her skills both personal and professional to the advance of ASOR's goals.

ASOR has been fortunate to have people with the same kind of dedication on its Jerusalem staff. Inna Pommerantz served the School as secretary, business manager, and librarian for ten years, until the 1948 War made it impossible for her to cross from West to East Jerusalem. In 1967 Munira Said assumed those responsibilities in Jerusalem; she continues to perform them with efficiency and graciousness.

During the past several years Thomas W. Beale, an anthropologist by degree, has been ASOR's executive director, overseeing the administrative office, writing excellent grant proposals, and doing a myriad of other tasks that have helped to keep ASOR in the forefront of archaeological research. His professional knowledge of archaeology has been a great asset to the organization. At an earlier stage Thomas D. Newman performed similar administrative duties with unusual skill and efficiency.

ASOR Trustees

The ASOR trustees are a special group of magnanimous men and women who give generously of their talents, time, and resources; without them ASOR could accomplish little. In recent years this body has been especially active in all of ASOR's programs, encouraging the scholars with their wise counsel, abiding interest, and constant support. ASOR is solidly established today because of its lay trustees; comparable organizations are struggling because they lack this asset. Scholars are in the front-line of a learned society, but without the support of trustees from the business and professional world, they would fall short.[9]

Foreign Service Officers

Thanks must be expressed to the United States foreign service officers, who have since 1900 stood ready to assist ASOR in fulfilling its scholarly mandate. Agencies of the government in Washington, D.C. have also been encouraging and supportive; without their help ASOR may not have survived for eighty years.

ASOR Benefactors

During ASOR's lifetime many benefactors, both institutional and individual, through their generous gifts have enabled deserving scholars to undertake research in the Mideast. The first manifestation of this kind was the Joseph Henry Thayer Fellowship,[10] supported by the Archaeological Institute of America. It enabled W. F. Albright and numerous others to spend a year in Jerusalem pursuing research projects of relevance to the Mideast. The first recipient of the Thayer Fellowship was Martin A. Meyer of Hebrew Union College, Cincinnati, in the academic year 1901-1902; he was the only student of the School that year.

More recently a fellowship endowed by George A. Barton, early director of the Jerusalem School, has become available, affording annual recipients the opportunity to do research in Jerusalem while residing at the Albright Institute. Other unendowed fellowships honoring the memory of prominent ASOR pioneers become available in occasional years, according to the state of ASOR's annual operating budget.

The Zion Research Foundation of Boston has set an admirable example by annually funding a large number of research grants and travel scholarships, which are accessible to students from educational

---

[9]ASOR's lay trustees never seek the limelight; to say more about them here might be cause for embarrassment. The names of the officers and trustees appear in the appendixes.

[10]A sample examination for the Thayer Fellowship appears in the appendixes.

institutions affiliated with ASOR. Most recipients spend the summer participating in fieldwork in Israel, Jordan and elsewhere in the Mideast; many of these projects afford the opportunity for earning academic credits. Were it not for the generosity of the Zion Research Foundation many students would never have made their first trip to the Mideast.

Conclusion

From the perspective of 1982, it is funny to recall that Albright as a young boy, reading Rogers's *History of Assyria and Babylonia*, feared that all the mounds of Palestine would have been excavated by the time he was old enough to go there. The history of archaeology makes it clear that much has been accomplished in the Mideast, but much still remains to be done, enough to engage several future generations.

In a 1963 article, "Palestine: Known but Mostly Unknown," Paul Lapp correctly observed, "Palestinian archaeology may be past infancy but has hardly gotten beyond childhood."[11] That remark is equally applicable to the American Schools of Oriental Research, a service organization that has been contributing to the understanding of the cultural heritage of the ancient Near East for eighty years. Its work has just begun.

[11]*Biblical Archaeologist* 26 (1963) 122.

Appendix I

Presidents of the American Schools of Oriental Research

1921-1933	James A. Montgomery, University of Pennsylvania
1934-1948	Millar Burrows, Yale University
1949-1954	Carl H. Kraeling, University of Chicago
1955-1965	A. Henry Detweiler, Cornell University
1966-1974	G. Ernest Wright, Harvard University
1974-1976	Frank Moore Cross, Harvard University
1976-1982	Philip J. King, Boston College
1982-	James A. Sauer, University of Pennsylvania

Appendix II
Directors of the Jerusalem School

1900-01	Charles C. Torrey	1948-49	Ovid R. Sellers
1901-02	Hinckley G. Mitchell	1949-50	James L. Kelso
1902-03	George A. Barton	1950-51	Fred V. Winnett
1903-04	Lewis B. Paton	1951-52	William L. Reed
1904-05	Nathaniel Schmidt	1952-53	A. Douglas Tushingham
1905-06	Benjamin W. Bacon	1953-54	James Muilenburg
1906-07	David G. Lyon	1954-55	William H. Morton
1907-08	Francis Brown	1955-56	Patrick W. Skehan
1908-09	Robert F. Harper	1956-57	Robert C. Dentan
1909-10	Richard J. Gottheil	1957-58	H. Neil Richardson
1910-11	Charles R. Brown	1958-59	Fred V. Winnett
1911-12	J. F. McCurdy	1959-60	Marvin H. Pope
1912-13	Warren J. Moulton	1960-61	Oleg Grabar
1913-14	George L. Robinson	1961-65	Paul W. Lapp
1914-15	James A. Montgomery	1965-66	George E. Mendenhall
1919-20	William H. Worrell	1966-67	John H. Marks
1920-29	William F. Albright	1967-68	William Van Etten Casey
1929-31	Chester C. McCown	1968-69	Kermit Schoonover
1931-32	Millar Burrows	1969-70	David Noel Freedman
1932-33	Nelson Glueck	1970-71	Robert J. Bull
1933-36	William F. Albright	1971-75	William G. Dever
1936-40	Nelson Glueck	1975-76	Eric M. Meyers
1940-41	Clarence S. Fisher	1976-77	David Noel Freedman
1942-47	Nelson Glueck	1977-80	Albert E. Glock
1947-48	Millar Burrows	1980-	Seymour Gitin

Appendix III
Annual Professors of the Baghdad School

1923-24	Albert T. Clay	1951-52	Francis R. Steele
1924-25	Edward Chiera	1952-53	Alexander Heidel
1925-26	Raymond P. Dougherty	1953-54	Thorkild Jacobsen
1926-27	Ephraim A. Speiser	1954-55	Bruce Howe
1927-28	Leroy Waterman	1955-56	Albrecht Goetze
1928-29	Robert H. Pfeiffer	1956-57	Vaughn E. Crawford
1929-30	Henry F. Lutz	1958-59	Fred V. Winnett
1930-31	Theophile J. Meek	1959-60	Bruce Howe
1931-32	Ephraim A. Speiser	1960-61	Richard C. Haines
1932-33	Edward Chiera	1961-62	Stephen D. Simmons
1933-34	Nelson Glueck	1962-63	Donald Hansen
1936-37	Albert T. Olmstead	1963-64	Bruce Howe
1937-38	Elihu Grant	1965-66	Theresa H. Carter
1942-46	Nelson Glueck	1966-67	Robert McC. Adams
1946-47	Samuel N. Kramer	1967-68	Richard S. Ellis
1947-48	Albrecht Goetze	1968-69	John A. Brinkman
1948-49	George G. Cameron		Thorkild Jacobsen
1949-50	Francis R. Steele	1969-70	McGuire Gibson

Appendix IV
Trustees of the American Schools of Oriental Research
(January 1982)

Appendix V
Corporate Members of the
American Schools of Oriental Research
(January 1982)

American Baptist Seminary of
the West
Ancient Biblical Manuscript Center
for Preservation and Research
Anderson College
Andover Newton Theological School
Andrews University
Archaeological Institute of America
Asbury Theological Seminary
Associated Mennonite Seminary
Aurora College
Austin Presbyterian Theological
Seminary
Australian Institute of Archaeology
Bangor Theological Seminary
Baptist Bible College of
Pennsylvania
Bard College
Baylor University
Boston College
Boston University
Brandeis University
Brigham Young University
Brown University
Bryn Mawr College
Caesarea World Monument,
California
Calvin Theological Seminary
Catholic University of America
Central Baptist Theological Seminary
Central College

Christ Seminary-Seminex
Christian Theological Seminary
Claremont Graduate School
Colgate Rochester Divinity School
College of the Holy Cross
College of Wooster
Columbia Theological Seminary
Concordia College
Concordia College-Seward
Concordia Theological Seminary
Cornell University
Covenant Theological Seminary
DePaul University
Drew University
Duke University
Dumbarton Oaks
Emmanuel School of Religion
Emory University
Episcopal Divinity School
The Foundation for Biblical Research
Garrett-Evangelical Theological
Seminary
General Theological Seminary
Gettysburg Lutheran Theological
Seminary
Golden Gate Baptist Seminary
Grace Theological Seminary
Harvard University,
The Divinity School
Harvard University,
Fogg Art Museum

Harvard University, Peabody Museum of Archaeology and Ethnology
Harvard University, Semitic Museum
Hebrew Union College, Jewish Institute of Religion, Cincinnati
Iliff School of Theology
Indiana University of Pennsylvania
Institute for Advanced Study
Jesuit School of Theology
Johannes Gutenberg Universität
John Carroll University
Johns Hopkins University
Loma Linda University
Louisville Presbyterian Theological Seminary
Luther College
Luther Theological Seminary
Lutheran School of Theology
Lutheran Theological Seminary
Lycoming College
McCormick Theological Seminary
McGill University
Methodist Theological School
Miami University, Ohio
Metropolitan Museum of Art
Midwestern Baptist Theological Seminary
Milwaukee Public Museum
Mount Holyoke College
New York University
North Carolina State University
Northern Baptist Theological Seminary
Oberlin College
Oklahoma State University
Pacific Lutheran Theological Seminary
Palestine Institute, Pacific School of Religion
Phillips University
Pittsburgh Theological Seminary
Princeton Theological Seminary

Princeton University
Rice University
Rochester Institute of Technology
St. Francis Xavier University
St. John Fisher College
St. John's Seminary, Boston
St. Lawrence University
St. Mary's Seminary, Baltimore
St. Mary's University of San Antonio
St. Paul School of Theology
Samford University
Seabury-Western Theological Seminary
Seton Hall University
Smith College
Southeastern Baptist Theological Seminary
Southern Baptist Theological Seminary
Southern Methodist University
Southwest Missouri State University
Southwestern Baptist Theological Seminary
Southwestern at Memphis
Southwestern University
Texas Christian University
Trinity Lutheran Seminary
Union Theological Seminary, New York
Union Theological Seminary, Virginia
United Theological Seminary
Unity School of Christianity
University of Arizona
University of Chicago, Oriental Institute
University of California, Berkeley
University of Cincinnati
University of Connecticut
University of Kansas
University of Maryland

University of Melbourne

University of Michigan

University of Minnesota

University of Missouri-Columbia

University of Notre Dame

University of Pennsylvania

University of South Florida

University of Toronto

University of Vienna

Upsala College

Valparaiso University

Wake Forest University

Wartburg Theological Seminary

Wellesley College

Wesley Theological Seminary

Western Theological Seminary

Weston School of Theology

Wheaton College

Wilfrid Laurier University

Yale University

Appendix VI
The Archaeological Periods of Syria-Palestine*

Paleolithic	700,000 - 14,000 B.C.
Epipaleolithic	14,000 - 8000 B.C.
Neolithic	8000 - 4200 B.C.
Chalcolithic	4200 - 3300 B.C.
Early Bronze	3300 - 2000 B.C.
EB I	3300 - 3000 B.C.
EB II	3000 - 2800 B.C.
EB III	2800 - 2400 B.C.
EB IV	2400 - 2000 B.C.
Middle Bronze	2000 - 1550 B.C.
MB I (formerly MB II A)	2000 - 1800 B.C.
MB II (formerly MB II B)	1800 - 1650 B.C.
MB III (formerly MB II C)	1650 - 1550 B.C.
Late Bronze	1550 - 1200 B.C.
LB I	1550 - 1400 B.C.
LB II	1400 - 1200 B.C.
Iron	1200 - 539 B.C.
Iron I	1200 - 930 B.C.
Iron II A	930 - 721 B.C.
Iron II B	721 - 605 B.C.
Iron II C	605 - 539 B.C.
Persian	539 - 332 B.C.
Hellenistic	332 - 63 B.C.
Early Hellenistic	332 - 198 B.C.
Late Hellenistic	198 - 63 B.C.
Roman	63 B.C. - A.D. 324
Early Roman	63 B.C. - A.D. 135
Late Roman	A.D. 135 - 324

*These dates are only approximate. Scholars disagree about these dates which are constantly being refined in the light of new archaeological evidence. For this reason there are some differences between the dates within the text and those on this table.

Byzantine	A.D. 324 - 640
Early Byzantine	A.D. 324 - 491
Late Byzantine	A.D. 491 - 640
Early Islamic	A.D. 640 - 1174
Umayyad	A.D. 661 - 750
Abbasid	A.D. 750 - 878
Fatamid	A.D. 969 - 1174
Crusader	A.D. 1099 - 1291
Late Islamic	A.D. 1174 - 1918
Ayyubid	A.D. 1174 - 1250
Mamluk	A.D. 1250 - 1516
Ottoman	A.D. 1516 - 1918

Appendix VII

Examination Papers for the Thayer Fellowship
in the School at Jerusalem

HISTORY OF SYRIA AND PALESTINE

MARCH, 1906. (*Two hours*)

1. What were the conditions in Palestine about 1400 B.C., as shown by the Amarna Despatches? What is the bearing of these discoveries, and of the inscription of Mernephtah, on the date of the Israelite invasion of the country?

2. Give an outline of the history of Judah from the death of Josiah to the fall of Jerusalem 586 B.C.

3. Describe the principal Jewish sects and parties at the beginning of the Christian era.

4. What was the occasion of the rebellion against Hadrian? What measures did Hadrian take against the Jews at the end of the war? How were the relations of Christian Jews in Palestine to their countrymen affected by this war?

GEOGRAPHY OF PALESTINE

MARCH, 1906. (*One and one-half hours*)

1. Name the chief Phoenician cities in order from south to north, beginning at Mt. Carmel. What is the southernmost city of Palestine, commanding the road to Egypt?

2. Name the principal cities on or near the Great Plain, giving a brief description of their position.

3. Describe the course of the Jordan, and name its tributaries on both sides, from north to south. Describe the Dead Sea.

4. In what direction from Jerusalem, and at what distances, are Hebron, Samaria, Jericho, Bethel?

5. What was the southern boundary of Judah in the days of David? Where was it in the Maccabaean age? What people occupied the old territory of southern Judah, and when did they come in?

ARCHAEOLOGY

MARCH, 1906. (*One and one-half hours*)

1. Describe the Siloam Tunnel and its inscription. Probable date of the tunnel, with the reasons for this determination.

2. Jewish tombs and burial customs at the beginning of our era. Name some conspicuous tombs of this period, and describe their arrangement. What is a sarcophagus? An ossuary?

3. What are the seasons of the agricultural year in Palestine? How do the Hebrew feasts correspond to them?

4. Describe the writing and writing materials in use among the Jews in Palestine at the beginning of our era. For what purposes was the "square" alphabet employed? The "old Hebrew" alphabet? When did the codex form of books come into use in the Roman world? What use did the Jews make of it? Form and material of sacred books in the synagogue at the present time.

GREEK

MARCH, 1906. (*One and one-half hours*)

(a) Translate: Josephus, *Antiquities*, xx. 8. 1-7.

Point out anything in this passage which is significant for the student of the New Testament.

(b) Translate: Wisdom of Solomon, xiv. 12-31.

What direct literary influence on the New Testament has the Book of Wisdom had?

HEBREW

MARCH, 1906. (*One and one-half hours*)

Translate I Kings xxii. 2-11 and 19-23.

In verse 7 explain the tense of נדרשה

In verse 9 what part of the verb is מהרה?

What is the usual narrative tense in Hebrew?

Explain the use of the bare perfect in prediction; what tense regularly follows if another verb is connected with the first by "and"?

ARABIC

MARCH, 1906. (*One hour*)

Translate, in the Breslau ed. of *Alif Leila we Laila*, vol. vi., from p. 217, middle, to p. 220, middle.

SYRIAC

MARCH, 1906. (*One hour*)

Translate, in Lagarde's ed. of the Syro-Hexaplar text, from Gen. 37, 17b to the end of the chapter (Lagarde, *Bibliothecae Syriacae quae ad philologiam sacram pertinent*, p. 41 f.).

NEW TESTAMENT

MARCH, 1906. (*Two hours*)

1. Discuss the Syriac versions of the New Testament.

2. Explain the term "Antilegomena."

3. The Enoch literature,—the existing books, their component parts, dates, origin, purpose, later use, etc.

4. The history of the Armenian version of the Bible.

5. Tell what you know of Papias and his work.

6. Who was Irenaeus? What did he write, and what is his significance for the study of the New Testament?

INDEX OF PERSONS

Adams, R. Mc., 134, 172-173, 219

Aharoni, Y., 136-137, 174, 176, 259-260

Albright, W. F., 19, 22, 49-58, 63-66, 72-86, 90, 92-96, 106, 115-117, 120-122, 124, 134, 144, 147, 153-154, 158, 160-161, 164-167, 189, 195-196, 205, 229-235, 240, 243, 263, 270, 273-274

Alt, A., 4, 24-25, 65, 231

Amiran, R., 167, 176, 239

Anderson, B. W., 144, 155

Andrae, W., 62

Avigad, N., 105, 117, 174, 210

Aviram, J., 136, 174

Avi-Yonah, M., 173, 214

Bacon, B. W., 36-38, 87, 108

Badè, W. F., 77, 79

Bahnassi, A., 242, 244

Bar-Adon, P., 174

Baramki, D. C., 129

Barton, G. A., 12, 16, 33, 63, 67, 83, 273

Bea, A., 233

Beale, T. W., 272

Bechtel, E. H., 120-121, 160

Bell, G., 68

Ben Dor, I., 135

Bennet, C-M., 201-202

Biran, A., 130, 136, 177

Bliss, F. J., 5, 19-23, 42, 58, 152, 205

Bloomhardt, P. F., 147

Boling, R. G., 195, 236

Boraas, R. S., 194-195, 198, 258

Botta, P. E., 62

Bounni, A., 242

Braidwood, R. J., 133, 172, 236

Breasted, J. H., 16, 42-43, 52-53, 77-78, 245

Briggs, C. A., 16

Brinkman, J. A., 219-220

Brown, C. R., 44

Brown, F., 15-16, 41-42, 108

Brown, R. M., 253-254

Brownlee, W. H., 116

Buccellati, G., 242

Buckingham, J. S., 249

Buitron, D., 224

Bull, R. J., 144-146, 189, 209, 211, 214

Bullard, R., 170, 185

Burckhardt, J. L., 4, 249

Burrows, M., 34, 103, 107-109, 114-118, 121

Butler, H. C., 155, 249, 257

Callaway, J. A., 150-152, 186, 235

Cameron, G. G., 132-133

Campbell, E. F., 108, 145, 155, 168, 185, 195, 236, 240, 262, 265, 269

Carpenter, J., 223

Casey, W. V. E., 182-184

Chiera, E., 12, 68-72

Clark, K. W., 121, 123-124

Clay, A. T., 12, 51, 56, 58-59, 63, 67

Clermont-Ganneau, C., 9, 152

Clifford, R. J., 240

Cohen, R., 261

Cole, D. P., 217

Coleman, J. E., 223

Colt, H. D., 235

Conder, C. R., 5, 7-9, 19, 205, 249

Coogan, M. D., 252, 262

Cooley, R. E., 131, 186

Cooper, J. S., 132

Corbo, V., 211

Coughenour, R. A., 162, 198

Crawford, V. E., 132-134, 172

Cresson, B., 266

Cross, F. M., 108, 117, 122, 144, 160, 199, 225, 228-229, 235-238, 240, 262

Crowfoot, J. W., 87, 89, 92, 147, 152

Dajani, A., 148, 200

Dalman, G. H., 24-25, 65, 158

Dentan, R. C., 139

Detweiler, A. H., 70, 129, 146-147

Dever, W. G., 167-168, 170-171, 186, 189-190, 235, 261, 263, 269-271

De Vries, B., 256-257

Dickie, A. C., 22, 152

Dikaios, P., 221

Dornemann, R. H., 154, 197, 243

Dothan, M., 176

Dothan, T., 174, 267

Dougherty, R. P., 70, 240

Driver, S. R., 16

Dunayevsky, I., 137, 174
Eakins, J. K., 207
Eichhorn, J. G., 13
Eitan, A., 136
Ellenberger, L. C., 108, 144
Ellis, M deJ., 132
Ennabli, A., 225
Estey, H., 272
Filson, F. V., 108
Fisher, C. S., 12, 39-41, 44, 75-82, 87-89, 91-93, 231
Fitzgerald, G. M., 77
Foerster, G., 210-211
Frank, F., 98
Frank, H. T., 263
Franken, H. J., 149
Free, J. P., 130
Freedman, D. N., 117, 120, 176, 189, 231, 233, 262-264, 269
Fritz, V., 260
Frova, A., 214
Funk, R. W., 140, 150, 209
Galling, K., 80
Gardiner, A., 246
Gardiner, F., 11
Garstang, J., 57, 91-92, 96, 140, 150, 161
Gelat, A. T., 43, 60, 74
Geraty, L. T., 190-191
Gesenius, W., 2
Gitin, S., 267
Gjerstad, E., 221
Glock, A. E., 164, 186
Glueck, N., 20, 46, 76, 87-88, 91, 93, 96-104, 113, 148, 154, 158, 182, 189, 194, 198, 249, 254, 258
Goedicke, H., 235
Goetze, A., 131-132, 172
Goodwin, D. R., 11
Gordon, C. H., 71
Gordon, R. L., 258
Gottheil, R. J. H., 43
Grabar, O., 140, 241
Graf, D. F., 254, 263
Grant, E., 90-91
Greenfield, J. C., 235
Groh, D. E., 213
Guérin, V., 5
Gunkel, H., 15

Güterbock, H. G., 132
Guy, P. L. O., 78
Hadidi, A., 200
Hanfmann, G. M. A., 146
Hansen, D. P., 172
Harden, D. B., 227
Harding, G. L., 20, 87, 118-119, 200
Harper, R. F., 42-43
Harper, W. R., 16-17, 42, 52
Hartman, L. F., 150
Hassan bin Talal, 202, 259
Hatch, W. H. P., 66
Haupt, P., 52, 85, 232
Haynes, J. H., 12
Hennessy, J. B., 150, 209
Henry, D. O., 253
Herbert, S. C., 219
Herr, L. G., 239
Hill, D. K., 195
Hillers, D. R., 168, 235, 263
Hilprecht, H. V., 12-13, 59
Hitchcock, R. D., 8
Holladay, J. S., 186, 246-247
Holland, T. A., 153
Holm-Nielsen, S., 94
Horn, S. H., 182, 190, 198-199
Horsfield, G., 87, 200
Howe, B., 133, 172
Huesman, J. E., 149
Hulbert, H. W., 25
Humphrey, J. H., 225, 227-228
Ingholt, H., 241
Irby, C., 155
Jacobsen, T., 131-133, 172, 219
Jamieson, H. M., 159
Jastrow, M., 12, 59, 68
Jibrin, O., 103, 139-140, 182-184
Kaplan, J., 106
Karageorghis, V., 224
Kee, H. C., 123, 209
Kelsey, F. W., 227
Kelso, J. L., 76, 90, 129-130, 161-162
Kempinski, A., 260
Kenyon, K., 19, 91-92, 94, 125-128, 135, 141-142, 144-145, 150, 152-153, 161, 167
King, P. J., 238, 269
Kitchener, H. H., 7, 8, 211
Kjaer, H., 93-94

Klein, F. A., 124
Kochavi, M., 176, 260
Koeppel, R., 150
Koester, H., 264
Kohl, H., 210-211, 213
Koldewey, R., 62
Kraeling, C. H., 89, 121-122
Kramer, S. N., 172
Krueger, E., 202
Kyle, M. G., 72-73, 80-84, 90, 162, 165
Lagrange, M-J., 23-24, 59, 65
Lance, H. D., 108, 168, 271
Lapp, N., 150, 162, 167
Lapp. P. W., 66, 150, 153-168, 182-184, 189, 222, 249, 252, 274
Lawlor, J. I., 191
Layard, A. H., 62
Lehavy, Y., 221
Leichty, E. V., 132
Levy, J. M., 59, 84
Loffreda, S., 211
Loftus, W. K., 62
Loud, G., 78
Lux, U., 202
Lynch, W. F., 6, 35
Lyon, D. G., 38-40, 166
Lyons, M. K., 264-265
Macalister, R. A. S., 22-23, 32-33, 152, 168, 170-171
MacDonald B., 255
Mackay, E. G. H., 57, 69
Malamat, A., 234
Mallon, A., 48, 72, 92, 150, 165
Mangles, J., 155
Mare, W. H., 255-256
Marks, J. H., 182, 195
Marquet-Krause, J., 95-96, 150-152
Masry, A., 187
Mathews, K., 120
Matthiae, P., 241-242
Mazar, B., 105-106, 136, 174, 207
McCown, C. C., 79, 86-87, 89
McCreery, D. W., 255
McCurdy, J. F., 44
McFadden, G., 224
McGovern, P. E., 253-254
McKenzie, J. L., 150
Mellaart, J., 249
Mendenhall, G. E., 198, 239

Merrill, S., 8-9, 30, 38, 249, 257
Meyer, M. A., 31, 273
Meyers, E. M., 211-213, 269
Miles, J. A., 263
Milik, J. T., 228-229
Miller, J. M., 254
Mitchell, H. G., 26, 32-33, 58
Montgomery, J. A., 12, 16, 31, 48-51, 55, 58, 60-61, 108
Moore, G. F., 16, 31
Moran, W. L., 235
Morton, W. M., 125
Moulton, W. J., 45, 58
Mowry, L., 123
Muilenburg, J., 112-113, 129, 147
Naveh, J., 267
Naville, E., 246-247
Negev, A., 173, 214
Newell, E. T., 60
Newman, T. D., 179, 273
Nies, J. B., 31, 66
North, R., 150
Norton, C. E., 10
Norton, R., 63
Oren, E. D., 218
Oweis, Y., 200
Owens, T. R., 67
Parker, S. T., 253
Parr, P. J., 243, 258
Parrot, A., 231
Paton, L. B., 16, 33-34, 58
Pedley, J. G., 225
Perrot, J., 137
Peters, F., 242
Peters, J. P., 12-13, 26, 55-59, 68
Petrie, W. M. F., 11, 17-22, 94, 119, 205, 207, 231, 234, 245-246
Pettinato, G., 241-242
Pfeiffer, R. H., 69
Phythian-Adams, W. J., 57, 231
Pickering, T. R., 198
Place, V., 62
Pommerantz, I., 272
Pope, M. H., 140
Prince, J. D., 31
Pritchard, J. B., 129, 147-149, 188-189
Rabinowitz, L. M., 113
Rainey, A., 218, 261
Rast, W. E., 164, 249, 251-252

Rawlinson, H. C., 62, 133
Redford, D. B., 258
Reed, W. L., 118, 124, 154, 187
Reisner, G. A., 39-41, 76-77, 91-93, 141, 144, 245
Renan, E., 6
Richard, S., 258
Richardson, H. N., 140, 150, 209
Riley, F. B., 67
Ripley, S. D., 245
Ritter, C., 2, 5
Robinson, E., 1-8, 13, 65, 90, 93, 129, 148, 177, 208, 210, 231, 249
Robinson, G. L., 45-46
Rockefeller, J. D., Jr., 16, 52, 77-78, 108
Rogers, R. W., 52, 274
Rollefson, G. O., 258
Rose, D. G., 206, 266
Rothenberg, B., 261
Rowe, A., 77, 168
Saad, Y., 139
Sachs, A. J., 132
Said, M., 272
Samuel, A. Y., 114-116
Sanders, J. A., 104, 117, 120, 155
Sarzec, E. de, 62
Sauer, J. A., 149, 158, 195, 198, 201, 204, 239, 244, 269
Sayce, A. H., 14
Schaeffer, C. F. A., 231
Schaub, R. T., 249, 251-252
Scheuer, R. J., 269
Schiff, J. H., 38-39
Schmidt, A., 93-94
Schmidt, N., 34-36, 108
Schoff, W. H., 60
Schoonover, K., 189
Schumacher, G., 9-10, 39, 47-48, 249
Scott, R. B. Y., 155
Seetzen, U. J., 4, 87, 249
Seger, J., 186, 217-218
Seger, K., 217-218
Sellers, O. R., 89, 111-112, 149
Sellin, E., 14-15, 46-48, 91, 93, 144, 162, 164
Shiloh, Y., 240
Shutler, M. E., 217
Skehan, P. W., 122

Slousch, N., 104-105
Smith, E., 4-6, 175
Smith, R. H., 209
Soren, D., 223-224
South, A., 223
Speiser, E. A., 70-71, 76, 107, 132, 233
Stager, L. E., 206, 222, 225-229
Starkey, J. L., 20, 94-95, 119, 235
Starr, R. F. S., 69
Steckeweh, H. H., 93, 144
Stekelis, M., 137
Stewart, M., 268
Stuart, M., 1-2, 5, 7, 13
Sukenik, E. L., 72, 92, 105, 117, 140, 210
Swauger, J. L., 176
Swiny, S., 223-224
Thayer, J. H., 8, 25-28, 31, 264
Thompson, H. O., 198-199
Tobler, T., 5
Todd, I., 221-224
Toombs, L. E., 145, 168, 206-207
Torrey, C. C., 16, 28-31, 42-43, 50-51, 58, 65, 108, 188, 229, 263
Toueir, K., 242
Toy, C. H., 38
Trever, J. C., 114-117
Tufnell, O., 20, 24, 94-95
Tushingham, A. D., 125-128, 153
Ungerleider-Mayerson, J., 269
Urice, S., 256
Van Beek, G. W., 207-208
Van Elderen, B., 198-199
Vaux, R. de, 118-120, 130, 152-153, 167, 184, 237, 254
Veliotes, N., 198
Vincent, L. H., 64-65, 90, 105, 210, 231, 234
Vogel, E. K., 104
Wade, W., 123
Walker, A., 222-224
Wallace, P. W., 223
Walton, G. R., 272
Ward, W. H., 8, 12, 26, 68
Warren, C., 7, 22, 65, 129, 152
Waterman, L., 71
Watzinger, C., 47, 91, 129, 210-211, 213
Weinberg, S. S., 218

Weippert, M., 261
Weiss, H., 243
Welker, M. H., 198
Wellhausen, J., 13-15
Welter, G., 93
Wheeler, M., 127
Williams, P. H., 154
Wilson, C. W., 7
Wilson, E. L., 45
Winnett, F. V., 124, 129, 140, 187
Wolf, C. U., 123

Wolfe, C. L., 12
Woolley, C. L., 57, 69
Worrell, J. E., 206
Worrell, W. H., 51, 55-56, 58
Wright, G. E., 91, 93, 106-107, 127-
    128, 141-145, 150, 153, 168, 177-179,
    181, 186-187, 200, 204-205, 211, 222,
    224, 234-237, 270
Yadin, Y., 105-106, 140-142, 170-171,
    174-175, 184, 234
Yeivin, S., 135-136

SELECTED INDEX OF PLACES

Abila, 255-256
Ai, 95-96, 150-152
Anafa, Tell, 218-219
Arad, 175-176
Araq el Emir, 155, 157-158
Ashdod, 176-177
Ashkelon, 57
Avdat, 173-174
Bab edh Dhra, 72-73, 165-166, 249, 251-252
Beer Resisim, 261-262
Beit Mirsim, Tell, 79-82
Bethel, 90, 130
Beth-shan, 77
Beth-shemesh, 90-91
Beth-zur, 89-90, 149-150
Caesarea Maritima, 214-215
Capernaum, 210-211
Carthage, 225-228
Daliyeh, Wadi ed, 159-160
Dan, 177
Dhahr Mirzbaneh, 166-167
Dibon, 124-125
Dothan, 130-131
Ebla, 241-242
Ekron, 267
En-gedi, 174-175
Gawra, Tepe, 71
Gezer, 23, 168, 170-171
Ghassul, Tuleilat el, 92, 150
Gibeah, 65-66, 160-161
Gibeon, 148
Gilgal, 129
Gush Halav, 213
Hazor, 140-141
Heshbon, 190-191, 193-194
Hesi, Tell el, 17-20, 22, 205-207
Idalion, 222-223
Ira, Tell, 261
Iskander, Khirbet, 258
Jemmeh, Tell, 207-208

Jerash, 87-89
Jericho (Tell es Sultan), 47, 91-92, 125, 127-128
Jericho (Herodian), 129
Jerusalem, 7, 152-153
Judean Desert Caves, 140, 174
Kheleifeh, Tell el, 98-99
Khorsabad, 69-70
Lachish, 94-95
Lagash, 172
Lahav (Tell Halif), 217-218
Malhata, Tell, 260-261
Masada, 175
Maskhuta, Tell el, 246-247
Masos, Tell, 260-261
Megiddo, 9-10, 47, 77-79
Meiron, 212
Mizpah, 79-80
Nabratein, Khirbet en, 213
Nippur, 11-13, 131-132
Numeira, 252
Nuzi, 69
Opis, 71
Pella, 208-210
Qumran, 118-120
Raddana, Khirbet, 186
Ras, Tell er, 145-146
Rumeith, Tell er, 158-159
Saidiyeh, Tell es, 148-149
Samaria, 39-41, 92-93
Sardis, 146
Shechem, 47, 93, 141-142, 144-145, 185-186
Shema, Khirbet, 211-212
Shiloh, 93-94
Taanach, 47, 162, 164-165
Tannur, Khirbet et, 98, 107
Tarkhalan, 71
Tirzah, 120
Umm el Jimal, 256-257
Zarephath, 188-189